Consumption Tax Trends 2016

VAT/GST AND EXCISE RATES, TRENDS AND POLICY ISSUES

OECD
BETTER POLICIES FOR BETTER LIVES

Please cite this publication as:
OECD (2016), *Consumption Tax Trends 2016: VAT/GST and excise rates, trends and policy issues*, OECD Publishing, Paris.
http://dx.doi.org/10.1787/cct-2016-en

ISBN 978-92-64-26404-5 (print)
ISBN 978-92-64-26405-2 (PDF)

Series: Consumption Tax Trends
ISSN 1562-8752 (print)
ISSN 1999-0979 (online)

The statistical data for Israel are supplied by and under the responsibility of the relevant Israeli authorities. The use of such data by the OECD is without prejudice to the status of the Golan Heights, East Jerusalem and Israeli settlements in the West Bank under the terms of international law.

Corrigenda to OECD publications may be found on line at: *www.oecd.org/about/publishing/corrigenda.htm*.

Foreword

This is the eleventh edition of Consumption Tax Trends, *a biennial OECD publication. It presents cross-country comparative data relative to consumption taxes in OECD member countries, as at 1 January 2016. Tables using data from the* National Accounts *and data on tax revenue from* Revenue Statistics 1965-2015 *are updated up to and including 2014. Price levels for fuel oils are updated as at 4th Quarter 2015 from* Energy Prices and Taxes – Quarterly Statistics *issued by the International Energy Agency. The country data for the report have, for the most part, been provided by delegates to Working Party No. 9. The exchange rates used to convert national currencies into US dollars (USD) are average market rates for 2015 taken from the OECD* Monetary and Financial Statistics, *except for Tables 1.A1.10 (Chapter 1), and 2.A2.3 (Chapter 2) where the Purchase Power Parity (PPP) rates are used as they provide for a better comparison of the value of VAT relief thresholds (PPP rates for GDP 2015 are extracted from the OECD Statistics Database).*

This publication illustrates the evolution of consumption taxes as instruments for raising tax revenue. It identifies and documents the large number of differences that exist in respect of the consumption tax base, rates and implementation rules while highlighting the features underlying their development. It looks, in particular, at developments in the Value Added Tax/Goods and Services Tax (VAT/GST) area (referred to as "VAT" in this publication). It notably presents an updated estimate of the VAT Revenue Ratio (VRR) for OECD countries, providing an indicator of the loss of VAT revenue as a consequence of exemptions and reduced rates, fraud, evasion and tax planning. It notes the completion of the OECD International VAT/GST Guidelines and its worldwide acceptance as the emerging international standard for the application of VAT to cross-border trade in services and intangibles. Chapter 1 summarises trends in consumption taxes and their main features. It shows the evolution of consumption tax revenues between 1965 and 2014 and looks in some more detail at the application of VAT to international trade, more particularly at the challenges of applying VAT to cross-border trade in services and intangibles and at the OECD International VAT/GST Guidelines. It also considers the recent evolutions concerning VAT fraud. Chapter 2 describes the key features of VAT regimes in OECD countries, i.e. tax rates, exemptions, specific restrictions to input tax credit, registration and collection thresholds, VAT relief arrangements for goods imported by final consumers and special tax collection methods. It is complemented with a technical note on the rationale and impact of reduced VAT rates. Chapter 3 describes how the VAT Revenue Ratio (VRR) provides an indicator of the effect of exemptions, reduced rates and non-compliance on government revenues and explains how it is calculated and should be interpreted. It is complemented with technical notes on measurement issues. Chapter 4 describes the main features of excise duties and their impact on revenue, customer behaviour and markets. It shows the detailed excise tax rates on beer, wine, alcoholic beverages, tobacco, and mineral oil products in OECD countries. It also provides, for the first time, an estimate of the total tax burden in a pack of cigarettes in OECD countries. Chapter 5 describes the main features of vehicle taxes and their use for influencing customer behaviour. It provides detailed information on taxes on sale and registration of vehicles and recurrent taxes.

This publication was prepared under the auspices of the Working Party N° 9 on Consumption Taxes, of the Committee on Fiscal Affairs. It was written by Stéphane Buydens of the OECD Centre for Tax Policy and Administration (CTPA).

Table of contents

Tables

Figures

Acknowledgements

Aknowledgements are due to: David Bradbury (Head, Tax Policy and Statistics Division); Piet Battiau (Head, Consumption Taxes Unit), Kurt Van Dender (Head, Tax and Environment Unit); Michele Harding (Head, Statistical Unit); Bert Brys (Head, Tax Policy Unit); Alastair Thomas (Tax Economist), Florens Flues (Tax Economist), Michel Lahittete (Statistician), Michael Sharrat (Statistician) and Martine Monza (Assistant), CTPA; Mariano Berkenwald, International Energy Agency; Professor Walter Hellerstein (Distinguished Research Professor & Francis Shackelford Distinguished Professor in Taxation Law, University of Georgia).

Executive summary

Consumption taxes generally consist of *general taxes on goods and services* ("taxes on general consumption"), consisting of value-added tax (VAT) and its equivalent in several jurisdictions (goods and services tax, or GST), sales taxes, and other general taxes on goods and services; and *taxes on specific goods and services*, consisting primarily of excise taxes, customs and import duties, and taxes on specific services (such as insurance premiums and financial services).

Consumption taxes accounted for 30.5% of total tax revenues in OECD countries in 2014, on average. While the share of all taxes on consumption (taxes on general consumption plus taxes on specific goods and services) as a percentage of total tax revenue has remained relatively stable since 1975, the composition of consumption taxes has fundamentally changed. Over time, OECD countries have relied increasingly on taxes on general consumption. Since 1965, the share of these taxes as a percentage of GDP in OECD countries has more than doubled, from 3.2% to 7.0%. They presently raise 20.7% of total tax revenue on average, compared with 11.9% in 1965. VAT has become the largest source of taxes on general consumption, accounting on average for 6.8% of GDP and 20.1% of total tax revenue in OECD countries in 2014. While revenues from taxes on general consumption fell between 2005 and 2009, as a consequence of the global economic crisis, they have now returned to the pre-crisis levels largely due to the rise in standard VAT rates in many countries. In contrast to this increase, revenues from taxes on specific goods and services, the bulk of which are excise taxes, have fallen over time as a percentage of GDP (from 5.6% in 1965 to 3.3% in 2014) and as a percentage of total tax revenue (from 24.3% in 1965 to 9.6% in 2014).

Key trends

- VAT revenues are at an all-time high in OECD countries at 6.8% of GDP and at 20.1% of total tax revenue on average (excl. the United States which do not have a VAT system), up from respectively 6.6% of GDP and 19.8% of total tax revenue in 2012. Revenues from VAT rose as a percentage of GDP in 22 of the 34 OECD countries that operate a VAT and fell, only slightly, in 5 countries compared to 2012.
- Standard VAT rates in the OECD reached a record level of 19.2% on average in 2015 and have remained stable since. Ten OECD countries now have a standard VAT rate above 22%, against only four in 2008. The average standard rate of the 22 OECD countries that are members of the European Union (21.7%) is significantly above the OECD average.
- Countries increasingly look at base broadening measures to raise additional revenue from VAT, notably by increasing reduced VAT rates and/or narrowing their scope in line with OECD recommendations.

- Most OECD countries have implemented or announced measures to collect the VAT on the ever-rising volume of online sales by offshore sellers in line with the International VAT/GST Guidelines and the BEPS Action 1 Report on *Addressing the Tax Challenges of the Digital Economy*.
- The International VAT/GST Guidelines are the first-ever global standard for the application of VAT to cross-border trade. They were completed in 2015 and were endorsed by over 100 countries, jurisdictions and international organisations at the OECD Global Forum on VAT in November 2015. They were adopted as a Recommendation by the OECD Council in September 2016.
- The total tax burden on cigarettes is now above 50% of the consumer price in almost all OECD countries and has reached 80% or more in 10 countries. Countries increasingly use excise duties to influence customer behaviour.

Key findings

- Many OECD countries continue to apply reduced rates to a broad range of products such as basic essentials, pharmaceuticals and healthcare services, cultural and sporting events, etc. to pursue equity or other non-distributional goals (e.g. supporting cultural objectives, promoting locally supplied labour-intensive activities or correcting environmental or other externalities). This notwithstanding evidence that reduced rates are not an effective tool to achieve redistribution or to pursue the other non-distributional goals as mentioned above. They also continue to make considerable use of exemptions to pursue distributional objectives (such as exemptions for basic health, charities and education) and for activities that are considered hard to tax (for example, financial services).
- The VAT Revenue Ratio (VRR) for OECD countries suggests that there is still potential for additional revenue by improving the performance of VAT. The VRR provides a comparative measure of how exemptions and reduced rates affect tax revenues and countries' ability to secure effectively the potential tax base for VAT. It measures the difference between the VAT revenue collected and what would theoretically be raised if VAT was applied at the standard rate to the entire potential tax base in a "pure" VAT regime. Across the OECD, the unweighted average VRR has remained relatively stable at 0.56 in 2014, compared to 0.55 in 2012, meaning that 44% of the potential VAT revenue is not collected. Although the VRR has to be interpreted with care and tax base erosion may be caused by a variety of factors, this VRR estimate suggests that there is significant potential for raising additional revenues by improving VAT systems' performance.
- The share of excise duties in total tax revenue has been subject to a long decline since 1965, when they accounted for 14.2% on average, compared to 7.6% in 2014. Excise duties are increasingly used to influence consumer behaviour, in particular to reduce pollution through taxes on motor fuels and improve health by heavier taxation of tobacco products.
- Car taxation is increasingly used to influence customer behaviour and encourage the use of low polluting vehicles. In 2016, more than three quarters of OECD countries apply lower taxes or exemptions on purchase or use/ownership for vehicles according to environmental or fuel efficiency criteria.

Chapter 1

Taxing consumption

This chapter describes the relative importance of consumption taxes as a source of tax revenues and the main features of these taxes. It shows the evolution of consumption tax revenues between 1965 and 2014. It describes the functioning of value added taxes (VAT) and of retail sales taxes (in the United States) and the main characteristics of consumption taxes on specific goods and services. It looks in some more detail at the application of VAT to international trade, more particularly at the challenges of applying VAT to cross-border trade and at the International VAT/GST Guidelines that the OECD has developed as the global standard to address these challenges. Finally, it considers the recent developments concerning VAT fraud and evasion and outlines some of the countermeasures that have been implemented in some countries or that may be implemented in the future.

The statistical data for Israel are supplied by and under the responsibility of the relevant Israeli authorities. The use of such data by the OECD is without prejudice to the status of the Golan Heights, East Jerusalem and Israeli settlements in the West Bank under the terms of international law.

1.1. Introduction

Consumption taxes account for approximately one third of the total taxes collected in OECD countries. They have two common forms: taxes on general consumption (value added taxes and retail sales taxes) and taxes on specific goods and services (mainly excise duties).

Since the mid-1980s, VAT[1] (also called Goods and Services Tax – GST) has become the main consumption tax both in terms of revenue and geographical coverage. VAT is designed to be a tax on final consumption that is broadly neutral towards the production process and international trade. It is widely seen as a relatively growth-friendly tax. As a result many countries have sought to raise additional revenues from VAT (rather than other taxes) as part of their fiscal consolidation strategies in the aftermath of the global financial and economic crisis. Many developing countries have introduced a VAT during the last two decades to replace lost revenues from trade taxes following trade liberalisation. Some 166 countries operate a VAT today (see Annex A), including 34 of the 35 OECD member countries, the only exception being the United States although most states within the US employ some form of retail sales tax. VAT raises approximately a fifth of total tax revenues in the OECD and worldwide.

The combination of the global spread of VAT, the rapid globalisation of economic activity and the developments of the digital economy, which has resulted in an increased interaction between VAT systems, along with increasing VAT rates, have raised the profile of VAT as an increasingly significant issue in cross-border trade since the turn of the century. In contrast with the taxation of income (where there are the OECD Model Tax Convention and the Transfer Pricing Guidelines) there was no internationally agreed framework for the application of VAT to cross-border trade, which led to increasing uncertainty and complexity for tax authorities and businesses and to growing risks of double taxation and unintended double non-taxation. This was a matter of special concern with respect to international trade in services and intangibles, which has grown particularly strong over the last decades. In response, the OECD's Committee on Fiscal Affairs (CFA) developed the *International VAT/GST Guidelines*. These Guidelines present a set of internationally agreed standards and recommended approaches for the consistent application of VAT/GST to international trade, with a particular focus on trade in services and intangibles. Their main objective is to reduce the uncertainty and the risks of double taxation and unintended non-taxation that result from inconsistencies in the application of VAT in a cross-border context. The *International VAT/GST Guidelines* were endorsed as a global standard by over one hundred countries, jurisdictions and international organisations at the OECD Global Forum on VAT in November 2015. They were adopted as a Recommendation by the Council of the OECD in September 2016. This Recommendation is the first OECD legal instrument in the area of VAT (as the other OECD legal instruments in the area of taxation, such as the OECD Model Tax Convention and the Transfer Pricing Guidelines, relate essentially to the taxation of income).

Whilst VAT was first introduced about 60 years ago, excise duties have existed since the dawn of civilisation. They are levied on a specific range of products and are assessed by reference to various characteristics such as weight, volume, strength or quantity of the product, combined in some cases with *ad valorem* taxes. Although they generally apply to alcoholic beverages, tobacco products and fuels in all OECD countries and beyond, their tax base, calculation method and rates vary widely between countries, reflecting local cultures and historical practice. Excise duties are increasingly being used to influence consumer behaviour to achieve health and environmental objectives.

This chapter first provides an overview of the statistical classification of consumption taxes (Section 1.2) and shows the evolution of consumption tax revenues between 1965 and 2014 (Section 1.3). It then describes the geographical spread of VAT (Section 1.4) and outlines the main features of VAT design (Section 1.5). This is followed by a high-level description of the main design features of retail sales taxes (Section 1.6) and of the main characteristics of consumption taxes on specific goods and services (Section 1.7). This chapter then looks in some more detail at the challenges of applying VAT to cross-border trade in services and intangibles and at the International VAT/GST Guidelines developed by the OECD as the global standard to address these challenges. It also looks at the available options for collecting VAT on cross-border trade in low value goods (Section 1.8). It finally considers the recent developments concerning VAT fraud and evasion and outlines some of the countermeasures that have been implemented in some countries or that may be implemented in the future (Section 1.9). For ease of reference, the tables which are referred to below are included at the end of the chapter.

1.2. Classification of consumption taxes

In the OECD classification, "taxes" are confined to compulsory, unrequited payments to general government. According to the OECD nomenclature, taxes are divided into five broad categories: taxes on income, profits and capital gains (1000); social security contributions (2000); taxes on payroll and workforce (3000); taxes on property (4000); and taxes on goods and services (5000) (OECD, 2016a).

Consumption taxes (Category 5100 "Taxes on production, sale, transfer, leasing and delivery of goods and rendering of services") fall mainly into two sub-categories:

- *General taxes on goods and services* ("taxes on general consumption"), which includes value added taxes (5111), sales taxes (5112) and other general taxes on goods and services (5113).
- *Taxes on specific goods and services* consisting primarily of excise taxes (5121), customs and import duties (5123) and taxes on specific services (5126, e.g. taxes on insurance premiums and financial services).

Consumption taxes such as VAT, sales taxes and excise duties are often categorised as *indirect taxes* as they are generally not levied directly on the person who is supposed to bear the burden of the tax. They are rather imposed on certain transactions, products or events (OECD Glossary of Tax Terms). They are not imposed on income or wealth but rather on the expenditure that the income and wealth finance. Governments generally collect the tax from producers and distributors at various points in the value chain, while the burden of the tax falls in principle on consumers assuming that it will be passed on to them in the prices charged by suppliers.

1.3. Evolution of consumption tax revenues

On average, consumption taxes produce 31% of the total tax revenue and account for 10% of the GDP in the OECD member countries (unweighted average, see Tables 1.A1.1 and 1.A1.2). In 2014, approximately two thirds of revenue from consumption taxes was attributable to taxes on general consumption and one third to taxes on specific goods and services (see Tables 1.A1.4 and 1.A1.6).

Figure 1.1. **Average tax revenue as a percentage of total taxation, by category of tax 2014**

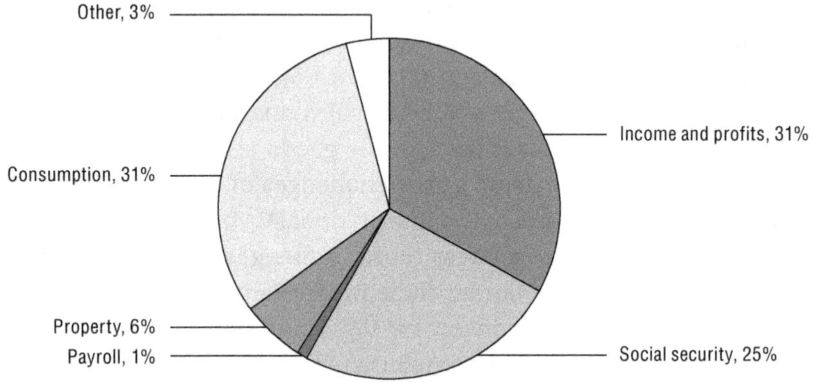

Source: Adapted from OECD (2016a), *Revenue Statistics 2016*, OECD Publishing, Paris. DOI: *http://dx.doi.org/10.1787/rev_stats-2016-en-fr*.

StatLink http://dx.doi.org/10.1787/888933419904

Tables 1.A1.3 and 1.A1.4 respectively present revenues from taxes on general consumption as a percentage of Gross Domestic Product (GDP) and as a percentage of total taxation in 2014. These taxes include VAT, sales taxes and other general taxes on goods and services. These ratios vary considerably between countries both in percentage of GDP and of total taxation. In Australia, Japan, Mexico, Switzerland, and the United States, taxes on general consumption account for less than 4% of GDP while they account for more than 9.5% in Hungary, Israel and New Zealand. Revenues from those taxes account for less than 15% of total taxation in Australia, Canada, Italy, Japan, Switzerland and the United States and for more than 30% in Chile, Hungary and Israel. Taxes on general consumption account for more than 20% of total taxation in 20 of the 35 OECD countries, with an OECD unweighted average of 20.7%.

Over the longer term, OECD member countries have relied increasingly on taxes on general consumption. Since 1965, the share of these taxes as a percentage of GDP in OECD countries has more than doubled, from 3.2% to 7.0% in 2014.They accounted for only 11.9% of total tax revenue in OECD countries in 1965 compared to 20.7% in 2014. While the global financial and economic crisis had an effect on consumption tax revenues, which fell between 2005 and 2009, they have generally returned to the pre-crisis levels, largely due to the rise in standard VAT rates in many countries during and in the aftermath of the crisis (21 of the OECD member countries raised their standard rate between 2009 and 2014 – see Chapter 2).

VAT is now the largest source of taxes on general consumption in OECD countries on average. Revenues from VAT as a percentage of GDP increased from 6.8% in 2012 to 7.0% in 2014 on average; and from 20.5% in 2012 to 20.7% in 2014 as a share of total taxation (see Tables 1.A1.7 and 1.A1.8). VAT is operated in 34 of the 35 OECD countries, the United States being the only OECD country not to have adopted a VAT. In 1975, thirteen of the current OECD member countries had a VAT (see Table 2.A2.1 in Chapter 2). Greece, Iceland, Japan, Mexico, New Zealand, Portugal, Spain and Turkey introduced VAT in the 1980s while Switzerland followed shortly afterwards. The Central European economies introduced VAT in the late 1980s and early 1990s, often based on the European Union (EU) model in anticipation of their future EU membership. Revenues from VAT as a percentage of GDP compared to 2012 rose in 21 of the 34 OECD countries that operate a VAT and fell, only slightly, in 4 countries (see Table 1.A1.7). The largest increase was in Japan (1.2 percentage points explained by the increase of the VAT rate from 5% to 8% in April 2014). Other countries with substantial rises of VAT revenue as a percentage of GDP between 2012 and 2014 were Spain and Israel (0.7), the Slovak Republic (0.6) and Slovenia (0.5). These countries are also those where the standard VAT rate was increased the most during the same period. The share of VAT in total tax revenues in the 34 OECD countries that operate a VAT shows a considerable spread, from 12-13% (Japan, Australia, Switzerland, Canada, Italy) to 25-26% (Estonia, Latvia, Mexico) and to 29.9% in New Zealand and 41.6% in Chile (see Figure 1.2 and Table 1.A1.8). VAT produces 15% or more of total tax revenues in 30 of the 34 OECD countries that operate a VAT and it exceeds 20% of total taxation in 20 of these countries.

Figure 1.2. **Share of VAT as a percentage of total taxation 2014**

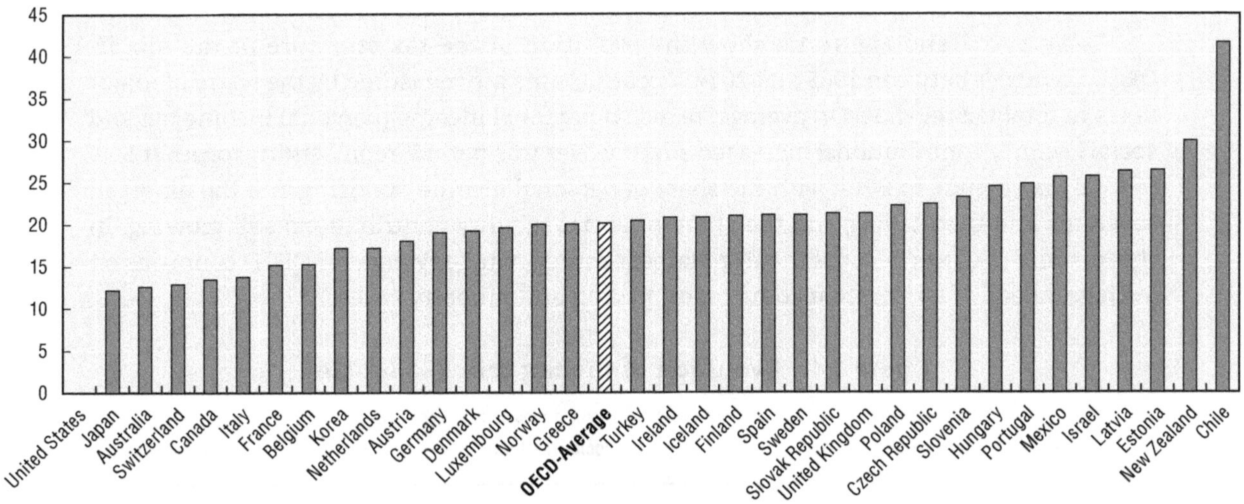

Source: Adapted from OECD (2016a), *Revenue Statistics 2016*, OECD Publishing, Paris. DOI: *http://dx.doi.org/10.1787/rev_stats-2016-en-fr*.

StatLink *http://dx.doi.org/10.1787/888933419914*

Tables 1.A1.5 and 1.A1.6 show that revenues from taxes on specific goods and services, the bulk of which are excise taxes, have decreased steadily as a percentage of GDP between 1965 and 2010 (from 5.6% in 1965 to 3.3% in 2010) and have remained stable at 3.3% of GDP on average since then. The share of taxes on specific goods and services total taxation has continued to fall between 2012 and 2014 (from 10.7% in 1965 to 9.6% in 2014 on average). The share of taxes on specific goods and services in total tax revenues fell in 23 OECD countries in increased in 7. Excise taxes are discussed in greater detail in Chapter 4.

As a result, the composition of consumption taxes has fundamentally changed over time. The substantially increased importance of VAT has effectively balanced the diminishing share of taxes on specific goods and services (see Figure 1.3). Only Turkey still collects a significant part of its revenues by way of taxes on specific goods and services, i.e. 22% of its total tax revenue against an OECD average of 9.6%.

Figure 1.3. **Share of consumption taxes as percentage of total taxation 1966-2014**

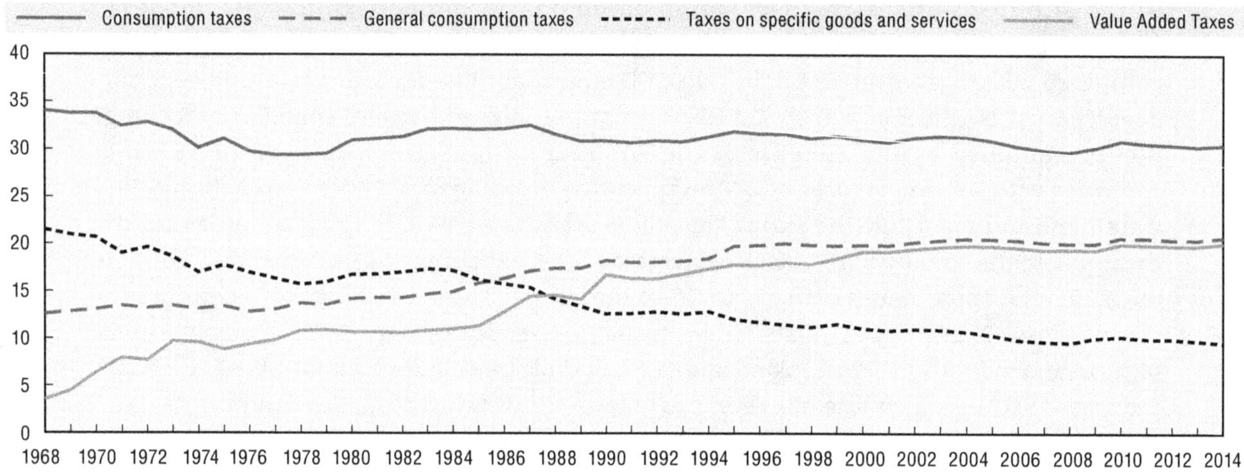

Source: Adapted from OECD (2016a), *Revenue Statistics 2016*, OECD Publishing, Paris. DOI: *http://dx.doi.org/10.1787/rev_stats-2016-en-fr*.

StatLink http://dx.doi.org/10.1787/888933419925

Table 1.A1.7 and Figure 1.4 show the evolution of the tax structure or tax mix in OECD countries between 1965 and 2014. Tax structures are measured by the share of major taxes in total tax revenue. On average, taxes on personal income (personal income tax and social security contributions) increased slightly over this period, representing together 50% of total tax revenue in 2014, with the share of personal income tax rising into the nineteen seventies and then falling and the share of social security contributions still growing. In this tax mix, VAT has become the third largest source of tax revenue for OECD countries on average, ahead of corporate income taxes, payroll and property taxes.

Figure 1.4. **Evolution of the tax mix 1965-2014**

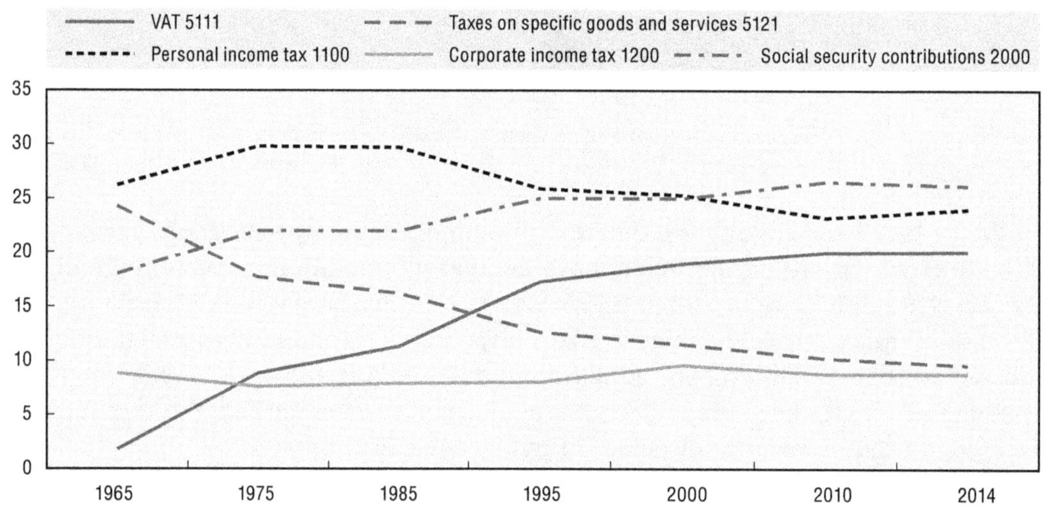

Source: Adapted from OECD (2016a), *Revenue Statistics 2016*, OECD Publishing, Paris. DOI: *http://dx.doi.org/10.1787/rev_stats-2016-en-fr*.

StatLink http://dx.doi.org/10.1787/888933419936

1.4. Spread of VAT

The spread of VAT has been among the most important development in taxation over the last half century. Limited to less than 10 countries in the late 1960s, it is today an important source of revenue in more than 166 countries worldwide (see Figure 1.5 and Annex A).

The domestic and international neutrality properties of the VAT have encouraged its spread around the world. Many developing countries have introduced a VAT during the last two decades to replace lost revenues from trade taxes following trade liberalisation. In the EU, VAT is directly associated with the development of its internal market. The adoption of a common VAT framework in the EU was intended to remove the trade distortions associated with cascading indirect taxes that it replaced and to facilitate the creation of a common market in which Member States cannot use taxes on production and consumption to protect their domestic industries and investment (Ebrill et al., 2001). A VAT is operated in 34 of the 35 OECD countries, the only exception being the United States.

Figure 1.5. **Number of countries having implemented a VAT 1960-2016**

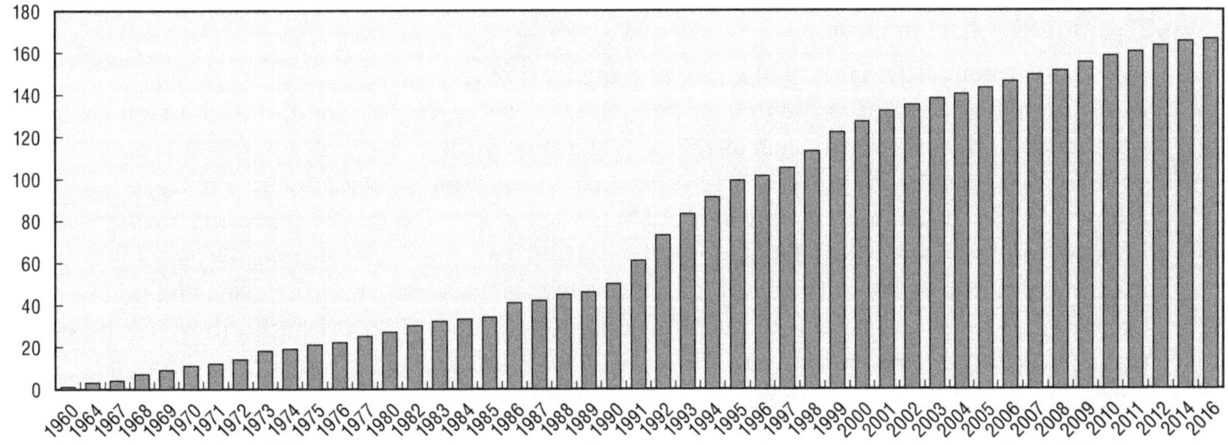

Source: F. Annacondia, International – Overview of General Turnover Taxes and Tax Rates, 27 International VAT Monitor 2 (2016), Journals IBFD.

StatLink http://dx.doi.org/10.1787/888933419943

1.5. The main features of VAT design

Although there is a wide diversity in the way VAT systems are implemented, the VAT can be defined by its purpose and its specific tax collection mechanism. The OECD *International VAT/GST Guidelines* (OECD, 2016b) provide an overview of the core features of VAT, which are summarised below.

A tax on final consumption

VAT is a broad-based tax on consumption by households as, in principle, only private individuals, as distinguished from businesses, engage in the consumption at which a VAT is targeted. In other words "*businesses buy and use capital goods, office supplies and the like – but they do not consume them in this sense*" (Keen and Hellerstein, 2010). In practice, however, many VAT systems impose VAT burden not only on consumption by private individuals, but also on various entities that are involved in non-business activities.

From a legal and practical standpoint, VAT is essentially a transaction tax. In "real life" things can be consumed in many ways. Some can be consumed fully and immediately (like a taxi ride); some can be bought and fully consumed later (like a sandwich); some can be consumed over a longer period of time (like a desk or a subscription to an on-line database). However, VAT does not actually tax such material consumption. Rather, it aims at taxing the sale to the final consumer through a staged payment process along the supply chain.

VAT is collected by businesses through a staged process but, since it is a tax on final consumption by households, the burden of the VAT should not rest on businesses, except when they acquire goods, services or intangibles for private consumption by their owners or their employees.

It can be argued, however, that the economic burden of the VAT can lie in variable proportion on business and consumers. Indeed, the effective incidence of VAT, like that of any other tax, is determined not only by its formal nature but also by market circumstances, including the elasticity of demand and the nature of competition between suppliers (Ebrill et al., 2001).

The staged collection process

The central design feature of a VAT, and the feature from which it derives its name, is that the tax is collected through a staged process on the value added at each stage of production and distribution. Each business in the supply chain takes part in the process of controlling and collecting the tax, remitting the proportion of tax corresponding to its margin, i.e. on the difference between the VAT imposed on its taxed inputs and the VAT imposed on its taxed outputs. Businesses collect VAT on the value of their outputs from their customers and are entitled to deduct the tax they have paid on purchases and must account and remit the difference (or receive a refund from) to the tax authorities. In this respect, the VAT differs from a retail sales tax ("RST"), which taxes consumption through a single-stage levy imposed in theory only at the point of final sale.

This mechanism reflects the central design feature of the VAT as a tax collected by businesses through a staged payment process coupled with the fundamental principle that the burden of the tax does not rest on businesses but on final consumers. This requires a mechanism for relieving businesses of the burden of the VAT they pay when they acquire goods, services or intangibles.

There are two main approaches for operating the staged collection process:

- Under the ***invoice credit method*** (which is a "transaction based method"), each trader charges VAT at the rate specified for each supply and passes to the purchaser an invoice showing the amount of tax charged. The purchaser is in turn able to credit that input tax against the output tax it charges on its sales, remitting the balance to the tax authorities and receiving refunds when there are excess credits. This method is based on invoices that could, in principle, be cross-checked to pick up any overstatement of credit entitlement. By linking the tax credit on the purchaser's inputs to the tax paid by the purchaser, the invoice credit method is designed to discourage fraud.
- Under the ***subtraction method*** (which is an "entity based method"), the tax is levied directly on an accounts-based measure of value added, which is determined for each business by subtracting the VAT calculated on allowable purchases from the VAT calculated on taxable supplies.

Almost all jurisdictions that operate a VAT use the invoice-credit method. In the OECD, only Japan uses the subtraction method.

Neutrality

The staged collection process, whereby tax is in principle collected from businesses only on the value added at each stage of production and distribution, gives to the VAT its essential character in domestic trade as an economically neutral tax. The full right to deduct input tax through the supply chain, except by the final consumer, ensures the neutrality of the tax, whatever the nature of the product, the structure of the distribution chain, and the means used for its delivery (e.g. retail stores, physical delivery, Internet downloads). As a result of the staged payment system, VAT "flows through the businesses" to tax supplies made to final consumers.

Where the deductible input VAT for any period exceeds the output VAT collected, there is an excess of VAT credit, which should in principle be refunded. This is generally the case in particular for exporters, since their output is in principle free of VAT under the destination principle, and for businesses whose purchases are larger than their sales in the same period (such as new or developing businesses or seasonal businesses). These are especially important groups in terms of wider economic development, so it is important that VAT systems provide for an effective treatment of excess credits to avoid the risk that VAT introduces significant and costly distortions for these groups of business. At the same time, however, the payment of refunds evidently can create significant opportunities for fraud and corruption. It is important therefore that an effective refund system is also closely connected to the proper implementation of a comprehensive audit program (Ebrill et al., 2001).

When the right of deduction covers all business inputs, the final burden of the tax does not lie on businesses but on consumers. This is not always the case in practice, as restrictions on the right to deduct input tax may be restricted in a number of ways. Some are deliberate and some result from imperfect administration (see Chapter 2).

Deliberate restrictions to the deduction of input VAT result in particular from the application of VAT exemptions. When a supply is VAT-exempt, no VAT is charged on the supply and the supplier is not entitled to deduct the related input VAT. Many VAT systems apply exemptions for social (health, education and charities), practical (financial services, insurance) or historical (immovable property, land) reasons.

Another set of restrictions to the right of deduction of input VAT relates to purchases used, or deemed to be used, for the private consumption of the owners of a business, or of its employees or clients (e.g. cars and entertainment). Restrictions to the deduction of input VAT have also often been imposed in relation to investment goods or capital assets. This implies that an irrecoverable tax is embedded in the VAT base of final consumption and leads to a form of cumulative tax. However, most VAT systems accept the principle of full deduction and refunding of input VAT on investment goods.

Chapter 2 of the OECD's *International VAT/GST Guidelines* presents the key principles of VAT-neutrality and a set of internationally agreed standards to support neutrality of VAT in international trade.

1.6. Main design features of Retail Sales Taxes

A retail sales tax is a tax on general consumption charged only once on products at the last point of sale to the end user. In principle, only consumers are charged the tax; resellers are exempt if they are not final end users of the products. To implement this principle, business purchasers are normally required to provide the seller with a "resale certificate," which states that they are purchasing an item to resell it. The tax is charged on each item sold to purchasers who do not provide such a certificate. The retail sales tax covers not only retailers, but all businesses dealing with purchasers who do not provide a resale or other exemption certificate signifying that no tax is due (e.g. a public body or a charity, unless specific exemption applies).

The basis for taxation is the sales price. Unlike multi-stage cumulative taxes and like the VAT, this system allows the tax burden to be calculated precisely and it does not in principle discriminate between different forms of production or distribution channels. In practice, however, at least in the United States, the failure of the retail sales tax to reach many services and the limitation of the resale exemption to products that are resold in the same form that they are purchased, or are physically incorporated into products that are resold, leads to substantial taxation of business inputs.

In theory, the final outcomes of VAT and retail sales tax should be identical: they both ultimately aim to tax final consumption of a wide range of products where such consumption takes place. They also both tax the consumption expenditure i.e. the transaction between the seller and the buyer rather than the actual consumption. In practice, however, the end result is somewhat different given the fundamental difference in the way the tax is collected. Unlike VAT where the tax is collected at each stage of the value chain under a staged payment system (see Section 1.5 above), sales taxes are collected only at the very last stage i.e. on the sale by the retailer to the final consumer. The latter method has significant disadvantages: the higher the rate the more pressure is placed on the weakest link in the chain – the retailer, especially numerous small retailers; all the revenue is at risk if the retailer fails to remit the tax and the audit and invoice trail is poorer than under a VAT, especially for services; there are inevitably troublesome "end-use exemptions"; and revenue is not secured at the easiest stage, that is at the time of importation and this can be crucial for many developing countries. As a result, a single point resale sales tax is efficient at relatively low rates, but is increasingly difficult to administer as rates rise (Tait, 1988).

The United States is the only OECD country that employs a retail sales tax as the principal consumption tax. However, the retail sales tax in the United States is not a federal tax. Rather, it is a tax imposed at the state and local government levels. Currently, 45 of the 50 States as well as thousands of local tax jurisdictions impose general retail sales taxes. In general, the local taxes are almost identical in coverage to the state-level tax, are administered at the state level and amount in substance simply to an increase in the state rate, with the additional revenues distributed to the localities. Retail sales taxes are complemented in every state by functionally identical "use" taxes imposed on goods purchased from out-of-state vendors, because the state has no power to tax out-of-state "sales" and therefore imposes a complementary tax on the in-state "use" (Hellerstein, Hellerstein and Swain, 2016).

Combined state and local sales tax rates vary widely in the United States, from 1.78% (Alaska), 4.35% (Hawaii) and 5.41% (Wisconsin) to 9.46% (Tennessee), 9.30% (Arkansas) and

9.00% (Louisiana). Five states do not have a state-wide sales tax (Alaska, Delaware, Montana, New Hampshire, and Oregon and of these, two allow localities to charge local sales taxes (Alaska and Montana) (Tax Foundation 2016). These rates are much lower than the applicable VAT rates in OECD countries (except Canada, Japan and Switzerland). This is due to two main factors: the compliance risks associated with the sales tax collection method (see above) and the competition between jurisdictions (see below).

Retail sales and use taxes in force in the United States are subject to significant competitive pressure, especially in the context of interstate and international trade. Supreme Court rulings prohibit states from requiring vendors to collect tax with respect to cross-border sales when they are not physically present in the purchaser's state. States have therefore been unable effectively to collect use taxes with respect to cross-border sales from remote sellers. This problem has become increasingly significant with the advent of the Internet and online sales. To address this problem, as well as others caused by the lack of harmonisation in state sales and use taxes, a number of states have entered into the Streamlined Sales and Use Tax Agreement (SSUTA available at *www.streamlinedsalestax.org*). This agreement aims at establishing a uniform set of definitions of potentially taxable items that states can choose to tax or not (e.g. digital products). The Streamlined member states have also developed a Streamlined Sales Tax Registration System (SSTRS) that enables taxpayers to register voluntarily in order to participate in SSUTA. Voluntary registration requires sellers to collect sales and use taxes in all states into which they make sales, regardless of their physical presence there, and it permits sellers to benefit from increased legal certainty as regards their tax liability. Vendor collection of use taxes due on cross-border sales could become mandatory if the US Congress approves proposed legislation authorising states to require such collection if they have adopted SSUTA or similar measures to ease compliance burdens for vendors.

1.7. Main characteristics of consumption taxes on specific goods and services

In the OECD nomenclature, taxes on specific goods and services (5120) include a range of taxes such as excises, customs and import duties, taxes on exports and taxes on specific services. Consumption Tax Trends focuses on excise duties only.

A number of general characteristics differentiate excise duties from value added taxes:

- They are levied on a limited range of products.
- They are not normally due until the goods enter free circulation, which may be at a late stage in the supply chain.
- Excise charges are generally assessed by reference to the weight, volume, strength or quantity of the product, combined in some cases, with *ad valorem* taxes.

Consequently, and unlike VAT, the excise system is characterised by a small number of taxpayers at the manufacturing or wholesale stage (although, in some cases they can also be levied at the resale stage).

As with VAT, excise taxes aim to be neutral internationally. As the tax is normally collected when the goods are released into free circulation, neutrality is often ensured by holding exports under controlled regimes (such as bonded warehouses) and certification of final export (again under controlled conditions) by Customs. Similarly, imported excise goods are levied at importation although frequently the goods enter into controlled tax-free regimes until released into free circulation.

Excise taxes may cover a very wide range of products like salt, sugar, matches, fruit juice or chocolates. However, the range of products subject to excise has declined with the expansion of taxes on general consumption. Excise taxes on alcohol, tobacco and hydrocarbon oils continue to raise significant revenues for governments (see Chapter 4).

There has been a discernible trend in recent decades to ascribe to these taxes characteristics other than simply revenue-raising. A number of excise duties have been adjusted with a view to discouraging certain behaviours considered harmful, especially for health reasons. This is particularly the case for excise duties on tobacco and alcohol whose rates have been increased with the aim of reducing consumption of these products. The structure of certain excise duties has also gradually changed to encourage more responsible behaviour towards the collective welfare, especially the environment. This is the case for taxes on fuels, cars and other products which produce environmentally harmful emissions.

Such a trend can be regarded as a change in tax policy of governments. Governments have long been conscious that the tax system has an influence on the decisions of firms and individuals. They know the impact of the tax system on employment, business formation and expansion, and consumption patterns but have generally considered behavioural responses by taxpayers undesirable. In other cases, changing behaviour e.g. to reduce pollution or discourage consumption of products considered harmful to health can be a policy objective, along with revenue raising. Environmentally related taxes, although they are often not levied for environmental reasons alone, are effective instruments for pursuing environmental objectives (OECD 2015a). Health related taxes are also considered as an efficient means to achieve health outcomes and reduce health inequalities (see Chapter 4).

1.8. VAT and international trade – The destination principle

The overarching purpose of the VAT as a levy on final consumption coupled with its central design feature of a staged collection process lays the foundation for the core VAT principles bearing on international trade. The fundamental issue of economic policy in relation to the international application of the VAT is whether the levy should be imposed by the jurisdiction of origin or destination. Under the destination principle, the tax is fully levied on the final consumption that occurs within the taxing jurisdiction. Under the origin principle, the tax is levied in the various jurisdictions where the value is added. The key economic difference between the two principles is that the destination principle places all firms competing in a given jurisdiction on an even footing whereas the origin principle places consumers in different jurisdictions on an even footing.

The application of the destination principle in VAT achieves neutrality in international trade. Under the destination principle, exports are exempt with refund of input taxes (that is, free of VAT[2]) and imports are taxed on the same basis and at the same rates as domestic supplies. Accordingly, the total tax paid in relation to a supply is determined by the rules applicable in the jurisdiction of its consumption and therefore all revenue accrues to the jurisdiction where the supply to the final consumer occurs.

By contrast, under the origin principle each jurisdiction would levy the VAT on the value created within its own borders[3]. Under an origin-based regime, exporting jurisdictions would tax exports on the same basis and at the same rate as domestic supplies while importing jurisdictions would give a credit against their own VAT for the hypothetical tax that would have been paid at the importing jurisdiction's own rate. Tax paid on a supply would then reflect the pattern of its origins and the aggregate revenue would be distributed in that pattern. This would run counter to the core features of a VAT: as a tax on consumption, the revenue should accrue to the jurisdiction where the final consumption takes place. Under the origin principle these revenues are shared amongst jurisdictions where value is added. Moreover, by imposing tax at the various rates applicable in the countries where value is added, the origin principle could influence the economic or geographical structure of the value chain and undermine neutrality in international trade.

For these reasons, there is widespread consensus that the destination principle with revenue accruing to the country of import where final consumption occurs is preferable to the origin principle from both a theoretical and practical standpoint. In fact, the destination principle is the international norm. It is sanctioned by the World Trade Organisation rules and it is one of the key principles on which the OECD's *International VAT/GST Guidelines* are grounded.

Sales tax systems, although they work differently in practice, also set out to tax consumption of goods, and to some extent services, within the jurisdiction of consumption. Exported goods are usually relieved from sales tax to provide a degree of neutrality for cross-border trade. However, in most sales tax systems, businesses do incur some irrecoverable sales tax and, if they subsequently export goods, there will be an element of sales tax embedded in the price.

The application of the destination principle is not without its own difficulties. First, as already noted, the usual way of implementing this principle for VAT involves exemption of exports, which means that goods and services circulate free of tax in cross-border trade. The possibilities of fraud are evident. Second, although most of the rules currently in force are generally intended to tax supplies of goods and services within the jurisdiction where consumption takes place in application of the destination principle, practical means of implementing this intention are diverse across countries. This can, in some instances, lead to double taxation or unintended non-taxation and create uncertainties for both business and tax administrations. The adoption of the OECD International VAT/GST Guidelines responds to these challenges (see below).

Implementing the destination principle

While the destination principle has been widely accepted as the basis for applying VAT to international trade, its implementation is nevertheless diverse across jurisdictions. This can lead to double taxation or unintended non-taxation and to complexity and uncertainty for businesses and tax administrations.

In order to apply the destination principle, VAT systems must have a mechanism for identifying the destination of supplies. Because VAT is generally applied on a transaction-by-transaction basis, VAT systems contain "place of taxation" rules that address all transactions, building on "proxies" that indicate where the good or service supplied is expected to be used by a business in the production and distribution process (if the supply is made to a business) or consumed (if the supply is made to a final consumer).

The following paragraphs provide a concise overview of the mechanisms for identifying the destination of a supply, focusing on supplies of goods first and then on supplies of services.

Application of the destination principle to the cross-border trade in goods

The term "goods" generally means "tangible property" for VAT purposes. The VAT treatment of supplies of goods normally depends on the location of the goods at the time of the transaction and/or their location as a result of the transaction. The supply of a good is in principle subject to VAT in the jurisdiction where the good is located at the time of the transaction. When a transaction involves goods being moved from one jurisdiction to another, the exported goods are generally "free of VAT" in the origin's jurisdiction (and are freed of any input VAT via successive businesses' deductions of input tax), whilst imports are subject to the same VAT as equivalent domestic goods in the importing jurisdiction. The VAT on imports is generally collected at the same time as customs duties, although in some countries collection is postponed until declared on the importer's next VAT return. Deduction of the VAT incurred at importation, in the same way as input tax deduction on a domestic supply, ensures neutrality and limits distortions in relation to international trade.

Within the European Union, which abolished internal customs barriers and tax frontiers in 1993, the system of intra-Community delivery (free of VAT in the Member State of origin) and intra-Community acquisition (taxed in the Member State of destination) for business-to-business supplies allows the application of the destination principle even in the absence of customs procedures.

Many VAT systems apply an exemption for the importation of relatively low value goods. These exemptions are generally motivated by the consideration that the administrative costs of bringing these low value items into the customs and tax system would likely to outweigh the revenue gained. Most OECD countries currently apply such a VAT relief arrangement, with thresholds varying widely across countries, from USD 11 in Denmark to USD 671 in Australia (see Table 1.A1.7). However, 20 out of these countries belong to the EU where legislation[4] provides that Member States must exempt from VAT the import of goods whose value does not exceed EUR 10, and are permitted to grant an exemption for imported goods with a value of more than EUR 10 but not exceeding EUR 22. All EU Member States that are members of the OECD have opted for the higher threshold of EUR 22, except Denmark that applies the lower threshold of EUR 10. This exemption in the EU does not apply to tobacco or tobacco products and alcoholic products. EU Member States may also exclude from the low value import exemption goods imported on mail order (France and Poland make use of this option). Outside the EU, two OECD countries (Chile and Turkey) do not apply any threshold and tax all imports of goods regardless of their value.

The exemptions for low value imports have become increasingly controversial in the context of the growing digital economy. This was one of the findings of Action 1 of the OECD/G20 Base Erosion and Profit Shifting (BEPS) project, on *Addressing the Tax Challenges of the Digital Economy* (OECD 2015b). At the time when most low value import relief provisions were introduced, internet shopping did not exist and the level of imports benefitting from the relief was relatively small. In recent years, however, many countries have seen a significant and rapid growth in the volume of low value imports of physical goods from online sales on which VAT is not collected. This results in potentially unfair competitive pressures on domestic retailers who are required to charge VAT on their sales to domestic consumers and in decreased VAT revenues. It also creates an incentive for domestic suppliers to relocate to an offshore jurisdiction in order to sell their low value goods free of

VAT. The report on Addressing the Tax Challenges of the Digital Economy recognised that the difficulty lies in finding the balance between the need for appropriate revenue protection and avoidance of distortions of competition, which tend to favour a lower threshold, and the need to keep the cost of collection proportionate to the relatively small level of VAT collected, which favours a higher threshold. The report observed that tax authorities could be in a position to remove or lower the exemption threshold for imports of low value goods, if they were able to improve the efficiency of processing such low value imports and of collecting the VAT on such imports. The report then outlines and assesses the main available approaches for a more efficient collection of VAT on the import of low value goods, which may allow governments to reduce or remove the VAT exemption thresholds, should they decide to do so. The report explores models for collecting import VAT that would limit or remove the need for customs authorities to intervene in the VAT collection for imports that are not subject to customs duties (noting that most countries apply a de minimis threshold for customs duties, which is often higher than the VAT exemption threshold). This is expected to lower the cost of collection of VAT on low imports considerably. The report identifies four broad models for collecting VAT on low value imports: (1) the traditional collection model; (2) the purchaser collection model; (3) the vendor collection model; and (4) the intermediary collection model. The distinction between these collection models is essentially based on the person liable to account for the VAT. The traditional collection model is the model that is generally applied currently for the collection of duties and taxes at importation, and that is often combined with a VAT exemption for imports of low value goods. The three other models present possible alternative approaches, which essentially rely on specific parties involved in the supply chain for online sales to intervene in the collection and remittance of the import VAT. The report concludes that jurisdictions could opt for a combination of models. For instance, an optional vendor collection regime could be combined with the collection through intermediaries such as e-commerce platforms and express carriers (which may notably allow small and medium size businesses to comply more easily), whereby vendors as well as intermediaries could benefit from a simplified registration and compliance regime to facilitate compliance. Both approaches could be combined with further simplification arrangements, such as fast-track processing and/or a bulk-shipper scheme. To increase compliance, these approaches could be combined with a fall-back rule whereby VAT would be collected under the traditional collection processes, possibly from the final consumer. The report notes that any reform in this area would need to be complemented with appropriate risk assessment and enhanced international administrative co-operation between tax authorities to enforce compliance.

A number of OECD jurisdictions are currently considering the possible removal or limitation their VAT exemption thresholds and possible implementation approaches for a more efficient collection of import VAT as outlined in the report *Addressing the Tax Challenges of the Digital Economy* (OECD 2015b). Notably the Australian government has announced that, subject to the unanimous agreement of its States and Territories, the GST (i.e. VAT) will be collected from 1 July 2017 on low value physical goods imported by consumers under a vendor/platform registration model, where non-resident businesses with an Australian turnover of AUD 75 000 or more would be required to register and charge the tax (Australian Treasury 2016). The European Commission has also announced in a recent Communication (European Commission 2016a) its intention to propose legislation for extending its One Stop Shop vendor registration mechanism, for the collection of VAT on ttelecommunications, broadcasting and e-services, to the online sale of low value goods to final consumers.

VAT systems also generally exempt from VAT the imports of goods in the personal luggage of travellers. Although such an exemption applies in all OECD countries, differences exist on the applicable thresholds and conditions, except within the European Union where common rules apply. These differences are illustrated in Table 1.A1.13 showing the thresholds for tax-free import of goods in the luggage of individual travellers. Table 1.A1.13 also shows the thresholds for refunds of VAT on export to individual travellers.

Application of the destination principle to the cross-border trade in services and intangibles

The VAT legislation in many countries tends to define a "service" negatively as "anything that is not otherwise defined", or to define a "supply of services" as anything other than a "supply of goods". While this generally also includes a reference to intangibles, some jurisdictions regard intangibles as a separate category. For the purposes of this section references to "services" include "intangibles" unless otherwise stated.

A wide range of proxies can be used by VAT systems to identify the place of taxation of services, including the place of performance of the service, the place of establishment or actual location of the supplier, the residence or the actual location of the consumer, and the location of tangible property (for services connected with tangible property, such as repair services). Many systems use multiple proxies before the place of taxation is finally determined and may use different rules for inbound, outbound, wholly foreign, and wholly domestic supplies (Cockfield et al., 2013).

In the European Union, the determination of the "place of supply" (i.e. the place of taxation) depends on the status of the customer receiving the service and the nature of the service supplied. Supplies of services between businesses (B2B supplies) are in principle taxed at the customer's place of establishment (or at the fixed establishment of the customer to which it is provided), implementing the destination principle for both supplies within the EU and with customers in third countries. On the other hand, supplies of services to final consumers (B2C supplies) are still, in principle, taxed at the supplier's place of establishment. This latter rule does not reflect a will to apply the "origin principle" to B2C supplies but rather the historical reality that most services were consumed where they were provided and it was technically difficult to provide services at a distance to final consumers. There are, however, many exceptions aiming at aligning the place of taxation with the place where consumption is likely to take place. These exceptions include notably the services connected with immovable property (taxed where the property is located); services relating to cultural, artistic, sporting, scientific, educational, entertainment etc. (taxed at the place where they are physically carried out) and the B2C electronically supplied services, that are taxed where the customer resides (since 2003 for services provided by non-EU suppliers and since 2015 also for EU suppliers).

To facilitate compliance by non-EU suppliers, a web portal ("Mini One Stop Shop") was created, allowing these suppliers to register at a distance in only one Member State and account in this Member State for the VAT due in all the Member States of the EU where their customers are located.

Although the EU model for determining the place of supply applies to the 28 Member States of the Union and to a number of other countries such as Norway, Switzerland, and Russia, it is far from being the international norm. A number of countries (e.g. Australia, Canada, New Zealand, Singapore, South Africa) have adopted different models. While the EU model is based on an approach by category, where a "place of supply" (which is also the place of taxation) is determined for each category of supplies, according to their nature and the status (business or consumer) of the customer, other models systematically apply a series of proxies for place of consumption or use to all kinds of services. Such systems work in steps: first a connection with the country is established (e.g. the supplier or the customer are established there; the service is performed or can be acquired there). Then, a number of proxies are applied to determine the actual place of taxation, e.g. a connection with a tangible property; the customer location and/or residence; the location of the person to whom the services are delivered or who uses the service.

For example, in New Zealand (which adopted the GST in 1986) the place of taxation for supplies made by non-residents is generally presumed to be outside New Zealand, except when the service is performed in New Zealand or supplied to a customer who is resident in New Zealand and the recipient is either a final consumer or a registered business who has agreed to have the transaction treated as being made in New Zealand. In contrast, the place of taxation for supplies by residents is presumed to be New Zealand, unless the supply is a zero-rated export of services. These services include international transport and related services; services physically performed outside New Zealand; services supplied to a non-resident who is outside New Zealand at the time the services are performed; services directly in connection with land or goods located outside New Zealand and supplies in relation to intellectual property rights for use outside New Zealand. From 1 October 2016, New Zealand applies GST to supplies of services and intangibles made by non-resident suppliers to final consumers who are usually resident in New Zealand (see section below).

In Australia (which adopted GST in 2000), supplies are taxable (unless GST-free) in Australia and the GST collected through the supplier when the supplies are "connected with Australia". Supplies made through an Australian based business or performed in Australia for a final consumer are connected with Australia. To prevent GST applying to services not consumed or used in Australia, the Australian GST law includes broad, proxy-based zero-ratings ("GST-free") similar to those used in New Zealand. The Australian GST rules have been amended and from 1 July 2017 supplies of services and intangibles made by non-residents to final consumers who are residents of Australia will be connected with Australia and generally taxable unless the GST-free provisions apply (see Section below).

The different ways in which the VAT systems have attempted to bring consumption within the scope of the tax during the second half of the 20th century and the new interactions between national VAT systems have become increasingly problematic as volumes of cross-border trade in services and intangibles were growing. VAT systems have experienced considerable difficulties in determining where services are deemed to be consumed, to monitor these transactions and to ensure collection of the tax, particularly where businesses sell services in jurisdictions where they do not have a physical presence. In the absence of adjustment, from a government's viewpoint there is a risk of under-taxation and loss of revenue, or distorting trade through double taxation; from a business viewpoint, there are large revenue risks and high compliance costs.

The OECD developed the *International VAT/GST Guidelines* as the international standard for applying VAT to cross-border trade in services and intangibles, to minimise the risks of double taxation and unintended double non-taxation resulting from mismatches between national VAT systems.

The International VAT/GST Guidelines

The OECD released its completed *International VAT/GST Guidelines* in November 2015 at the occasion of the third meeting of its Global Forum on VAT, where these Guidelines were endorsed as the international standard for the application of VAT to the international trade in services and intangibles by over 100 countries, jurisdictions and international organisations (see the Statement of Outcomes in Annex B). These Guidelines were subsequently adopted as a Recommendation by the Council of the OECD in September 2016 (OECD 2016b), making this the first OECD legal instrument in the area of VAT (since the other OECD legal instruments in the area of taxation, such as the OECD Model Tax Convention and the Transfer Pricing Guidelines, relate essentially to the taxation of income).

The *International VAT/GST Guidelines* present a set of global standards and recommended approaches for the consistent VAT treatment of international transactions, focusing in particular on trade in services and intangibles. They build on the internationally agreed principles of VAT neutrality and the destination principle for determining the place of taxation

The OECD first developed international standards on consumption taxation in the context of electronic commerce, on the basis of the Ottawa Taxation Framework Conditions that were approved by OECD Ministers in 1998 (OECD, 1998). This work resulted in the Guidelines on Consumption Taxation of Cross-Border Services and Intangible Property in the Context of E-commerce (OECD, 2001). These E-commerce Guidelines provided that for business-to-business transactions, the place of consumption should be "the jurisdiction in which the recipient has located its business presence"; and for business-to-consumer transactions, the place of consumption should be "the jurisdiction in which the recipient has its usual place of residence". These Guidelines were complemented with three Consumption Tax Guidance Series (OECD, 2003), which looked at various aspects of the implementation of the E-commerce Guidelines in practice. This work has now been superseded by the *International VAT/GST Guidelines.*

The *International VAT/GST Guidelines* first present six guidelines on VAT neutrality (Chapter 2 of the Guidelines). The first three guidelines on neutrality (Guidelines 2.1 to 2.3) look at the basic neutrality principles, which are equally relevant in a domestic and an international context, while the next three guidelines set out additional principles for achieving neutrality in an international context (Guidelines 3.4 to 3.6). Guideline 2.1 sets out the basic principle that VAT should not be a burden on business. VAT should normally "flow through the business" to tax the final consumers. Two corollaries of Guideline 2.1 are that "businesses in similar situations carrying out similar transactions should be subject to similar levels of taxation" (Guideline 2.2) and that "VAT rules should be framed in such a way that they are not the primary influence on business decisions" (Guideline 2.3). Guideline 2.4 confirms that the neutrality principles set out in Guideline 2.1 to 2.3 apply equally to both domestic and foreign businesses. VAT systems should be designed and applied in such a way that there is no unfair competitive advantage for domestic businesses compared to foreign competitors. This means that domestic legislation should not discriminate against a foreign business when it comes to the right to deduct or recover input VAT. Guideline 3.5 provides that "to ensure foreign businesses do not incur irrecoverable VAT, governments may choose from a number of approaches". Guideline 2.6 finally recognises that dealing with foreign businesses with no legal presence in a jurisdiction inevitably brings an element of risk for tax administrations and that they may take specific measures to protect their tax base against evasion and avoidance. But where there is an element of additional compliance burden associated with doing business in a foreign jurisdiction, this should not be disproportionate or inappropriate when assessed against the additional risk involved in dealing with a foreign business.

The guidelines on neutrality are followed by a set of guidelines for determining the place of taxation of cross-border supplies of services and intangibles in accordance with the destination principle (Chapter 3). Guideline 3.1 provides that "for consumption tax purposes internationally traded services and intangibles should be taxed according to the rules of the jurisdiction of consumption". To achieve this, exports are zero rated (i.e. no tax is levied but the associated input tax is deductible according to the normal rules) and imports are taxed. Guideline 3.2 provides that, for business-to-business (B2B) supplies, the taxing rights should accrue to the jurisdiction where the customer is located. This is the jurisdiction where the business customer has located its permanent business presence (for single location entities) or where the customer's establishment(s) using the service or intangible is (are) located (for businesses that are established in more than one jurisdiction – multiple location entities). For business-to-consumer (B2C) supplies, the Guidelines recommend that the taxing rights over "on-the-spot supplies" (e.g. restaurant services) be allocated to the jurisdiction in which the supply is physically performed; and that the taxing rights over all other supplies and services (including digital supplies) be allocated to the jurisdiction in which the customer has its usual residence. The Guidelines also provide guidance on the circumstances in which the implementation of a proxy other than the place customer's location or physical performance might be justified (Guideline 3.7). For supplies of services directly connected with a specific immovable property, they recommend to allocate the taxing rights to the jurisdiction where the immovable property is located (Guideline 3.8).

The Guidelines also provide recommended approaches for collecting the VAT on cross-border supplies. For B2B supplies, they recommend the application of the reverse charge mechanism, where this is compatible with the design of the local legislation. For B2C supplies the Guidelines recommend that non-resident suppliers be required to register and remit the VAT in the jurisdiction of taxation and suggest that countries implement a simplified registration and compliance regime to facilitate compliance for non-resident suppliers. They present the key features of such a simplified registration and compliance regime. The Guidelines do not recommend jurisdictions to make a distinction between B2B and B2C supplies, but provide guidance for their application where this distinction is made.

Table 1.A1.11 presents a broad overview of the approaches adopted by OECD countries for collecting VAT on cross-border supplies of services and intangibles from foreign suppliers (i.e. on "inbound supplies"). This overview shows that the EU framework determines the place of taxation for cross-border supplies of services and intangibles (i.e. transactions with non-EU Member States) in principle by reference to the customer's location (B2B) and to the customer's usual residence (B2C). The VAT on inbound supplies is collected through a reverse charge mechanism, for B2B supplies, and through a simplified vendor registration and compliance regime ("Mini One Stop Shop") for B2C supplies of telecommunication, broadcasting and electronic services. This regime is operated by the 22 OECD member countries that belong to the EU (Austria, Belgium, Czech Republic, Denmark, Estonia, Finland, France, Germany, Greece, Hungary, Ireland, Italy, Latvia, Luxembourg, Netherlands, Poland, Portugal, Slovak Republic, Slovenia, Spain, Sweden and the United Kingdom) Eight other OECD countries use the customer location (usual residence, head office, etc.) as the main proxy for determining the place of taxation for cross-border supplies of services and intangibles (Canada, Iceland, Israel, Japan, Korea, New Zealand, Norway and Switzerland) and three countries (Australia, Mexico and Turkey) apply other proxies, such as place of performance or place of effective use and enjoyment. Australia, has announced the implementation of new GST rules on 1 July 2017 according to which the place of taxation for inbound B2C supplies of services will be determined in accordance with the customer's usual residence and a simplified registration and compliance regime will be available for foreign suppliers to remit the GST on such supplies.

Most OECD countries apply a reverse charge mechanism to collect VAT on inbound B2B supplies of services and intangibles. In Australia, Canada and New Zealand this mechanism only applies when the customer has a limited right to deduct the input tax, and no tax is due when the customer has a full right to deduction. In Switzerland, the application of the reverse charge mechanism is limited to situations where the place of taxation is determined according to the customer's residence proxy. When the supply is taxed in Switzerland according to other proxies (e.g. the location of the immovable property to which the supply is connected), the reverse charge mechanism does not apply and the supplier must register and account for VAT. In addition, foreign suppliers that are registered in the Switzerland to account for VAT on their B2C supplies must also account for their B2B supplies under their local registration and the reverse charge does not apply. In Korea, inbound B2B supplies are considered out of scope and no VAT is due on such supplies. In Iceland, inbound supplies of services are VAT exempt if the customer has a full right to deduction; where this is not the case the supplier must register for VAT in the country

For B2C supplies, many OECD countries (28 of 35 countries i.e. the 22 EU Member States, Iceland, Japan, Korea, New Zealand, Norway and Switzerland) require the foreign supplier to register and account for VAT in the jurisdiction where the customer is located. A simplified registration and collection regime (without right to deduct input taxes in the taxing jurisdiction – "pay-only registration") applies in the vast majority of these countries (the option of standard registration is also available in most of these countries). Only two countries (Switzerland and Iceland) require the supplier to register under the standard regime (with the right to deduct the input tax incurred in the country). Japan and Switzerland require the supplier to appoint a tax agent in the country to account for VAT. Five countries (Canada, Chile, Israel, Mexico and Turkey) operate a self-assessment regime that requires the private customer to remit the VAT on services and intangibles acquired from foreign suppliers and Australia currently does not tax inbound B2C supplies of services, but has announced its plan to introduce a simplified "pay-only" supplier registration to tax B2C supplies. Israel also intends to amend its VAT law to require non-resident suppliers of digital B2C services to register for VAT in Israel under a simplified registration procedure.

Five among the countries requiring foreign suppliers to register to account for VAT on their B2C supplies (Iceland, Japan, New Zealand, Norway and Switzerland) do not impose such requirement when the turnover of the suppliers in the country is below a certain threshold. In these five countries the same threshold applies for both domestic and foreign suppliers. These thresholds vary between USD 5000 (Norway) and USD 100 000 (Switzerland).

1.9. Tackling the VAT compliance gap

Losses of VAT revenue from non-compliance can be caused by a number of factors. In addition to "traditional" VAT avoidance (i.e. arrangements intended to reduce the tax liability that could be strictly legal but in contradiction with the intent of the law) and evasion (illegal arrangements where liability to tax is ignored or hidden) there has been a significant and worrying trend in recent years of increasing criminal attacks on the VAT system. The most common type of organised VAT fraud is the "missing trader" or "carousel" fraud. It arises when a business makes a purchase without paying VAT (typically a transaction for which tax self-assessment applies), then collects VAT on an onward supply and disappears without remitting the VAT collected. Originally, the fraud developed with high-value goods sold across borders, such as computer chips and cell phones but it expanded to services that can be bought and sold like goods. For instance, the development of markets for trading CO^2 emission allowances has created opportunities for organised crime. Using the weaknesses in the market registration procedures and the zero-rating of cross-border supplies followed by taxed transactions in domestic markets, fraudulent traders have caused billions of Euros of tax losses in some countries. Europol estimated that in some countries, up to 90% of the whole CO^2 allowances market volume was fraudulent (Europol, 2009). The fraud also developed on the energy markets In 2014, a joint statement from the European energy regulators, energy trading firms and gas and electricity operators warned tax authorities about the very serious danger of VAT fraud for the functioning of Europe's gas and electricity markets, reporting signs of "a major penetration of the gas and electricity markets by VAT fraudsters". There are also some indications that new types of acquisition fraud have developed in the telecommunication market (Voice over the Internet Protocol; VoIP) and recent research showed that a large number of accounting software products contained hidden tools (zappers) for manipulation of VAT receipts (OECD, 2013). In addition to the revenue losses, VAT criminal fraud is often connected with other criminal activities such as terrorism and money laundering.

Reducing the revenue losses from VAT non-compliance remains a key challenge and a priority for countries around the world. An increasing number of tax administrations carry out research to estimate the VAT compliance gap, i.e. the revenue loss due to fraud and evasion, tax avoidance, bankruptcies, financial insolvencies, miscalculations, etc. The EU's updated VAT gap estimates for 2016 (CASE 2016) suggest that this gap amounted to EUR 159.5bn in the EU in 2014, i.e. a loss of VAT revenue of 14.06%. The smallest gaps were observed in Sweden (1.24%), Luxembourg (3.80%) and Finland (6.92%), and the largest gaps were registered in Romania (37.89%), Lithuania (35.94%) and Malta (35.32%). Although these figures should not be directly associated with fraud and evasion as they also include the effects of simple (statistical or reporting) errors as well as insolvencies and payment problems, they provide some illustration of the problem that VAT fraud still represents in the EU (European Commission 2014a). The United Kingdom estimated its VAT gap at GBP 13.1 billion in 2013-14, i.e. 11.1% of the estimated net VAT total theoretical liability (HM Revenue & Customs 2015). This estimate includes GBP 1 billion for the missing Trader Intra-Community fraud (i.e. carrousel fraud) alone although there is a downward trend in this fraud from GBP 3.5 billion in 2005-06. According to figures published by the Australian Taxation Office in 2015, the Australian GST gap for 2013-14 is at AUD 2.7 billion or 4.9% of revenue (ATO 2015).

In response, governments are increasingly developing strategies to counter the losses. The European Commission recently issued a VAT reform package (European Commission 2016a) and a set of 20 measures to tackle this gap, including extending the automated access to data; reinforcing administrative co-operation within the European Union; developing anti-fraud tools to combat VAT fraud in the e-commerce sector and building synergies with third countries and with the OECD to "establish an international system of administrative cooperation" (European Commission 2016b).

One countermeasure is the adoption of a reverse charge mechanism for collecting the VAT in relation to domestic B2B supplies of certain goods and services susceptible to fraud i.e. mobile phones, integrated circuit devices, gas and electricity, telecom services, game consoles, tablet PCs and laptops, cereals and industrial crops and raw and semi-finished metals. Since 2013 EU Member States, after the authorisation of the European Council, are allowed to apply the reverse charge to any kind of supply in case of sudden and massive VAT fraud. Member States can also apply, on an optional and temporary basis, a domestic reverse charge mechanism to a determined list of supplies.

This reverse charge mechanism shifts the liability to pay the VAT from the supplier to the customer. If he is a normal taxable business, the customer will deduct the VAT due on the supplies as input tax, and no net tax will be payable on the transactions covered. In this mechanism, no taxpayer can claim a credit for input VAT without being liable for its payment, thus removing the scope for fraudsters to disappear with the VAT without paying it and/or to claim an input tax credit for input VAT that was not remitted to the tax authorities earlier in the distribution chain. It is recognised, however, that the implementation of a domestic reverse-charge mechanism needs to be considered with care. One concern is that it would transform the VAT into a sales tax with the inherent weaknesses of such a system if applied too extensively.

Table 1.A1.12 shows that the use of domestic reverse charge as a means to combat fraud is widely used in the 22 OECD countries that are Member States of the EU. They all use it to some extent, in particular for the supply of CO_2 emission certificates (all except Latvia); scrap materials and waste (all except Belgium, Luxembourg and the United Kingdom); and construction work (all except Estonia, Luxembourg, Poland and the United Kingdom). The domestic reverse charge also applies to the supply of gold (14 countries on 22); electronic devices such as laptops, chips, cell phones etc. (11 countries on 22) and the supply of gas and electricity to taxable dealers (7 countries on 22). Certain other OECD countries do use that mechanism but to a much lesser extent i.e. Canada (supplies of real property by non-residents and some supplies between provinces); Chile (supplies of rice, construction works, waste and certain plants and animals); Israel (metal debris); Mexico (waste, some supplies made by individuals); New Zealand (supplies of land incorrectly zero rated); Norway (supply of CO_2 emission allowances and investment gold) and Turkey (some supplies made by non-taxable persons). By contrast this mechanism in not in use in Australia, Japan Korea and Switzerland.

Another means of combatting (domestic) VAT fraud is the use of a so-called *split payment mechanism* (or *withholding tax*) whereby the supplier remains liable to charge the VAT on its domestic supplies to the customer, but where the customer directly remits (part of) the VAT directly to the tax authorities rather than to the supplier. In practice, such a system has the same effects as a domestic reverse charge mechanism (requiring the customer to pay the VAT rather than the supplier) when the customer is liable to pay the full VAT amount, but with some legal differences in terms of invoicing and liability. According to Table 1.A1.12, this system is used in Italy for the supplies of goods and services made to public authorities; in Korea for the supply of gold, copper and iron; and in the Czech Republic to allow the customer to avoid the joint and several liability with the supplier.

There is also a growing recognition that effective strategies to tackle VAT fraud and evasion require strongly enhanced international co-operation in tax administration and enforcement between tax authorities in the field of indirect taxes. The criminal attacks against the VAT system are not limited to the European Union and there is growing consensus among tax authorities worldwide that international co-operation is needed in this area (OECD 2015b; European Commission, 2014b and European Court of Auditors, 2016). A number of instruments already exist that provide the legal foundation for such an international administrative co-operation including the Multilateral Convention on Mutual Administrative Assistance in Tax Matters, the bilateral treaties implementing the current Articles 26 and 27 of the OECD and UN Model Tax Conventions, the Tax Information Exchange Agreements (TIEAs) based on the OECD Model Agreement and regional agreements such as the European Union Directives, the Nordic Mutual Assistance Convention on Mutual Administrative Assistance in Tax Matters, the CIAT Model Agreement on the Exchange of Tax Information, and the African Tax Administration Forum Agreement on Mutual Assistance in Tax Matters.

Amongst these instruments, the *Multilateral Convention on Mutual Administrative Assistance in Tax Matters* (the Convention) is considered the most promising. The Convention was developed jointly by the Council of Europe and the OECD and opened for signature by the member states of both organisations in 1988. It was aligned to the internationally agreed standard on transparency and exchange of information and opened to all countries in 2011. It provides for all possible forms of administrative co-operation between the Parties in the assessment and collection of taxes, in particular with a view to combating tax avoidance and evasion. The Convention has a very wide scope and covers all forms of compulsory payments to general governments (i.e. the central government and its political subdivisions) including VAT (although the obligations set forth in the Convention are subject to any reservations by the Parties). As of 25 August 2016, 103 jurisdictions participate in the Convention. A multilateral instrument is likely to offer the most efficient solution for the development of the actual administrative co-operation on VAT given its key advantages: it provides for all forms of administrative co-operation in the VAT area, including on demand, spontaneous and automatic exchange of information, it has potentially a global reach and adjustments and updates are easier to implement in practice. The regional frameworks and bilateral agreements clearly also have a role to play since the legal instruments for administrative co-operation are not exclusive from each other and can be used in parallel.

Notes

1. For ease of reading, all value added taxes will be referred to as VAT in this chapter.
2. "Free of VAT" may be termed zero-rated, exempt with credit, or some other local terminology depending on the jurisdiction. Whatever the description used, the effect should be the same – no VAT is added by the supplier but the supplier is entitled to input tax credits, to the extent that the jurisdiction allows, in respect of such supplies.
3. This should be distinguished from the term used in the EU for a proposed system (that was never implemented) in which the VAT would have been collected by the Member State of origin and the revenue later channelled to the Member State of destination for transactions within the EU.
4. Article 143 paragraph 1 b) of Directive 2006/112/EC of 28 November 2006 in connection with Article 23 of Directive 2009/132/EC of 19 October 2009 (formerly article 22 of Directive 83/181/EEC of 28 March 1983).

References

ATO (2015), *Measuring tax gaps in Australia 2014-15*, Australian Taxation Office, November 2015. *www.ato.gov.au/About-ATO/Research-and-statistics/In-detail/Tax-gap/Measuring-tax-gaps-in-Australia, 2014-15.*

Australian Treasury (2016), *Budget Paper No. 2*, Budget 2016-17, 3 May 2016.

CASE (2016), *Study and Reports on the VAT Gap in the EU 28 Member States: 2016 Final Report*, Institute for Advances Studies, Warsaw, August 2016.

Cockfield, A. et al. (2013), *Taxing Global Digital Commerce*, Kluwer, Netherlands.

Ebrill, L. et al. (2001), *The Modern VAT*, International Monetary Fund, Washington DC.

European Commission (2016a), *Communication from the Commission to the European Parliament, the Council and the European Economic and Social Committee on an action plan on VAT – towards a single EU VAT area*, COM(2016) 148 final, Brussels.

European Commission (2016b), *20 measures to tackle the VAT gap*, ec.europa.eu/taxation_customs.

European Commission (2014a), *Report from the Commission to the Council and the European Parliament*, COM(2014)71 final, Brussels.

European Commission (2014b), *Tackling tax fraud: Commission proposes stronger cooperation with non-EU countries on VAT*, Press Communiqué IP/14/121, Brussels.

European Court of Auditors (2015), *Tackling intra-Community VAT fraud: More action needed, Luxembourg.*

EUROPOL (2009), Press Communiqué of 9 December 2009, The Hague, (*www.europol.europa.eu/content/press/carbon-credit-fraud-causes-more-5-billion-euros-damage-european-taxpayer-1265*).

Hellerstein, W. (2003), *Jurisdiction to Tax Income and Consumption in the New Economy: A Theoretical and Comparative Perspective*, Georgia Law REView 1, 28 2003.

Hellerstein, J., W. Hellerstein and J. Swain (2016), *State Taxation*, 3d ed., Thomson Reuters Tax & Accounting, Carrollton, TX.

HM Revenue and Customs (2015), *Measuring tax gaps*, London.

Keen, M. and W. Hellerstein, (2010), "Interjurisdictional issues in the design of a VAT", *Tax Law Review*, Vol. 63, No. 2, New York University, New York.

Millar, R. (2016), *Looking Ahead: Potential Solutions and the Framework to Make Them Work,*

Legal Studies Research Paper No. 16/30, Sydney Law School, April 2016.

Millar, R. (2007), "Cross-border services – A survey of the Issues", in *GST in Retrospect and Prospect*, Thompson, Wellington.

OECD (2016a), *Revenue Statistics 2016, OECD Publishing, Paris*, DOI: *http://dx.doi.org/10.1787/rev_stats-2016-en-fr.*

OECD (2016b), *Recommendation of the Council on the application of value added tax/goods and services tax to the international trade in services and intangibles*, C(2016)120, *http://webnet.oecd.org/oecdacts/.*

OECD (2015a), *Taxing Energy Use*, OECD Publishing, Paris, *http://dx.doi.org/10.1787/9789264232334-en.*

OECD (2015b), *Addressing the Tax Challenges of the Digital Economy*, Action 1 2015 Final Report, OECD Publishing, Paris, *http://dx.doi.org/10.1787/9789264218789-en.*

OECD (2013b), *Electronic Sales Suppression: a Threat to Tax Revenues*, OECD, Paris, *www.oecd.org/ctp/crime/ElectronicSalesSuppression.pdf.*

OECD (2011), *Environmental Taxation – A Guide for Policy Makers*, OECD, Paris. *http://dx.doi.org/10.1787/9789264087637-en.*

OECD (2010), *Taxation, Innovation and the Environment*, OECD Publishing, Paris, *http://dx.doi.org/10.1787/9789264087637-en.*

OECD (2003), Consumption Tax Guidance Series, *www.oecd.org/tax/consumption/consumptiontaxguidanceseries.htm*

OECD (2001), Consumption Taxation of Cross-Border Services and Intangible Property in the Context of E-Commerce *www.oecd.org/ctp/consumption/5594831.pdf.*

OECD (1998), *"A Borderless World: Realising the Potential of Electronic Commerce"*, Report by the Committee on Fiscal Affairs presented to Ministers at the OECD Ministerial Conference on 8 October 1998. *https://www.oecd.org/ctp/consumption/1923256.pdf.*

OECD Glossary of Tax Terms, *www.oecd.org/ctp/glossaryoftaxterms.htm.*

Tait, A. (1988), *Value added tax, international practice and problems*, International Monetary Fund, Washington.

Tax Foundation (2016), *States and Local Tax Rates in 2016*, Washington.

ANNEX 1.A1

Data on taxing consumption

Table 1.A1.1. **Consumption taxes (5100) as percentage of GDP**

	1965	1975	1985	1995	2000	2005	2010	2011	2012	2013	2014	Difference 2010-14
Australia	6.2	6.6	7.9	6.5	8.0	7.6	6.5	6.3	6.4	6.5	6.5	-0.0
Austria	12.3	12.3	12.6	11.2	11.4	11.1	10.8	10.9	11.1	11.0	10.9	0.1
Belgium	10.4	10.1	10.3	10.0	10.1	10.1	10.1	10.0	10.4	10.3	10.1	0.0
Canada	8.7	8.2	8.3	8.3	7.9	7.6	6.9	6.8	6.8	6.7	6.7	-0.1
Chile				11.0	11.4	10.1	9.5	9.9	10.1	10.1	10.3	0.8
Czech Republic				10.3	9.5	10.0	10.2	10.6	10.8	11.1	10.3	0.1
Denmark	11.5	12.1	14.9	14.6	14.7	15.1	13.9	14.0	14.0	13.9	13.8	-0.1
Estonia				12.4	11.7	12.0	13.0	12.8	13.0	12.6	13.0	0.0
Finland	12.6	11.4	13.1	13.3	13.0	12.9	12.6	13.4	13.7	14.0	13.9	1.3
France	12.6	11.3	12.0	11.2	10.8	10.6	10.1	10.4	10.5	10.5	10.7	0.5
Germany	9.8	8.7	8.9	9.8	9.8	9.5	10.0	10.0	9.9	9.8	9.8	-0.2
Greece	7.5	7.9	9.8	10.9	11.0	9.9	11.2	12.0	12.1	12.7	14.3	3.1
Hungary				16.5	15.4	14.2	15.7	15.5	16.6	16.3	16.4	0.7
Iceland	15.7	18.2	16.4	13.9	14.3	15.0	11.1	11.3	11.8	11.5	11.5	0.4
Ireland	12.0	12.4	14.3	12.2	11.2	10.6	9.0	8.5	8.6	8.6	8.8	-0.2
Israel				12.3	10.7	11.0	11.2	11.1	10.7	11.0	11.5	0.3
Italy	9.1	6.9	7.7	9.6	10.1	9.3	9.9	10.1	10.4	10.1	10.4	0.6
Japan	4.4	3.1	3.2	3.6	4.5	4.7	4.6	4.7	4.8	4.8	5.8	1.2
Korea		8.9	9.2	7.4	7.9	7.5	7.6	7.1	7.2	7.0	6.9	-0.7
Latvia				11.2	10.8	11.1	10.5	10.4	10.6	10.8	11.1	0.6
Luxembourg	6.2	6.5	9.1	8.8	9.7	10.8	10.2	10.4	10.8	10.6	10.9	0.7
Mexico			9.8	4.3	5.1	4.3	4.8	4.5	4.6	4.3	5.0	0.2
Netherlands	8.4	8.6	9.3	9.7	9.7	10.1	9.9	9.6	9.5	9.7	9.8	-0.1
New Zealand	6.1	6.3	6.5	11.1	10.5	10.8	11.2	11.3	11.5	11.2	11.7	0.5
Norway	11.7	14.2	15.2	14.7	12.3	11.1	11.0	10.6	10.4	10.5	10.5	-0.5
Poland				13.4	11.4	12.2	11.9	12.1	11.3	11.2	11.2	-0.7
Portugal	6.9	7.6	10.2	12.3	12.2	13.2	11.8	12.4	12.4	12.0	12.4	0.6
Slovak Republic				13.2	11.5	11.5	9.3	9.7	9.1	9.6	9.7	0.5
Slovenia				14.6	13.1	12.5	13.2	13.1	13.5	13.9	13.8	0.6
Spain	5.8	4.3	7.4	8.2	9.1	9.2	7.8	7.6	8.1	8.8	9.1	1.3
Sweden	9.3	8.8	11.4	12.6	11.8	11.8	12.2	11.9	11.9	11.8	11.7	-0.5
Switzerland	5.3	4.6	4.8	5.0	5.5	5.4	5.3	5.3	5.3	5.3	5.3	-0.0
Turkey	5.6	4.9	4.1	6.2	9.8	11.5	12.0	12.1	11.9	13.0	12.2	0.2
United Kingdom	9.1	8.1	10.4	10.0	10.0	9.5	9.6	10.4	10.4	10.3	10.3	0.7
United States	4.7	4.2	4.0	4.2	3.9	3.8	3.6	3.7	3.7	3.8	3.8	0.2
Unweighted average												
OECD-Average	**8.8**	**8.6**	**9.7**	**10.4**	**10.3**	**10.2**	**9.9**	**10.0**	**10.1**	**10.2**	**10.3**	**0.3**

Israel: The statistical data for Israel are supplied by and under the responsibility of the relevant Israeli authorities. The use of such data by the OECD is without prejudice to the status of the Golan Heights, East Jerusalem and Israeli settlements in the West Bank under the terms of international law.

Unweighted averages: All member counties are taken into account for the calculation of the unweighted averages, including countries that had not implemented the relevant taxes for the year considered. They are counted with a value of zero in the numerator and 1 in the denominator. However, countries that did not exist at the time considered (Czech and Slovak Republics before 1993; Slovenia before 1991) are not included in the calculation of the averages. Are also excluded from the calculation of the averages the countries for which no data is available for the time considered (Chile before 1990, Estonia, Hungary and Israel before 1995, Korea before 1975; Mexico before 1980; Poland before 1995; and Slovak Republic before 2000).

Source: Revenue Statistics 2016, OECD Publishing, Paris DOI: *http://dx.doi.org/10.1787/rev_stats-2016-en-fr*

StatLink *http://dx.doi.org/10.1787/888933419981*

Table 1.A1.2. **Consumption taxes (5100) as percentage of total taxation**

	1965	1975	1985	1995	2000	2005	2010	2011	2012	2013	2014	Difference 2010-14
Australia	30.0	25.8	28.6	23.1	26.2	25.4	25.5	24.1	23.3	23.7	23.3	-2.2
Austria	36.6	33.9	31.0	27.3	27.1	27.0	26.5	26.7	26.5	25.8	25.4	-1.0
Belgium	34.1	26.0	23.7	23.5	23.1	23.3	23.8	23.2	23.6	22.8	22.5	-1.2
Canada	34.7	26.0	26.1	23.9	22.8	23.7	22.5	22.3	22.0	21.6	21.6	-0.9
Chile				59.8	60.6	48.7	48.2	46.4	47.1	50.7	51.9	3.7
Czech Republic				29.6	29.3	29.0	31.2	31.8	32.0	32.5	31.2	-0.1
Denmark	39.6	32.7	34.0	31.3	31.4	31.4	30.8	31.0	30.6	29.8	27.8	-3.0
Estonia				34.5	37.7	40.0	39.1	40.6	41.4	40.1	40.2	1.1
Finland	41.9	31.6	33.4	29.9	28.3	30.6	30.8	31.9	32.1	32.1	31.7	0.9
France	37.5	32.4	28.7	26.8	25.2	24.8	24.2	24.0	23.7	23.3	23.4	-0.7
Germany	31.1	25.4	24.6	26.9	27.1	27.9	28.4	28.1	27.4	27.0	26.7	-1.8
Greece	44.1	42.2	40.0	39.4	33.0	31.9	34.8	35.7	34.2	35.7	39.9	5.1
Hungary				40.3	39.9	38.8	41.8	42.6	42.9	42.9	42.9	1.2
Iceland	61.7	62.2	59.5	45.7	39.5	37.8	33.1	32.9	33.3	31.8	29.5	-3.6
Ireland	49.1	44.4	42.6	38.4	36.5	36.2	33.3	31.4	31.4	30.6	30.7	-2.6
Israel				34.7	30.8	32.9	36.7	36.2	36.1	35.9	36.7	0.1
Italy	37.0	28.3	23.6	25.0	25.0	23.8	23.6	24.0	23.6	23.1	23.9	0.3
Japan	25.0	15.1	12.1	13.8	17.0	17.2	16.7	16.5	16.2	15.9	18.2	1.5
Korea		60.0	58.5	38.6	36.7	33.3	32.6	29.2	29.2	28.8	28.1	-4.6
Latvia				37.6	37.0	39.7	37.4	37.3	37.4	38.0	38.4	1.0
Luxembourg	23.5	20.6	24.1	25.2	26.0	28.4	26.8	27.5	27.9	27.7	28.3	1.5
Mexico			64.5	38.1	37.2	33.8	33.7	32.3	33.2	29.6	32.8	-0.9
Netherlands	27.1	22.5	23.4	25.6	26.1	28.6	27.4	26.7	26.5	26.5	26.2	-1.2
New Zealand	26.2	22.8	22.0	31.3	32.4	30.0	37.1	37.3	35.9	35.9	36.0	-1.1
Norway	39.9	36.6	36.4	36.7	29.4	26.1	26.2	25.1	25.1	26.2	27.2	1.0
Poland				35.5	34.5	36.8	38.3	38.2	35.4	35.3	35.0	-3.3
Portugal	44.0	40.1	42.3	42.1	39.2	42.7	38.8	38.3	39.1	35.3	36.3	-2.5
Slovak Republic				33.4	34.1	36.6	33.1	33.9	32.2	31.5	31.2	-1.9
Slovenia				37.9	35.8	33.1	35.7	36.0	36.6	37.9	37.8	2.1
Spain	40.6	24.0	27.6	26.1	27.2	26.0	24.8	24.2	24.9	26.4	26.8	2.0
Sweden	29.5	22.7	25.5	27.7	24.1	25.3	28.3	28.1	27.9	27.5	27.4	-0.9
Switzerland	31.9	20.6	20.2	19.6	20.1	20.5	20.0	19.6	19.9	19.8	19.4	-0.6
Turkey	53.5	40.9	35.7	37.1	40.6	47.4	45.8	43.5	43.2	44.3	42.4	-3.4
United Kingdom	31.1	23.7	29.7	33.5	30.5	29.1	29.5	31.3	31.7	31.7	32.0	2.5
United States	19.9	17.1	16.3	15.7	13.9	14.8	15.4	15.5	15.4	14.8	14.7	-0.7
Unweighted average												
OECD-Average	**36.2**	**31.1**	**32.1**	**31.9**	**31.0**	**30.9**	**30.9**	**30.7**	**30.5**	**30.4**	**30.5**	**-0.4**

Israel: The statistical data for Israel are supplied by and under the responsibility of the relevant Israeli authorities. The use of such data by the OECD is without prejudice to the status of the Golan Heights, East Jerusalem and Israeli settlements in the West Bank under the terms of international law.

Unweighted averages: All member counties are taken into account for the calculation of the unweighted averages, including countries that had not implemented the relevant taxes for the year considered. They are counted with a value of zero in the numerator and 1 in the denominator. However, countries that did not exist at the time considered (Czech and Slovak Republics before 1993; Slovenia before 1991) are not included in the calculation of the averages. Are also excluded from the calculation of the averages the countries for which no data is available for the time considered (Chile before 1990, Estonia, Hungary and Israel before 1995, Korea before 1975; Mexico before 1980; Poland before 1995; and Slovak Republic before 2000).

Source: Revenue Statistics 2016, OECD Publishing, Paris DOI: *http://dx.doi.org/10.1787/rev_stats-2016-en-fr*.

StatLink *http://dx.doi.org/10.1787/888933419993*

Table 1.A1.3. **Taxes on general consumption (5110) as percentage of GDP**

	1965	1975	1985	1995	2000	2005	2010	2011	2012	2013	2014	Difference 2010-14
Australia	1.5	1.7	2.2	2.5	3.7	4.0	3.5	3.4	3.4	3.6	3.6	0.1
Austria	6.3	7.2	8.5	7.6	7.9	7.7	7.7	7.6	7.8	7.7	7.7	-0.0
Belgium	6.5	6.3	6.8	6.5	7.1	7.0	7.0	6.9	7.0	7.0	6.9	-0.1
Canada	4.5	3.9	4.2	4.9	4.9	4.8	4.3	4.3	4.3	4.3	4.3	0.0
Chile				7.5	7.9	7.8	7.6	7.9	8.1	8.1	8.2	0.7
Czech Republic				5.8	6.0	6.6	6.7	6.9	7.0	7.4	7.4	0.7
Denmark	3.0	6.5	9.1	9.1	9.2	9.7	9.5	9.6	9.6	9.4	9.5	0.0
Estonia				9.6	8.4	8.1	8.6	8.3	8.4	8.2	8.6	-0.0
Finland	5.5	5.6	7.2	7.7	8.0	8.4	8.3	8.8	9.0	9.3	9.2	0.9
France	7.8	8.2	8.4	7.4	7.4	7.4	7.0	7.1	7.1	7.1	7.2	0.1
Germany	5.2	5.0	5.7	6.3	6.7	6.1	7.0	7.0	7.0	7.0	7.0	-0.0
Greece	1.8	3.4	4.2	6.4	7.2	6.9	7.4	7.6	7.5	7.4	7.5	0.1
Hungary				8.0	10.1	10.3	11.1	10.9	11.7	11.4	11.6	0.5
Iceland	4.3	8.4	9.1	9.7	10.4	10.8	7.6	7.7	8.0	8.0	8.1	0.5
Ireland	1.4	4.1	6.9	6.7	7.1	7.3	6.0	5.6	5.8	5.8	6.0	-0.1
Israel				10.8	9.2	9.3	9.1	9.1	8.8	9.2	9.7	0.5
Italy	3.2	3.5	4.7	5.3	6.3	5.7	6.1	6.0	6.0	5.9	6.0	-0.1
Japan	0.0	0.0	0.0	1.4	2.4	2.6	2.6	2.7	2.7	2.8	3.9	1.3
Korea		1.9	3.3	3.4	3.7	3.9	4.1	4.1	4.3	4.1	4.2	0.1
Latvia				8.4	7.0	7.4	6.7	6.8	7.2	7.4	7.7	1.0
Luxembourg	3.3	3.8	4.8	4.3	5.0	6.1	6.5	6.7	7.2	7.2	7.5	1.1
Mexico			2.4	2.5	3.1	3.4	3.8	3.7	3.7	3.5	3.9	0.1
Netherlands	3.8	5.5	6.4	6.1	6.4	6.8	6.8	6.5	6.5	6.5	6.4	-0.3
New Zealand	1.8	2.5	3.1	8.1	8.1	8.6	9.3	9.4	9.6	9.4	9.7	0.4
Norway	6.3	8.0	7.6	8.5	8.3	7.7	7.8	7.6	7.6	7.7	7.8	-0.0
Poland				6.1	6.9	7.7	7.6	7.8	7.1	7.0	7.1	-0.5
Portugal	..	2.1	3.0	6.8	7.6	8.2	7.5	8.1	8.3	8.1	8.5	0.9
Slovak Republic				8.2	6.9	7.7	6.2	6.7	6.0	6.4	6.6	0.4
Slovenia				11.3	8.7	8.4	8.1	8.1	8.0	8.5	8.5	0.4
Spain	3.2	2.7	4.0	5.0	5.9	6.2	5.3	5.2	5.4	5.9	6.1	0.9
Sweden	3.3	4.7	6.3	8.8	8.4	8.6	9.3	9.2	9.0	9.1	9.1	-0.2
Switzerland	1.8	2.0	2.6	3.1	3.7	3.6	3.4	3.5	3.6	3.6	3.5	0.1
Turkey	..	..	2.7	5.2	5.8	5.3	5.7	6.1	5.8	6.4	5.9	0.2
United Kingdom	1.7	3.0	5.6	5.7	5.9	6.0	6.1	6.8	6.8	6.8	6.8	0.7
United States	1.1	1.7	1.9	2.1	2.2	2.1	2.0	2.0	2.0	2.0	2.0	0.1
Unweighted average												
OECD-Average	**3.2**	**4.1**	**5.0**	**6.5**	**6.7**	**6.8**	**6.7**	**6.7**	**6.8**	**6.8**	**7.0**	**0.3**

Israel: The statistical data for Israel are supplied by and under the responsibility of the relevant Israeli authorities. The use of such data by the OECD is without prejudice to the status of the Golan Heights, East Jerusalem and Israeli settlements in the West Bank under the terms of international law.

Unweighted averages: All member counties are taken into account for the calculation of the unweighted averages, including countries that had not implemented the relevant taxes for the year considered. They are counted with a value of zero in the numerator and 1 in the denominator. However, countries that did not exist at the time considered (Czech and Slovak Republics before 1993; Slovenia before 1991) are not included in the calculation of the averages. Are also excluded from the calculation of the averages the countries for which no data is available for the time considered (Chile before 1990, Estonia, Hungary and Israel before 1995, Korea before 1975; Mexico before 1980; Poland before 1995; and Slovak Republic before 2000).

Source: Revenue Statistics 2016, OECD Publishing, Paris DOI: *http://dx.doi.org/10.1787/rev_stats-2016-en-fr*.

StatLink *http://dx.doi.org/10.1787/888933420001*

Table 1.A1.4. **Taxes on general consumption (5110) as percentage of total taxation**

	1965	1975	1985	1995	2000	2005	2010	2011	2012	2013	2014	Difference 2010-14
Australia	7.4	6.7	7.9	8.7	12.0	13.4	13.7	12.8	12.3	13.0	12.9	-0.7
Austria	18.7	19.8	21.0	18.6	18.8	18.8	18.9	18.6	18.6	18.2	18.0	-0.9
Belgium	21.1	16.2	15.7	15.3	16.2	16.2	16.4	16.1	15.8	15.5	15.4	-1.0
Canada	17.8	12.5	13.2	14.0	14.2	14.8	14.0	14.0	13.9	13.7	13.8	-0.2
Chile				40.6	41.8	37.8	38.5	37.0	37.7	40.8	41.6	3.2
Czech Republic				16.6	18.3	19.1	20.5	20.6	20.9	21.8	22.4	1.9
Denmark	10.3	17.5	20.7	19.5	19.5	20.2	21.1	21.2	21.0	20.2	19.2	-1.9
Estonia				26.6	27.1	26.9	25.8	26.3	26.6	26.0	26.4	0.6
Finland	18.5	15.6	18.3	17.4	17.4	19.9	20.4	20.9	21.1	21.3	21.0	0.7
France	23.3	23.4	20.0	17.7	17.1	17.3	16.7	16.4	16.0	15.7	15.8	-1.0
Germany	16.5	14.6	15.8	17.4	18.4	18.0	20.0	19.7	19.4	19.2	19.0	-1.0
Greece	10.3	18.3	17.2	23.0	21.5	22.2	23.0	22.7	21.2	20.7	21.0	-2.0
Hungary				19.4	26.1	28.0	29.7	30.0	30.4	29.8	30.5	0.8
Iceland	16.7	28.6	33.0	31.7	28.5	27.3	22.7	22.4	22.8	22.2	20.8	-1.9
Ireland	5.7	14.7	20.6	21.1	22.9	24.7	22.2	20.8	21.2	20.4	20.8	-1.5
Israel				30.3	26.5	27.6	29.9	29.7	29.7	30.1	30.9	1.0
Italy	12.9	14.3	14.5	13.8	15.4	14.6	14.5	14.4	13.6	13.3	13.8	-0.8
Japan	0.0	0.0	0.0	5.4	9.1	9.5	9.6	9.4	9.2	9.2	12.2	2.6
Korea		12.7	21.1	17.8	17.0	17.4	17.5	17.0	17.2	17.0	17.2	-0.3
Latvia				28.4	23.9	26.5	23.9	24.4	25.3	26.0	26.7	2.8
Luxembourg	12.4	12.1	12.8	12.4	13.4	16.1	17.0	17.7	18.4	19.0	19.6	2.6
Mexico			15.9	22.2	22.8	26.7	26.9	26.4	26.7	23.7	25.6	-1.4
Netherlands	12.4	14.4	16.2	16.2	17.3	19.2	18.7	18.1	18.0	17.8	17.2	-1.5
New Zealand	7.7	9.0	10.4	22.8	24.9	23.8	30.7	31.0	30.0	30.0	29.9	-0.8
Norway	21.5	20.5	18.2	21.2	19.8	18.2	18.6	18.0	18.2	19.2	20.1	1.5
Poland				16.2	21.0	23.2	24.4	24.8	22.4	22.1	22.2	-2.1
Portugal	..	11.2	12.6	23.3	24.4	26.6	24.7	25.0	26.2	23.6	24.8	0.0
Slovak Republic				20.8	20.4	24.7	22.1	23.4	21.1	21.0	21.3	-0.8
Slovenia				29.5	23.7	22.2	21.9	22.3	21.8	23.1	23.2	1.3
Spain	22.2	15.3	14.7	15.9	17.6	17.7	16.7	16.4	16.6	17.8	18.1	1.4
Sweden	10.4	12.0	14.0	19.4	17.1	18.5	21.5	21.5	21.3	21.1	21.3	-0.2
Switzerland	10.6	8.7	10.7	12.1	13.4	13.7	13.0	13.1	13.3	13.3	13.1	0.1
Turkey	..	..	23.3	31.1	24.2	21.8	21.7	21.8	20.8	22.0	20.4	-1.3
United Kingdom	5.9	8.9	15.9	19.0	18.1	18.6	18.8	20.5	20.8	20.9	21.3	2.5
United States	4.8	7.0	7.9	8.1	7.6	8.1	8.4	8.3	8.2	7.9	7.9	-0.5
Unweighted average												
OECD-Average	**11.9**	**13.4**	**15.8**	**19.8**	**19.9**	**20.6**	**20.7**	**20.6**	**20.5**	**20.5**	**20.7**	**0.0**

Israel: The statistical data for Israel are supplied by and under the responsibility of the relevant Israeli authorities. The use of such data by the OECD is without prejudice to the status of the Golan Heights, East Jerusalem and Israeli settlements in the West Bank under the terms of international law.

Unweighted averages: All member counties are taken into account for the calculation of the unweighted averages, including countries that had not implemented the relevant taxes for the year considered. They are counted with a value of zero in the numerator and 1 in the denominator. However, countries that did not exist at the time considered (Czech and Slovak Republics before 1993; Slovenia before 1991) are not included in the calculation of the averages. Are also excluded from the calculation of the averages the countries for which no data is available for the time considered (Chile before 1990, Estonia, Hungary and Israel before 1995, Korea before 1975; Mexico before 1980; Poland before 1995; and Slovak Republic before 2000).

Source: Revenue Statistics 2016, OECD Publishing, Paris DOI: *http://dx.doi.org/10.1787/rev_stats-2016-en-fr*.

StatLink *http://dx.doi.org/10.1787/888933420018*

Table 1.A1.5. **Taxes on specific goods and services (5120) as percentage of GDP**

	1965	1975	1985	1995	2000	2005	2010	2011	2012	2013	2014	Difference 2010-14
Australia	4.7	4.9	5.7	4.1	4.3	3.6	3.0	3.0	3.0	3.0	2.9	-0.1
Austria	6.0	5.1	4.0	3.5	3.5	3.3	3.1	3.3	3.3	3.2	3.2	0.1
Belgium	4.0	3.8	3.5	3.5	3.0	3.1	3.1	3.1	3.4	3.3	3.2	0.1
Canada	4.2	4.3	4.1	3.4	3.0	2.9	2.6	2.5	2.5	2.4	2.4	-0.2
Chile				3.5	3.5	2.3	1.9	2.0	2.0	2.0	2.0	0.1
Czech Republic				4.5	3.6	3.4	3.5	3.7	3.7	3.7	2.9	-0.6
Denmark	8.5	5.6	5.8	5.5	5.5	5.4	4.4	4.4	4.4	4.5	4.3	-0.1
Estonia				2.8	3.3	3.9	4.4	4.5	4.6	4.4	4.5	0.0
Finland	7.0	5.8	5.9	5.6	5.0	4.5	4.3	4.6	4.7	4.7	4.7	0.4
France	4.8	3.1	3.7	3.8	3.5	3.2	3.1	3.3	3.4	3.5	3.5	0.4
Germany	4.6	3.7	3.2	3.4	3.2	3.4	2.9	3.0	2.9	2.8	2.8	-0.2
Greece	5.8	4.5	5.1	4.6	3.8	3.0	3.7	4.2	4.1	4.4	4.5	0.7
Hungary				8.5	5.3	3.9	4.5	4.6	4.8	5.0	4.8	0.2
Iceland	11.5	9.8	7.3	4.3	4.0	4.2	3.5	3.6	3.7	3.5	3.4	-0.1
Ireland	10.6	8.3	7.4	5.5	4.2	3.4	3.0	2.9	2.8	2.9	2.9	-0.2
Israel				1.5	1.5	1.8	2.1	2.0	1.9	1.8	1.8	-0.3
Italy	5.9	3.4	3.0	4.3	3.9	3.6	3.8	4.0	4.4	4.3	4.4	0.6
Japan	4.4	3.1	3.2	2.2	2.1	2.1	2.0	2.0	2.0	2.0	1.9	-0.0
Korea		7.0	5.9	4.0	4.2	3.6	3.5	2.9	3.0	2.9	2.7	-0.9
Latvia				2.7	3.8	3.7	3.8	3.6	3.4	3.4	3.4	-0.4
Luxembourg	2.9	2.7	4.3	4.5	4.7	4.7	3.7	3.7	3.7	3.3	3.3	-0.4
Mexico			7.4	1.8	2.0	0.9	0.9	0.8	0.9	0.9	1.1	0.1
Netherlands	4.5	3.1	2.9	3.6	3.3	3.4	3.1	3.1	3.1	3.2	3.4	0.2
New Zealand	4.3	3.8	3.4	3.0	2.5	2.2	1.9	1.9	1.9	1.8	2.0	0.0
Norway	5.4	6.3	7.6	6.2	4.0	3.4	3.2	3.0	2.8	2.8	2.8	-0.5
Poland				7.3	4.5	4.5	4.3	4.2	4.2	4.2	4.1	-0.2
Portugal	6.9	5.5	7.2	5.5	4.6	5.0	4.3	4.3	4.1	4.0	3.9	-0.3
Slovak Republic				5.0	4.6	3.7	3.1	3.0	3.2	3.2	3.1	0.0
Slovenia				3.2	4.4	4.1	5.1	5.0	5.5	5.4	5.3	0.2
Spain	2.6	1.6	3.4	3.2	3.2	2.9	2.5	2.5	2.7	2.9	2.9	0.4
Sweden	6.0	4.2	5.2	3.8	3.4	3.2	2.9	2.8	2.8	2.7	2.6	-0.3
Switzerland	3.5	2.7	2.3	1.9	1.8	1.8	1.8	1.8	1.8	1.7	1.7	-0.1
Turkey	5.6	4.9	1.4	1.0	4.0	6.2	6.3	6.0	6.2	6.5	6.3	0.0
United Kingdom	7.4	5.1	4.9	4.3	4.1	3.4	3.5	3.6	3.6	3.5	3.4	-0.1
United States	3.6	2.5	2.1	2.0	1.8	1.7	1.7	1.7	1.7	1.8	1.8	0.1
Unweighted average												
OECD-Average	**5.6**	**4.6**	**4.6**	**3.9**	**3.6**	**3.4**	**3.3**	**3.3**	**3.3**	**3.3**	**3.3**	**-0.0**

Israel: The statistical data for Israel are supplied by and under the responsibility of the relevant Israeli authorities. The use of such data by the OECD is without prejudice to the status of the Golan Heights, East Jerusalem and Israeli settlements in the West Bank under the terms of international law.

Unweighted averages: All member counties are taken into account for the calculation of the unweighted averages, including countries that had not implemented the relevant taxes for the year considered. They are counted with a value of zero in the numerator and 1 in the denominator. However, countries that did not exist at the time considered (Czech and Slovak Republics before 1993; Slovenia before 1991) are not included in the calculation of the averages. Are also excluded from the calculation of the averages the countries for which no data is available for the time considered (Chile before 1990, Estonia, Hungary and Israel before 1995, Korea before 1975; Mexico before 1980; Poland before 1995; and Slovak Republic before 2000).

Source: Revenue Statistics 2016, OECD Publishing, Paris DOI: *http://dx.doi.org/10.1787/rev_stats-2016-en-fr*.

StatLink http://dx.doi.org/10.1787/888933420023

Table 1.A1.6. **Taxes on specific goods and services (5120) as percentage of total taxation**

	1965	1975	1985	1995	2000	2005	2010	2011	2012	2013	2014	Difference 2010-14
Australia	22.7	19.1	20.7	14.5	14.1	12.0	11.8	11.3	10.9	10.7	10.4	-1.5
Austria	18.0	14.0	9.9	8.6	8.2	8.2	7.5	8.1	7.9	7.6	7.4	-0.1
Belgium	13.0	9.8	8.0	8.3	6.9	7.2	7.4	7.2	7.8	7.2	7.1	-0.2
Canada	16.8	13.6	13.0	9.9	8.6	8.9	8.5	8.3	8.0	7.9	7.8	-0.7
Chile				19.2	18.8	10.9	9.8	9.4	9.4	9.9	10.3	0.5
Czech Republic				13.0	11.0	9.8	10.8	11.2	11.1	10.7	8.8	-2.0
Denmark	29.3	15.2	13.3	11.8	11.8	11.2	9.8	9.7	9.6	9.6	8.7	-1.1
Estonia				7.9	10.6	13.1	13.3	14.3	14.7	14.1	13.8	0.5
Finland	23.4	16.0	15.2	12.5	10.9	10.7	10.4	11.0	11.0	10.8	10.6	0.2
France	14.3	9.0	8.7	9.1	8.0	7.5	7.4	7.6	7.7	7.7	7.7	0.2
Germany	14.6	10.8	8.7	9.5	8.8	9.9	8.4	8.4	7.9	7.8	7.6	-0.8
Greece	33.8	23.9	20.9	16.4	11.5	9.6	11.5	12.4	11.6	12.4	12.5	0.9
Hungary				20.9	13.8	10.8	12.1	12.6	12.6	13.1	12.5	0.4
Iceland	45.0	33.6	26.5	14.0	11.0	10.6	10.5	10.5	10.5	9.7	8.8	-1.7
Ireland	43.4	29.7	22.0	17.4	13.6	11.5	11.1	10.6	10.3	10.2	9.9	-1.2
Israel				4.3	4.3	5.3	6.8	6.5	6.4	5.9	5.8	-1.0
Italy	24.1	14.0	9.1	11.1	9.6	9.2	9.1	9.7	10.0	9.8	10.1	1.0
Japan	25.0	15.1	12.1	8.3	8.0	7.7	7.2	7.1	6.9	6.7	6.0	-1.1
Korea		47.3	37.4	20.7	19.7	15.9	15.1	12.2	12.0	11.8	10.8	-4.3
Latvia				9.1	13.1	13.2	13.5	12.9	12.1	12.0	11.7	-1.8
Luxembourg	11.1	8.4	11.3	12.9	12.6	12.3	9.8	9.8	9.5	8.8	8.7	-1.1
Mexico			48.6	15.9	14.5	7.1	6.7	6.0	6.5	5.9	7.2	0.5
Netherlands	14.7	8.1	7.2	9.4	8.8	9.5	8.7	8.7	8.5	8.7	9.0	0.3
New Zealand	18.5	13.8	11.7	8.6	7.5	6.2	6.4	6.3	6.0	5.8	6.0	-0.3
Norway	18.4	16.1	18.2	15.5	9.6	7.9	7.7	7.1	6.9	7.0	7.1	-0.5
Poland				19.3	13.5	13.6	13.9	13.4	13.1	13.2	12.7	-1.2
Portugal	44.0	28.9	29.7	18.8	14.8	16.1	14.1	13.3	12.9	11.7	11.6	-2.6
Slovak Republic				12.6	13.7	11.9	11.0	10.5	11.1	10.5	9.9	-1.0
Slovenia				8.4	12.1	10.8	13.8	13.8	14.8	14.8	14.6	0.8
Spain	18.4	8.7	12.8	10.3	9.6	8.3	8.0	7.8	8.3	8.7	8.7	0.6
Sweden	19.2	10.7	11.6	8.3	7.0	6.8	6.8	6.6	6.7	6.4	6.1	-0.7
Switzerland	21.3	11.9	9.5	7.4	6.6	6.8	7.0	6.5	6.6	6.4	6.3	-0.7
Turkey	53.5	40.9	12.4	6.0	16.4	25.5	24.1	21.7	22.4	22.4	22.0	-2.1
United Kingdom	25.2	14.8	13.8	14.5	12.4	10.5	10.8	10.8	10.9	10.8	10.7	-0.0
United States	15.1	10.0	8.4	7.6	6.3	6.7	7.0	7.2	7.1	6.9	6.8	-0.2
Unweighted average												
OECD-Average	**24.3**	**17.7**	**16.2**	**12.6**	**11.5**	**11.1**	**10.8**	**10.7**	**10.7**	**9.8**	**9.6**	**-1.2**

Israel: The statistical data for Israel are supplied by and under the responsibility of the relevant Israeli authorities. The use of such data by the OECD is without prejudice to the status of the Golan Heights, East Jerusalem and Israeli settlements in the West Bank under the terms of international law.

Unweighted averages: All member counties are taken into account for the calculation of the unweighted averages, including countries that had not implemented the relevant taxes for the year considered. They are counted with a value of zero in the numerator and 1 in the denominator. However, countries that did not exist at the time considered (Czech and Slovak Republics before 1993; Slovenia before 1991) are not included in the calculation of the averages. Are also excluded from the calculation of the averages the countries for which no data is available for the time considered (Chile before 1990, Estonia, Hungary and Israel before 1995, Korea before 1975; Mexico before 1980; Poland before 1995; and Slovak Republic before 2000).

Source: Revenue Statistics 2016, OECD Publishing, Paris DOI: *http://dx.doi.org/10.1787/rev_stats-2016-en-fr*.

StatLink *http://dx.doi.org/10.1787/888933420033*

Table 1.A1.7. Value added taxes (5111) as percentage of GDP

	1965	1975	1985	1995	2000	2005	2010	2011	2012	2013	2014	Difference 2010-14
Australia	0.0	0.0	0.0	0.0	3.4	3.9	3.4	3.3	3.3	3.5	3.5	0.1
Austria	0.0	7.2	8.5	7.6	7.9	7.7	7.7	7.6	7.8	7.7	7.7	0.0
Belgium	0.0	6.3	6.8	6.5	7.0	6.9	6.9	6.9	6.9	6.9	6.9	0.0
Canada	0.0	0.0	0.0	2.9	3.2	3.2	4.2	4.2	4.2	4.1	4.2	0.0
Chile				7.5	7.9	7.8	7.6	7.9	8.1	8.1	8.2	0.7
Czech Republic				5.8	6.0	6.6	6.7	6.9	7.0	7.4	7.4	0.7
Denmark	3.0	6.5	9.1	9.1	9.2	9.7	9.5	9.6	9.6	9.4	9.5	0.0
Estonia				9.6	8.4	8.1	8.5	8.2	8.4	8.2	8.6	0.0
Finland	5.5	5.6	7.2	7.7	8.0	8.4	8.3	8.8	9.0	9.3	9.2	0.9
France	6.8	8.1	8.2	7.3	7.2	7.2	6.8	6.8	6.8	6.8	6.9	0.1
Germany	0.0	5.0	5.7	6.3	6.7	6.1	7.0	7.0	7.0	7.0	7.0	0.0
Greece	0.0	0.0	0.0	6.1	6.9	6.7	7.1	7.3	7.2	7.0	7.1	0.1
Hungary				7.3	8.7	8.3	8.6	8.5	9.2	9.0	9.4	0.8
Iceland	0.0	0.0	0.0	9.1	10.4	10.8	7.6	7.7	8.0	8.0	8.1	0.5
Ireland	0.0	4.1	6.9	6.7	7.1	7.3	6.0	5.6	5.8	5.8	6.0	-0.1
Israel				8.3	7.4	7.5	7.5	7.5	7.3	7.7	8.0	0.6
Italy	0.0	3.4	4.7	5.3	6.3	5.7	6.1	6.0	6.0	5.9	6.0	-0.1
Japan				1.4	2.4	2.6	2.6	2.7	2.7	2.8	3.9	1.3
Korea		0.0	3.3	3.4	3.7	3.9	4.1	4.1	4.3	4.1	4.2	0.1
Latvia				8.4	7.0	7.4	6.7	6.8	7.2	7.4	7.6	0.9
Luxembourg	0.0	3.8	4.8	4.3	5.0	6.1	6.5	6.7	7.2	7.2	7.5	1.1
Mexico			2.4	2.5	3.1	3.4	3.8	3.7	3.7	3.5	3.9	0.1
Netherlands	0.0	5.5	6.4	6.1	6.4	6.8	6.8	6.5	6.5	6.5	6.4	-0.3
New Zealand	0.0	0.0	0.0	8.1	8.1	8.6	9.3	9.4	9.6	9.4	9.7	0.4
Norway	0.0	8.0	7.6	8.5	8.2	7.7	7.8	7.6	7.5	7.7	7.7	0.0
Poland				6.1	6.9	7.7	7.6	7.8	7.1	7.0	7.1	-0.5
Portugal	0.0	0.0	0.0	6.8	7.6	8.2	7.5	8.1	8.3	8.1	8.5	0.9
Slovak Republic				8.2	6.9	7.7	6.2	6.7	6.0	6.4	6.6	0.4
Slovenia				0.0	8.5	8.4	8.1	8.1	8.0	8.5	8.5	0.4
Spain	0.0	0.0	0.0	5.0	5.9	6.2	5.3	5.2	5.4	5.9	6.1	0.9
Sweden	0.0	4.7	6.3	8.8	8.3	8.5	9.2	9.0	8.9	9.0	9.0	-0.1
Switzerland	0.0	0.0	0.0	3.1	3.6	3.6	3.4	3.5	3.5	3.5	3.5	0.1
Turkey			2.6	4.1	5.8	5.3	5.7	6.1	5.8	6.4	5.9	0.2
United Kingdom	0.0	3.0	5.6	5.7	5.9	6.0	6.1	6.8	6.8	6.8	6.8	0.7
United States	0.0	0.0	0.0	0.0	0.0	0.0	0.0	0.0	0.0	0.0	0.0	0.0
Unweighted average												
OECD-Average	**0.6**	**3.1**	**3.9**	**5.8**	**6.4**	**6.6**	**6.5**	**6.5**	**6.6**	**6.6**	**6.8**	**0.3**

Israel: The statistical data for Israel are supplied by and under the responsibility of the relevant Israeli authorities. The use of such data by the OECD is without prejudice to the status of the Golan Heights, East Jerusalem and Israeli settlements in the West Bank under the terms of international law.

Unweighted averages: All member counties are taken into account for the calculation of the unweighted averages, including countries that had not implemented the relevant taxes for the year considered. They are counted with a value of zero in the numerator and 1 in the denominator. However, countries that did not exist at the time considered (Czech and Slovak Republics before 1993; Slovenia before 1991) are not included in the calculation of the averages. Are also excluded from the calculation of the averages the countries for which no data is available for the time considered (Chile before 1990, Estonia, Hungary and Israel before 1995, Korea before 1975; Mexico before 1980; Poland before 1995; and Slovak Republic before 2000).

Source: Revenue Statistics 2016, OECD Publishing, Paris DOI: *http://dx.doi.org/10.1787/rev_stats-2016-en-fr*.

StatLink http://dx.doi.org/10.1787/888933420048

Table 1.A1.8. **Value added taxes (5111) as percentage of total taxation**

	1965	1975	1985	1995	2000	2005	2010	2011	2012	2013	2014	Difference 2010-14
Australia	0.0	0.0	0.0	0.0	11.1	13.1	13.3	12.5	12.1	12.7	12.6	-0.7
Austria	0.0	19.8	21.0	18.6	18.8	18.8	18.9	18.6	18.6	18.2	18.0	-0.9
Belgium	0.0	16.2	15.7	15.2	16.1	15.9	16.2	15.9	15.7	15.4	15.3	-1.0
Canada	0.0	0.0	0.0	8.4	9.2	9.9	13.7	13.7	13.7	13.4	13.5	-0.2
Chile				40.6	41.8	37.8	38.5	37.0	37.7	40.8	41.6	3.2
Czech Republic				16.6	18.3	19.1	20.5	20.6	20.9	21.8	22.4	1.9
Denmark	10.3	17.5	20.7	19.5	19.5	20.2	21.1	21.2	21.0	20.2	19.2	-1.9
Estonia				26.6	27.1	26.9	25.7	26.0	26.6	26.0	26.4	0.7
Finland	18.5	15.6	18.3	17.4	17.4	19.9	20.4	20.9	21.1	21.3	21.0	0.7
France	20.1	23.1	19.7	17.4	16.7	16.7	16.1	15.8	15.4	15.1	15.2	-0.9
Germany	0.0	14.6	15.8	17.4	18.4	18.0	20.0	19.7	19.4	19.2	19.0	-1.0
Greece	0.0	0.0	0.0	22.0	20.8	21.5	21.9	21.5	20.2	19.6	20.0	-1.9
Hungary				17.8	22.4	22.5	22.9	23.2	23.8	23.5	24.5	1.6
Iceland	0.0	0.0	0.0	29.9	28.5	27.3	22.7	22.4	22.8	22.2	20.8	-1.9
Ireland	0.0	14.7	20.6	21.1	22.9	24.7	22.2	20.8	21.2	20.4	20.8	-1.5
Israel				23.2	21.2	22.4	24.5	24.4	24.5	25.2	25.7	1.2
Italy	0.0	13.7	14.5	13.8	15.4	14.6	14.5	14.4	13.6	13.3	13.8	-0.8
Japan				5.4	9.1	9.5	9.6	9.4	9.2	9.2	12.2	2.6
Korea		0.0	21.1	17.8	17.0	17.4	17.5	17.0	17.2	17.0	17.2	-0.3
Latvia				28.4	23.9	26.5	23.9	24.4	25.3	26.0	26.3	2.4
Luxembourg	0.0	12.1	12.8	12.4	13.4	16.1	17.0	17.7	18.4	19.0	19.6	2.6
Mexico			15.9	22.2	22.8	26.7	26.9	26.4	26.7	23.7	25.6	-1.4
Netherlands	0.0	14.4	16.2	16.2	17.3	19.2	18.7	18.1	17.9	17.8	17.2	-1.5
New Zealand	0.0	0.0	0.0	22.8	24.9	23.8	30.7	31.0	30.0	30.0	29.9	-0.8
Norway	0.0	20.5	18.2	21.2	19.7	18.1	18.5	18.0	18.2	19.2	20.0	1.5
Poland				16.1	21.0	23.2	24.4	24.8	22.4	22.1	22.2	-2.1
Portugal	0.0	0.0	0.0	23.3	24.4	26.6	24.7	25.0	26.2	23.6	24.8	0.0
Slovak Republic				20.8	20.4	24.7	22.1	23.4	21.1	21.0	21.3	-0.8
Slovenia				0.0	23.3	22.2	21.9	22.3	21.8	23.1	23.2	1.3
Spain	0.0	0.0	0.0	15.9	17.6	17.7	16.7	16.4	16.6	17.8	18.1	1.4
Sweden	0.0	12.0	14.0	19.4	16.9	18.3	21.2	21.3	21.0	20.9	21.1	-0.1
Switzerland	0.0	0.0	0.0	12.1	13.2	13.5	12.8	12.8	13.1	13.1	12.9	0.1
Turkey			22.3	24.3	24.2	21.8	21.7	21.8	20.8	22.0	20.4	-1.3
United Kingdom	0.0	8.9	15.9	19.0	18.1	18.6	18.8	20.5	20.8	20.9	21.3	2.5
United States	0.0	0.0	0.0	0.0	0.0	0.0	0.0	0.0	0.0	0.0	0.0	0.0
Unweighted average												
OECD-Average	**2.2**	**8.8**	**11.3**	**17.8**	**19.2**	**19.8**	**20.0**	**20.0**	**19.8**	**19.8**	**20.1**	**0.1**

Israel: The statistical data for Israel are supplied by and under the responsibility of the relevant Israeli authorities. The use of such data by the OECD is without prejudice to the status of the Golan Heights, East Jerusalem and Israeli settlements in the West Bank under the terms of international law.

Unweighted averages: All member counties are taken into account for the calculation of the unweighted averages, including countries that had not implemented the relevant taxes for the year considered. They are counted with a value of zero in the numerator and 1 in the denominator. However, countries that did not exist at the time considered (Czech and Slovak Republics before 1993; Slovenia before 1991) are not included in the calculation of the averages. Are also excluded from the calculation of the averages the countries for which no data is available for the time considered (Chile before 1990, Estonia, Hungary and Israel before 1995, Korea before 1975; Mexico before 1980; Poland before 1995; and Slovak Republic before 2000).

Source: Revenue Statistics 2016, OECD Publishing, Paris DOI: *http://dx.doi.org/10.1787/rev_stats-2016-en-fr*.

StatLink *http://dx.doi.org/10.1787/888933420056*

Table 1.A1.9. **Tax structures in the OECD area**[1]

	1965	1975	1985	1995	2005	2010	2014
Personal income tax	26	30	30	26	23	23	24
Corporate income tax	9	8	8	8	10	9	9
Social security contributions[2]	18	22	22	25	25	27	25
(employee)	*(6)*	*(7)*	*(7)*	*(8)*	*(9)*	*(9)*	*(10)*
(employer)	*(10)*	*(14)*	*(13)*	*(15)*	*(15)*	*(15)*	*(15)*
Payroll taxes	1	1	1	1	1	1	1
Property taxes	8	6	5	5	6	5	6
General consumption taxes	12	13	16	20	21	21	21
(of which VAT)	*(2)*	*(9)*	*(11)*	*(18)*	*(20)*	*(20)*	*(20)*
Specific consumption taxes	24	18	16	12	10	10	10
All other taxes	2	2	2	3	4	4	4
Total	**100**	**100**	**100**	**100**	**100**	**100**	**100**

1. Percentage share of major tax categories in total tax revenue.
2. Including social security contributions paid by the self-employed and benefit recipients (heading 2300) that are not shown in the breakdown over employees and employers.

Source: Revenue Statistics 2016, OECD Publishing, Paris DOI: *http://dx.doi.org/10.1787/rev_stats-2016-en-fr*.

StatLink *http://dx.doi.org/10.1787/888933420061*

Table 1.A1.10. **VAT relief for low value imports**[1]

Country	Currency	Threshold in Local currency[2]	Threshold in USD[3]
Australia*	AUD	1 000	671
Austria	EUR	22	27
Belgium	EUR	22	27
Canada	CAD	20	16
Chile	CLP	0	0
Czech Republic	EUR	22	46
Denmark	EUR	10	11
Estonia	EUR	22	39
Finland	EUR	22	24
France*	EUR	22	27
Germany	EUR	22	28
Greece	EUR	22	36
Hungary	EUR	22	51
Iceland*	ISK	2 000	14
Ireland	EUR	22	26
Israel*	USD	75	75
Italy	EUR	22	29
Japan	JPY	10 000	95
Korea*	USD	150	150
Latvia	EUR	22	43
Luxembourg	EUR	22	24
Mexico*	USD	300/50	300/50
Netherlands	EUR	22	27
New Zealand*	NZD	400	282
Norway*	NOK	350	36
Poland*	EUR	22	51
Portugal	EUR	22	37
Slovak Republic	EUR	22	44
Slovenia	EUR	22	37
Spain	EUR	22	33
Sweden	EUR	22	23
Switzerland*	CHF	62	48
Turkey	TRY		0
United Kingdom*	GBP	15	22

* See country notes in Box 1.A1.10.

1. This table shows VAT collection thresholds for low value import items dispatched by a foreign supplier to a buyer in the given country. It does not cover other import scenarios such as imports of goods exchanged between private individuals or imports of goods in the personnal luggage of travellers (see Table 1.A1.13). Imports of exciseable goods are generally excluded from the tax reliefs.
2. Amounts in local currency: for Member States of the European Union, the threshold is mentioned in Euro (EUR) even for those that do not have the Euro as national currency (i.e. Czech Republic, Denmark, Hungary, Poland and Sweden), with the exception of the United Kingdom. Indeed the threshold applied in EU countries is determined in EUR by common EU legislation (Directive 2009/132/EC states that Member States shall exempt the import of goods whose value does not exceed EUR 10. They may grant an exemption for goods whose value does not exceed EUR 22). The amount in EUR is converted into USD as follows: it is first converted into local currency at market exchange rate (Eurostat average 2015) and then into USD at PPP exchange rate. For Mexico, the threshold is not provided in local currency in national legislation but in USD only. Except stated otherwise in the country notes, the amount reflects the intrinsic value of the goods (excluding freight, insurance and other costs and taxes).
3. Amounts are converted into USD at Purchase Parity Rates (PPPs). PPPs are the rates of currency conversion that equalise the purchasing power of different countries by eliminating differences in price levels between countries. They show the specified number of monetary units needed in each country to buy the same representative basket of consumer goods and services, which costs USD 1 in the United States. The currency conversion rates used in Consupltion Tax Trends are the PPP rates for GDP (see Annex A).

Source: National delegations Position as at 1 January 2016.

StatLink http://dx.doi.org/10.1787/888933420074

Box 1.A1.10. **Country notes**

Australia: The application of the GST will be extended to low value goods imported by consumers from 1 July 2017. Foreign suppliers that have an Australian turnover of AUD 75 000 or more will be required to register for collecting and remitting the GST for low value goods supplied to consumers in Australia, using a vendor registration model.

France: The threshold does not apply to goods imported on mail order.

Iceland: The threshold applies only to the importation of goods via "express deliveries". An exemption threshold of ISK 1 500 applies to imports of goods by importers registered for VAT purposes in Iceland.

Israel: The threshold is given in USD in national legislation. The statistical data for Israel are supplied by and under the responsibility of the relevant Israeli authorities. The use of such data by the OECD is without prejudice to the status of the Golan Heights, East Jerusalem and Israeli settlements in the West Bank under the terms of international law.

Korea: The threshold is given in USD in national legislation. Postal parcels and express consignments are exempt if their value does not exceed USD 150 and the quantity is such that the customs authorities recognise the goods as for personal use.

Mexico: The threshold is given in USD in national legislation. The threshold is of USD 300 if the importation is made by the postal service and USD 50 if the importation is made by courier services.

New Zealand: The threshold is not based on the value of the goods but on the amount of tax. Customs duty and VAT are not levied if the amount of tax due is NZD 60 or less. For ease of comparison, the equivalent threshold under the standard GST rate without applicable customs duties is shown in the table above i.e. NZD 400 x 15% GST = NZD 60.

Norway: Freight and insurance costs are included in the value of the threshold.

Poland: The threshold does not apply to goods imported on mail order.

Switzerland: The threshold is not based on the value of the goods but on the amount of tax. VAT is not levied if the amount of tax due is CHF 5 or less per declaration. For ease of comparison, the equivalent threshold under the standard VAT rate is shown in the table above i.e. CHF 62 x 8% VAT = CHF 5. For goods taxed under the reduced rate of 2.5% (e.g. books) the value of the threshold would be max. CHF 200 till the tax amount of 5 CHF is reached.

United Kingdom: There is no low value consignments relief on imports of goods into the UK from the Channel Islands purchased as part of a mail order/distance sale transaction.

Table 1.A1.11. Mechanisms for collecting VAT on cross-border supplies of services and intangibles from non-resident suppliers ("inbound supplies")

Country	VAT collection mechanism	Proxies for determining place of taxation	Threshold
Australia*	**B2C:** inbound supplies of services and intangibles are not taxed (unless supplies are made through a non-resident establishment in Australia). The rules will change as of 1 July 2017 (see country note). **B2B:** inbound supplies of services and intangibles are taxed only if the customer has limited right to deduct input GST. The business customer is liable to collect and pay any GST due under the reverse charge mechanism.	Place of supplier or place of performance in Australia, with exceptions for proxies that lead to a conclusion that the effective use or enjoyment is outside Australia. The rules will change as of 1 July 2017 (see country note).	Not applicable
Austria	European Union scheme (see below)		
Belgium	European Union scheme (see below)		
Canada	**B2C:** inbound supplies of services and intangibles are taxed. The consumer is liable to pay and remit the GST under the reverse charge mechanism. **B2B:** inbound supplies of services and intangibles are taxed only if the customer has limited right to deduct input GST. The business customer is liable to pay and remit any GST due under the reverse charge mechanism.	**B2C and B2B:** recipient's usual residence or location.	Not applicable
Chile	No distinction between **B2B and B2C:** the customer is liable to pay the VAT.	The service or intangible is used in Chile or is rendered in Chile.	No threshold
Czech Republic	European Union scheme (see below)		
Denmark	European Union scheme (see below)		
Estonia	European Union scheme (see below)		
Finland	European Union scheme (see below)		
France	European Union scheme (see below)		
Germany	European Union scheme (see below)		
Greece	European Union scheme (see below)		
Hungary	European Union scheme (see below)		
Iceland	**B2C:** inbound supplies of services and intangibles are subject to VAT. The supplier must register under standard procedure (no simplified registration and compliance scheme is available) for supplies of "electronic services" made to customers having their residency or fixed place of business (not registered for VAT purposes) in Iceland. No tax agent/fiscal representative is required. **B2B:** supplies of services and intangibles are VAT exempt if the customer has a full right of deduction. If not, the same procedure applies as for B2C supplies.	**B2C:** customer's usual residence. **B2B:** customer's permanent place of business.	ISK 1 million (USD 7 800) Same as for domestic suppliers
Ireland	European Union scheme (see below)		
Israel*	**B2C and B2B:** the customer is liable to report and pay the VAT on inbound supplies of services and intangibles.	**B2C and B2B:** the residence of the customer is in Israel or the supply is connected to an asset in Israel.	
Italy	European Union scheme (see below).		
Japan	**B2C:** suppliers of inbound "electronic services" to Japanese residents shall account for Japan Consumption Tax (VAT). Electronic services are services provided via electronic communication networks, – e.g. the Internet, such as the provision of e-books, music and advertisements. **B2B:** the reverse charge mechanism applies to inbound B2B "electronic services". A foreign business shall notify its Japanese customers that they (customers) shall account for VAT under the reverse charge mechanism.	**B2C and B2B:** the place of customer is in Japan (i.e. address or domicile for private customers and head office or principal office for businesses).	JPY 10 million (USD 95.000) Same as for domestic suppliers
Korea	**B2C:** inbound supplies of "electronic services" as defined by law are taxed. The supplier is required to register and account for VAT under a simplified registration through a fiscal representative ("pay only" registration). **B2B:** out of the scope.	**B2C:** customer location. **B2B:** not applicable.	No threshold
Latvia	European Union scheme (see below)		
Luxembourg	European Union scheme (see below)		

Table 1.A1.11. **Mechanisms for collecting VAT on cross-border supplies of services and intangibles from non-resident suppliers ("inbound supplies")** *(cont.)*

Country	VAT collection mechanism	Proxies for determining place of taxation	Threshold
Mexico	**B2C and B2B:** inbound supplies of services and intangibles are taxable. The customer (B or C) should self-assess the VAT. However, final consumers are not likely to report since there is no economic effect or sanctions imposed for non-reporting.	Services: consumption or physical presence of the customer in the country. Intangibles: residence of the acquirer or place of use.	No threshold
Netherlands	European Union scheme (see below)		
New Zealand	**B2C:** from 1 October 2016, non-resident suppliers that make cross-border supplies of services and intangibles to New Zealand consumers of more than NZD 60.000 in a 12-month period are required to register and account for GST. **B2B:** Non-resident suppliers are not required to return GST on cross-border supplies of services and intangibles to GST-registered businesses. The reverse charge may apply if GST-registered recipients use these cross-border services for non-taxable purposes.	**B2C:** customer's usual residence. **B2B:** Customer's location.	NZD 60 000 (USD 41 000) Same as for domestic suppliers
Norway	**B2C:** inbound supplies of electronic services are subject to VAT. The supplier must register for VAT. A simplified "pay only" registration (without tax representative) is available under a fully electronic procedure. Standard registration procedure (with right to deduct input tax) is also available. **B2B:** supplies of services and intangibles are taxed under the reverse charge mechanism.	**B2C:** Customer's usual residence. **B2B:** Customer's location.	NOK 50 000 (USD 5 000) Same as for domestic suppliers
Poland	European Union scheme (see below)		
Portugal	European Union scheme (see below)		
Slovak Republic	European Union scheme (see below)		
Slovenia	European Union scheme (see below)		
Spain	European Union scheme (see below)		
Sweden	European Union scheme (see below)		
Switzerland*	**B2C:** inbound supplies of services and intangibles are subject to VAT. The foreign supplier must register for VAT under the standard registration procedure (no simplified procedure is available; the appointment of a tax agent is required). The customer is liable to pay the VAT if the supplier has not registered and its on-line purchases exceed CHF 10 000 per year. **B2B:** most of the inbound supplies of services and intangibles are taxed under the reverse charge mechanism, unless the foreign supplier is registered for VAT to account for B2C supplies.	**B2C:** Customer's usual residence. **B2B:** Customer's location.	CHF 100 000 (USD 100 000)
Turkey	**B2C:** inbound supplies of services and intangibles are taxed. The consumer is liable to collect and pay the GST under a self-assessment procedure. **B2B:** inbound supplies of services and intangibles are taxed under the reverse charge mechanism.	Effective use and enjoyment.	No threshold
United Kingdom	European Union scheme (see below)		
European Union	**B2C:** inbound supplies of telecommunication, electronic and broadcasting services are subject to VAT. The non-EU supplier can opt to register for VAT under the "Mini One Stop Shop" mechanism. Through that mechanism, a simplified "pay only" registration (without tax representative) is available under a fully electronic procedure. **B2B:** supplies of services and intangibles are generally taxed under the reverse charge mechanism.	**B2C:** Customer's usual residence. **B2B:** Customer's location.	No threshold

* See country notes in Box 1.A1.11.

Notes: In the context of this table:

- "services and intangibles" refer to any supply of service or intangible by a non-resident supplier (with no establishment whatsoever in the customer's country).
- "pay only registration" refers to a VAT registration regime for non-resident suppliers that seeks only the collection of VAT on inbound supplies of services and intangibles from these suppliers, without granting the right for these suppliers to deduct any VAT incurred in the taxing jurisdiction (although a refund or other relief procedure may be available).

Box 1.A1.11. **Country notes**

Australia: From 1 July 2017, B2C suppliers of services and intangibles will be required to register for and charge GST on their sales to Australian consumers, if their Australian turnover exceeds AUD 75 000. Both a full and simplified (pay only) registration will be available. The proxy for determining the place of taxation for B2C supplies will be the customer's usual residence. The rules applicable to B2B supplies will not be changed.

Israel: A draft bill was published on 13 March 2016 to amend the VAT law to require, if passed, non-resident suppliers of digital B2C services to register for VAT in Israel (simplified registration procedure). The statistical data for Israel are supplied by and under the responsibility of the relevant Israeli authorities. The use of such data by the OECD is without prejudice to the status of the Golan Heights, East Jerusalem and Israeli settlements in the West Bank under the terms of international law.

Switzerland: For B2B supplies, the reverse charge mechanism only applies for supplies taxed in Switzerland according to the place of the customer. The reverse charge mechanism does not apply and the supplier must register for VAT for services taxed in Switzerland according to other proxies (e.g. the location of the immovable property to which the supply is connected). The law is currently under revision to determine the threshold for mandatory registration of the non-resident supplier with regard to its global turnover rather than its turnover made in Switzerland.

Table 1.A1.12. **Application of domestic reverse charge and split payment mechanisms**

	Domestic reverse charge system[1]	Domestic split payment mechanism[2]
Australia	-	-
Austria	Supply of laptops, tablets, PCs, game consoles, mobile phones and integrated circuit devices if the amount of the invoice is at least EUR 5 000. Supply of gas and electric energy to taxable dealers. Supply of gas and electric energy certificates. Supply of CO_2 emission allowances. Supply of certain metals and of taxable investment gold. Supply of scrap and industrial and non-industrial waste and recyclable waste. Construction services if the recipient is acting as general contractor or if he usually is rendering construction services. Supplies of staff engaged in the construction sector. Supply of goods provided as security by a VAT taxable person to another person in execution of that security. Supply of goods following the cession of the reservation of ownership to an assignee and the exercising of this right by the assignee. Supply of immovable property sold by the judgment debtor in a compulsory sale procedure to another person.	
Belgium	Some supplies of investment gold and of gold products of a purity of at least 325 thousands. Supply of work on immovable property under several conditions. Supplies of staff engaged in the construction sector. Supply of CO_2 emissions allowances.	
Canada	Certain purchasers of real property are required to self-assess (e.g. when the supplier is a non-resident; or when the purchaser is registered for GST/HST and, if he is an individual, the property is not a residential complex). In certain circumstances, persons may be required to self-assess the provincial part of the HST when certain property or services are moved from one province to another.	
Chile	Supplies of rice, construction works, waste, marine species, livestock, legumes, wood, wild products, wheat and berries. The customer (who must be a VAT taxpayer) acts as a withholding agent.	
Czech Republic	Supply of taxable investment gold and gold material of purity equal to or greater than 333 thousandths. Supply of designated categories of scrap and waste. Supply of CO_2 emission allowances. Supply of construction and assembly services provided between taxable persons registered for Czech VAT. Supply of mobile phones, integrated circuit devices, notebooks, tablets and videogame consoles. Supply of certain metals and basic products from metals. Supply of cereals and industrial crops, including oil seeds and sugar beet. Supply of immovable property under the option for taxation. Supply of gas and electric energy to taxable dealers (from 1 February 2016). Supply of gas and electric energy certificates (from 1 February 2016).	There is a special method for securing the payment of VAT that can be used when a recipient of a taxable supply wants to avoid being declared joint and severally liable for the unpaid taxes by the supplier. Similarly to the split payment mechanism, for these cases the recipient can pay the VAT due directly to the account of the supplier's tax office.
Denmark	Supply of CO_2 emission allowances. Supply of construction work, including repair, cleaning, maintenance and demolition services in relation to immovable property. Supply of scrap metals. Supply of investment gold. Supply of mobile phones, integrated circuit devices, games consoles, tablet PCs and laptops.	

Table 1.A1.12. Application of domestic reverse charge and split payment mechanisms (cont.)

	Domestic reverse charge system[1]	Domestic split payment mechanism[2]
Estonia	Supply of immovable property and investment gold, where the supplier has opted for taxation. Supply of gold material, including semi-finished gold products (purity of at least 325 thousandths). Supply of scrap metal and precious metals.	
Finland	Supply of taxable investment gold as well as gold material and semi-manufactured gold products of purity equal to or greater than 325 thousandths. Supply of CO_2 emission allowances. Supply of scrap metal and waste. Construction services, including supply of staff engaged in the construction sector.	
France	Supply of CO_2 emission allowances. Supply of used materials, scrap and waste. Supply of investment gold and gold products of a purity of at least 325 thousandths. Construction services (limited to certain services provided on a building when performed by a subcontractor on behalf of a taxable person). Supply of gas and electric energy to taxable dealers. Supply of certain telecommunication services.	
Germany	Supplies of pledged assets by the guarantor to the recipient of the security outside the framework of judicial liquidation. Supplies covered by the Real Property Transfer Tax Law (in particular transfers of real estate). If the customer is an entrepreneur: supplies of work or other services serving the construction, repair, maintenance, alteration or removal of structures (except for planning, engineering and supervision) and cleaning of buildings when the customer himself supplies such services. Supply of gold (unwrought or semi-finished of a purity of at least 325 thousandths). Supply of CO_2 emissions allowances. Supply of industrial scrap, ferrous and non-ferrous waste and other waste. Supply of mobile devices, integrated circuit devices, game consoles and tablet PC if the transaction value is or exceeds EUR 5 000. Supply of electricity (generally applicable only if supplier and recipient are both treated as resellers) and supply of gas (generally applicable only if the recipient is to be treated as reseller). Supply of precious metals as well as certain ignoble metals (e.g. copper, nickel, aluminium, lead, zinc), unwrought or semi-manufactured, if the transaction value is or exceeds EUR 5 000.	
Greece	Construction work assigned to public works' contractors by public authorities, provided the public authorities are owners of the works and taxable persons with the right to input tax deduction. Major projects as defined by EU Regulations are exempt from the reverse charge system. Provided the supply is intended for recycling, the following supplies of recyclable waste: a) Supply of ferrous and non-ferrous waste metals, scrap(clippings) and other used materials. b) Supply of semi-finished products made of ferrous and non-ferrous metals. c) Supply of residues and other recyclable materials consisting of ferrous and non-ferrous metals, alloys, slag, ash or scale and industrial residues containing metals or metal alloys. d) Supply of parings and scrap (clippings), waste and used recyclable material consisting of cullet, glass, paper, cardboard, rags, bone, leather (natural or artificial), diphtheria, raw hides and skins, tendons and sinews, twine, rope and trawl, cables, rubber and plastic materials. e) Supply of scrap (clippings) and waste from the working of base materials. f) Supply of the aforementioned materials after cleaning, polishing, selection, cutting, fragmenting and pressing. Supply of greenhouse gas emissions allowances according to EU Directive 2003/87/EC.	

Table 1.A1.12. **Application of domestic reverse charge and split payment mechanisms** *(cont.)*

	Domestic reverse charge system[1]	Domestic split payment mechanism[2]
Hungary	Supply of construction works regarded as a supply of goods. Construction or other alteration or repair activity qualifying as service, directed at the construction, expansion, rearrangement or other modification (including demolition) of immovable property and subject to acquiescence or authorisation by the building authority. Hiring-out of employees and the supply of staff. Supply of scrap and waste products. Supply of a building and the land on which it stands or of an inbuilt plot of land (with certain exceptions) if the supplier opted for taxation. In relation with debtors and creditors, the supply of goods that were pledged as collateral security to cover an overdue claim in execution of that security. Supply of goods with an open market value of more than HUF 100 000 (EUR 334) used by the taxable person for the purposes of his business if the supplier is adjudicated in liquidation proceedings or any similar insolvency proceedings. Supply of CO_2 emissions allowances. Supply of certain specific agricultural products such as wheat and meslin, rye, barley, oats, maize, triticale, soya beans whether or not broken; rape and colza seeds whether or not broken; sunflower seeds whether or not broken. Supply of certain iron and non-alloy steel products such as flat-rolled products of iron or non-alloy steel, bars and rods of iron or non-alloy steel, angles, shapes and sections of iron or non-alloy steel, wire of iron or non-alloy steel, tubes, pipes and hollow profiles of iron or non-alloy steel.	
Iceland	-	
Ireland	Supply of construction services supplied by sub-contractors to principal contractors. Supply of immovable property under the option for taxation (including sale by receiver, liquidator or mortgagee in possession. Supply of used material and scrap metal. Supply of CO_2 emissions allowances. Supply of gas and electricity by a business in Ireland to a taxable dealer carrying on business in Ireland. Supply of gas certificates or electricity certificates by a business in Ireland to another business in Ireland.	
Israel[3]	A person not liable for payment of the tax may, with the Director's consent and on conditions prescribed by him, take the payment upon himself, and after the date of that consent he shall be treated as the person liable for its payment. The tax levied on a buyer, if the buyer is a dealer, a non-profit organisation or a financial institution and has committed a real estate sale which is an occasional transaction. Sale of metal debris. A dealer, a non-profit organisation or a financial institution receives services of the types specified below from a person, whose main income is from wage, benefit or pension, shall pay the tax in respect of that service, unless a tax invoice was received from the person rendering the service; these are the services: 1. Artistic performance; construction or preparation of stage sets; preparation, checking, conducting and supervising exams; lectures etc. 2. Services of the following professionals: agronomist, architect; practical engineer; private investigator; rabbinical pleader; technician; dental technician; organizational, management, scientific or tax consultant; economist; engineer etc.	
Italy	Supplies carried out by subcontractors in the building sector. Supply of staff engaged in the construction sector. Supply of immovable property under the option for taxation. Supply of used materials, scrap, waste and specific services. Supply of investment gold, including supply of semi-finished products and of gold of a purity of at least 325 thousandths(so called industrial gold). Supply of scrap iron. Supply of mobile phones, tablets, personal computers and integrated circuit devices under certain conditions. Supply of CO_2 emission allowances. Supply of gas and electric energy to taxable dealers. Supply of gas and electric energy certificates.	Supplies of goods and services made to public authorities

Table 1.A1.12. **Application of domestic reverse charge and split payment mechanisms** *(cont.)*

	Domestic reverse charge system[1]	Domestic split payment mechanism[2]
Japan	-	
Korea	-	For supplies of gold bullion (99.5% or higher purity) and second hand gold products (with 58.5% or higher purity), copper, gold and iron scrap, the supplier must open a bank account designated for the gold or scrap transactions and the purchase price (without VAT) must be transferred to the supplier using the designated bank account. At the same time, the recipient must also deposit the relevant VAT amount into an account designated by the Director of the National Tax Services.
Latvia	Supply of timber and services related to the supply of timber. Supply of construction services. Supply of scrap metals and services related to the supply of scrap metals. Supply of mobile telephones, integrated circuit devices, tablet PC's and laptops (from 1 April 2016).	
Luxembourg	Supply of CO_2 emission allowances.	
Mexico	Domestic reverse charge applies to: • corporations that receive independent personal services from individuals or rent goods from them. acquire waste to be used for commercial or industrial activities; receive services rendered by commissionaires who are individuals; and receive land motor transportation services of goods lent to both individuals and corporations; • credit institutions acquiring assets through payments in kind or through legal or trust adjudication; and • individuals or entities acquiring or having temporary use or enjoyment of tangible assets transferred or granted by foreign residents who do not have a permanent establishment in Mexico.	
Netherlands	Supply of construction work (including shipbuilding), including repair, cleaning, maintenance, alteration and demolition services in relation to immovable property, including the handing over of construction works. Supply of staff engaged in the construction sector. Supply of immovable property under the option for taxation. Supply of used materials, scrap, waste and specific services. Supply of goods provided as security by one taxable person to another in execution of that security. Supply of immovable property sold by a judgement debtor in a compulsory sale procedure. Supply of CO_2 emission allowances. Supply of mobile phones, integrated circuit devices, laptops, game consoles and tablet pc's provided that the value of the transactions exceeds EUR 10 000.	
New Zealand	If the supply of land has been incorrectly zero rated and the incorrect treatment is discovered after settlement, the recipient of the supply is made responsible for paying GST.	
Norway	Supply of CO_2 emission allowances. Supply of investment gold (with purity equal to or greater than 325 thousandths).	
Poland	Supply of metal scrap, metal waste and metal materials. Supply of CO_2 emission allowances. Supply of mobile phones (including smart phones), video game consoles, tablets, notebooks, and laptops. Supply of unwrought non-ferrous metals (aluminium, lead, zinc, tin, nickel). Supply of raw and semi-finished metals, including gold materials and intermediate products containing gold, investment gold and selected steel products.	

Table 1.A1.12. **Application of domestic reverse charge and split payment mechanisms** *(cont.)*

	Domestic reverse charge system[1]	Domestic split payment mechanism[2]
Portugal	Supply of used material, scrap metal, waste and specific services. Supply of immovable property under the option for taxation. Work on immovable property (such as repair, cleaning, maintenance, alteration and demolition services, including the handing over of construction works). Supply of taxable investment gold and gold material of purity equal to or greater than 325 thousandths. Supplies of CO_2 emission allowances.	
Slovak Republic	Supply of certain construction works including supply of building (construction) and the supply of certain goods requiring installation or assembly. Supply of immovable property under the option for taxation. Supply of goods which are pledged as a security of a receivable of a creditor within the enforcement of such pledge. Supply of a building or a part of a building in the Slovak Republic which the supplier as a debtor recognised by a court or another relevant state authority sold within the statutory enforcement proceedings. Supply of goods following the cession of a reservation of ownership to an assignee and the exercising of this right by the assignee. Supply of investment gold and of gold material or semi-manufactured products of gold of a purity of at least 325 thousandths between taxable persons. Supply of metal scrap and metal waste. Supply of CO_2 emission allowances. Supply of cereals and oil seeds, grains, straw and fodder crops, which are not typically intended in the unaltered state for final consumption, if the taxable amount in the invoice for the supply of such goods is EUR 5 000 and more. Supplies of iron and steel if the taxable amount in the invoice for the supply is EUR 5 000 and more. Supply of mobile phones, being devices made or adapted for use in connection with a licensed network and operated on specified frequencies, whether or not they have any other use, if the taxable amount in the invoice for the supply of mobile telephones is EUR 5 000 and more. Supply of integrated circuit devices such as microprocessors and central processing units in a state prior to integration into end user products, if the taxable amount in the invoice for the supply is EUR 5 000 and more. Supply of construction work, including repair, cleaning, maintenance, alteration and demolition services in relation to immovable property as well as the handing over of construction works regarded as a supply of goods.	
Slovenia	Supply of construction work (including repair, cleaning, maintenance, alteration and demolition services in relation to immovable property). Supply of staff engaged in the mentioned activities. Supply of certain immovable property, where the supplier has opted for taxation of the supply. Supply of certain waste, scrap, used material and services. Supply of allowances to emit greenhouse gases.	
Spain	Construction works, including the supply of staff for its performance, in the framework of development, construction or renovation of immovable property. Supply of CO_2 emission allowances. Supply of metal scrap and metal waste. Supply of investment gold and supply of gold material or semi-finished products of a purity of at least 325 thousandths. Supply of buildings in certain situations. Supply of immovable property within bankruptcy proceedings. Supply of immovable property made under enforcement of a security or with the obligation for the acquirer to settle the securitized debt. Supply of mobile phones, videogame consoles, laptop and tablet PCs, only where the customer is a reseller of the goods (traders habitually engaging in the resale of these goods) or, otherwise, where the total amount of supplies to one trader exceeds EUR 10 000. Supply of silver, platinum and palladium.	

Table 1.A1.12. **Application of domestic reverse charge and split payment mechanisms** *(cont.)*

	Domestic reverse charge system[1]	Domestic split payment mechanism[2]
Sweden	Supply of construction work, including repair, cleaning, maintenance, alteration and demolition services in relation to immovable property, including the handing over of construction works. Supply of staff engaged in the construction sector. Supply of CO_2 emissions allowances. Supply of used materials, scrap, waste and specific services. Supply of investment gold and gold products of a purity of at least 325 thousandths.	
Switzerland	-	-
Turkey	Supply of lease of movable property by non-taxable persons to taxable persons. Supply of scientific, artistic and literary works provided to taxable persons. Supply of advertisement services provided by non-taxable persons to taxable persons.	Certain recipients of a number of specified services are required to withhold a percentage of the VAT charged to them by the service provider and remit it directly to the tax authorities (*partial withholding*). Among others, these services are (a) supervisory services for building construction, (b) scrap metal, glass, plastic and paper (in cases where the supplier waives the VAT exemption), (c) advisory, supervisory and audit services maintenance and (d) repair services for machinery, equipment and other fixed assets.
United Kingdom	Supply of investment gold and of gold products of a purity of at least 325 thousandths. Supply of CO_2 emissions allowances. Supply of mobile telephones and integrated circuit devices if the value of the goods supplied exceeds GBP 5.000 (VAT inclusive). The value limit does not apply to services. Supply of gas through a natural gas system situated in the United Kingdom or any network connected to such a system and to electricity.	

1. For the purpose of this table, are considered "domestic reverse charge" situations where the customer rather than the supplier of goods, services or intangibles is liable to remit the VAT to the tax authorities on a domestic supply (i.e. a supply where both the supplier and the customer are established in the same jurisdiction, where the supply takes place). The supplier does not charge the VAT to the customer.
2. For the purpose of this table, a "domestic split payment mechanism", is a mechanism whereby, on a domestic supply of goods, services or intangibles, the supplier remains liable to charge the VAT to the customer, but where the customer directly remits (part of) the VAT directly to the tax authorities rather than to the supplier.
3. Israel: the statistical data for Israel are supplied by and under the responsibility of the relevant Israeli authorities. The use of such data by the OECD is without prejudice to the status of the Golan Heights, East Jerusalem and Israeli settlements in the West Bank under the terms of international law.

Source: National delegates and IBFD – Situation as at 1 January 2016.

Table 1.A1.13. Import/export of goods by individual travellers

	Thresholds for tax-free import of goods by individual travellers			Refund for individuals upon export		
	Scheme	Max threshold		Scheme	Min Value	
		Nat.Curr.	USD[3]		Nat.Curr.	USD[3]
Australia	AUD 900 worth of general goods (or AUD 450 for people under the age of 18 and air and sea crew members); 2.25 litres of alcohol and 50 cigarettes or 50g of cigars or tobacco products may be imported without individuals needing to be assessed for GST and customs duty. If the individuals have in excess of this amount, they need to declare goods and be assessed.	AUD 900	605	Tourist Refund Scheme (TRS): individuals may claim a refund of GST on purchases made over AUD 300 from a single business within 60 days of departure which is worn or taken as hand luggage. GST refunds are available when goods are shown with the necessary documentation, on departure from Australia. The TRS applies to both residents and non-residents (except to crew, sea and air).	AUD 300	202
Austria	EU Scheme[1]			Refund to individuals exporting goods in their personal luggage to a destination outside the EU Minimum invoice amount EUR 75.	EUR 75	92
	In air and sea traffic	EUR 430	525			
	In land traffic	EUR 300	366			
Belgium	EU Scheme[1]			Refund to individuals exporting goods in their personal luggage to a destination outside the EU Minimum invoice EUR 125.	EUR 125	152
	In air and sea traffic	EUR 430	521			
	In land traffic	EUR 300	364			
	Restrictions of these thresholds apply depending on the age of the passenger, the nature of the products (excise products) staff of the means of transport.					
Canada	I) Goods acquired abroad and for personal or household use imported by Canadian residents, temporary residents or former residents returning to live in Canada: – Returning after an absence of not less than 24 hours, goods (except alcoholic beverages and tobacco products) valued at not more than CAD 200 and included in the baggage accompanying the person. – Returning after an absence of not less than 48 hours, goods (including either wine not exceeding 1.5 litres, beer not exceeding 8.5 litres or liquor not exceeding 1.14 litres and tobacco not exceeding fifty cigars, two hundred cigarettes, two hundred tobacco sticks and two hundred grams of manufactured tobacco) valued at not more than CAD 800 and included in the baggage accompanying the resident. – Returning after an absence of not less than seven days, goods (including either wine not exceeding 1.5 litres, beer not exceeding 8.5 litres or liquor not exceeding 1.14 litres and tobacco not exceeding fifty cigars, two hundred cigarettes, two hundred tobacco sticks and two hundred grams of manufactured tobacco)valued at not more than CAD 800 whether or not (except for alcoholic beverages and tobacco products) included in the baggage accompanying the person. II) Goods that are zero-rated when supplied domestically (for example, basic groceries) III) Conveyances and baggage temporarily imported by non-residents for use in Canada IV) Casual donations valued at CAD 60 or under sent by persons abroad to friends in Canada or imported personally by non-residents as gifts to friends in Canada (except advertising matter, tobacco or alcoholic beverages)	CAD 800 No max. for Items II, III, V-XI	521 idem		CAD 200	160

Table 1.A1.13. **Import/export of goods by individual travellers** *(cont.)*

	Thresholds for tax-free import of goods by individual travellers			Refund for individuals upon export		
	Scheme	Max threshold		Scheme	Min Value	
		Nat.Curr.	USD[3]		Nat.Curr.	USD[3]
	V) Personal effects of seasonal residents VI) Personal effects of returning former residents (resident in another country for at least one year) or residents who have been abroad for at least one year (goods must have been actually owned, possessed and used abroad by the individual for at least six months prior to the individual's return to Canada and accompany the individual upon return to Canada) VII) Personal effects of settlers VIII) Personal effects of settlers acquired with blocked currencies IX) Personal effects of deceased persons X) Foreign conveyances temporarily imported by a Canadian resident to be used in the international non-commercial transportation of the individual and accompanying the individual using the conveyance. XI) Medals, trophies and other non-resalable prizes that are: – won outside Canada or donated by persons outside Canada for heroic deeds, valour or distinction; – to be presented by the importer at awards ceremonies; or – bestowed or awarded abroad as marks of honour or distinction, won abroad in competitions, or won abroad in competitions and donated by persons abroad for bestowal or award in Canada.					
Chile	Goods acquired abroad and imported by: – Passengers regarding "travel baggage" exempted of Customs Duties limited to new and used goods for personal use and for gift; used goods exclusively intended to perform a profession or job; the quantity, not exceeding four hundred cigarettes, five hundred grams of tobacco, fifty cigars and 2.5 litres of alcoholic beverages; and some technological goods. The exemption excludes goods imported with commercial purpose. – Officers or employees of the Chilean Government who serve abroad and immigrants provided that the goods are personal effects, home appliances, tools and work equipment, provided these items do not require an import register. – Crew personnel of a ship, aircraft or another vehicle concerning travel baggage exempted of Customs Duties. – Travellers and Chilean residents from the First Region (Chile) under some circumstances.			Nonresident individuals who leave the country through the Chacalluta border crossing (on the First Region) can obtain a refund of VAT paid on merchandise acquired in Arica and Parinacota up to USD 319 daily.	CLP 3 268	8

Table 1.A1.13. **Import/export of goods by individual travellers** *(cont.)*

	Thresholds for tax-free import of goods by individual travellers			Refund for individuals upon export		
	Scheme	Max threshold		Scheme	Min Value	
		Nat.Curr.	USD[3]		Nat.Curr.	USD[3]
	– Travellers regarding goods subject to the customs classifications (goods owned by travellers coming from the Chilean duty-free zone up to USD 1 218; goods acquired by passenger from abroad, in Chilean tax duty free shop only, up to a value of USD 500; goods imported by Chilean residents of border places up to USD 150; home appliances of Chileans returning after an absence between six months and one year (up to USD 500); home appliances and work equipment of Chileans returning after an absence between one year and five years (up to USD 3 000); home appliances and work equipment of Chileans returning after an absence of not less than five years (up to USD 5 000); goods of foreign national with a temporary residence in Chile or with a job agreement not less than a one year term: home appliances (up to USD 5 000) and work equipment (up to USD 1 500). – National artists regarding their pieces of arts performed abroad under customs classification (drafts, painting, sculptures). Travellers and temporal visitors regarding goods for personal use during their visiting to Chile, and vehicles for their private transportation. Goods considered as: – Cultural or sport prizes and trophies won abroad without commercial nature, and non-commercial gifts occasionally awarded to individuals under customs classification (gifts cannot exceed the value of USD 50). – Prizes and gifts awarded to Chilean individuals, listed under the customs classification, who obtain highest distinction and under specific requirements					
Czech Republic	EU Scheme[1]			Refund to individuals exporting goods in their personal luggage to a destination outside the EU. Minimum invoice CZK 2 000 for one seller on one day.	CZK 2 000	152
	In air and sea traffic	EUR 430 (CZK 11 622)	890			
	In land traffic	EUR 300 (CZK 8 108)	621			
Denmark	EU Scheme[1]			Refund to individuals exporting goods in their personal luggage to a destination outside the EU. Minimum value: DKK 300. Refund to travellers from Norway and the Aland Islands exporting goods in their personal luggage. Minimum value DKK 1 200.	DKK 1 200	160
	In air and sea traffic	EUR 430 (DKK 3199)	428			
	In land traffic	EUR 300 (DKK 2232)	298			
Estonia	EU Scheme[1]			Refund to individuals exporting goods in their personal luggage to a destination outside the EU. The traveller's habitual residence must be outside the European Union.	EUR 38	68
	In air and sea traffic	EUR 430	775			
	In land traffic	EUR 300	540			
Finland	EU Scheme[1]			Refund to individuals exporting goods in their personal luggage to a destination outside the EU, minimum invoice EUR 40. Traveller from Norway and the Åland Islands can only get the refund if the value of the goods without VAT is at the minimum EUR 170.	EUR 40	43
	In air and sea traffic	EUR 430	462			
	In land traffic	EUR 300	322			

Table 1.A1.13. **Import/export of goods by individual travellers** *(cont.)*

	Thresholds for tax-free import of goods by individual travellers			Refund for individuals upon export		
	Scheme	Max threshold		Scheme	Min Value	
		Nat.Curr.	USD[3]		Nat.Curr.	USD[3]
France	EU Scheme[1]			Refund to individuals exporting goods in their personal luggage to a destination outside the EU. The traveller's habitual residence must be outside the European Union. The total value of the purchases (including VAT) in a single shop on the same day must be over EUR 175.	EUR 175	212
	In air and sea traffic	EUR 430	522			
	In land traffic	EUR 300	364			
Germany	EU Scheme[1]			Refund to individuals exporting goods in their personal luggage to a destination outside the EU. The traveller's habitual residence must be outside the European Union. The goods have to be exported within three months following the month of purchase. There is no threshold as to the amount. The VAT exemption is only valid for non-commercial purposes (except for the equipment and supply of private means of transport e.g. car, motorboat, aeroplane etc.)	-	-
	In air and sea traffic	EUR 430	546			
	In land traffic	EUR 300	382			
Greece	EU Scheme[1]			Refund to individuals exporting goods in their personal luggage to a destination outside the EU Minimum invoice EUR 120.	EUR 120	197
	In air and sea traffic	EUR 430	705			
	In land traffic	EUR 300	492	Limitations: foodstuffs; alcoholic beverages; tobacco products; goods for the provisioning and the equipping of means of transport for private use (motor vehicles, aircrafts or sea-going vessels); goods having commercial character.		
Hungary	EU Scheme[1]			Refund to individuals exporting goods in their personal luggage to a destination outside the EU. Minimum invoice EUR 175.	EUR 175	411
	In air and sea traffic	EUR 430	996			
	In land traffic	EUR 300	695			
	Limitation: tobacco, spirits/alcoholic beverages, fuel (free of VAT under a certain quantitative limit).					
Iceland	Food: travelers may import duty-free up to 3kg of food, including candy, not exceeding the value of ISK 25 000.	ISK 25 000	176	Refund for individuals when leaving the country for goods worth more than ISK 6 000.	ISK 6 000	42
	Alcoholic beverages and tobaccos: in addition to goods referred to above, travelers can import duty-free alcoholic beverages and tobacco products as follows: – 1 liter spirits and 1 liter wine and 6 liters beer or – 3 liters wine and 6 liters beer or – 1 liter spirits and 9 liters beer or – 1.5 liters wine and 9 liters beer or – 12 liters beer Spirits comprise alcoholic beverages containing more than 21% alcohol; wines comprise alcoholic beverages, other than beer, containing 21% alcohol or less. 200 cigarettes or 250g of other tobacco products.		-			
	Icelandic residents may bring duty free the luggage they brought with them abroad furthermore they can bring one or more items of duty free goods worth in total up to 88 000 ISK.	ISK 88 000	615			
Ireland	EU Scheme[1]			Refund to individuals exporting goods in their personal luggage to a destination outside the EU.	-	-
	In air and sea traffic	EUR 430	508			
	In land traffic	EUR 300	355	There is no threshold as to the amount.		

Table 1.A1.13. **Import/export of goods by individual travellers** *(cont.)*

	Thresholds for tax-free import of goods by individual travellers			Refund for individuals upon export		
	Scheme	Max threshold		Scheme	Min Value	
		Nat.Curr.	USD[3]		Nat.Curr.	USD[3]
Israel[2]	Import duty exemption: personal products, beverages and wines: liquor up to 1 litre and up to 2 litres of wine-for each entrant age 18. Alcoholic perfume- to 1/4 litres per entrant. Tobacco- weight not exceeding 250gr. Products other than those mentioned above up to USD 200.		200	A refund will be given to the visitor, a non-citizen holding a foreign passport. The arrangement does not apply to purchases of tobacco products, food and beverages, (except wineries). Minimum purchase amount for VAT refund is: 400 NIS including VAT, purchase at the same time in one business transaction. Providing a refund is subject to the purchase in a registered business.	ILS 400	103
Italy	EU Scheme[1] In air and sea traffic In land traffic	 EUR 430 EUR 300	 574 400	Refund to individuals exporting goods in their personal luggage to a destination outside the EU Minimum threshold is fixed at EUR 154.94.	EUR 155	207
Japan	(1) Goods which total taxable value do not exceed JPY 10 000. Goods other than those in (1), which total taxable value do not exceed JPY 200 000 Tax-free import of liquor, tobacco and perfume is limited to certain quantities	JPY 10 000 JPY 200 000 -	95 1900 -	On the time of the purchase at registered shops, foreign visitors who have temporarily stayed in Japan for less than 6 month are exempt from VAT (with the exceptions of gold, platinum, and other non-"daily life" items). There is also the maximum value of JPY 500 000 per shop per day for "consumable items" (such as foods, beverages, cosmetics, etc.).	JPY 5 000	47
Korea	The following personal goods (or goods arriving by separate post) of travellers that are exempted from customs duties. (1) Goods up to a total combined value of USD 600. (2) 1 bottle of alcoholic beverage (not exceeding 1liter and USD 400). (3) 200 cigarettes and 50 cigars. (4) Perfume that does not exceed 60ml.	KRW 710 000	797	Foreign travellers are exempted from VAT for exported goods when they are acquired in Tax-free shops only. Minimum invoice KRW 30 000.	KRW 30 000	34
Latvia	EU Scheme[1] In air and sea traffic In land traffic	 EUR 430 EUR 300	 847 591	Refund to individuals exporting goods in their personal luggage to a destination outside the EU. Minimum invoice EUR 35.57.	EUR 35.57	70
Luxembourg	EU Scheme[1] In air and sea traffic In land traffic	 EUR 430 EUR 300	 479 334	Refund to individuals exporting goods in their personal luggage to a destination outside the EU. Minimum invoice EUR 74.	EUR 74	82
Mexico	(1) Administrative Rule No. 3.2.3. includes a list of items that may be introduced to Mexico as part of the baggage of international passengers residing abroad or in Mexico. (2) When arriving to Mexico by ships or aircrafts it is possible to introduce tax free good which value does not exceed USD 500 or its equivalent in national or foreign currency. (3) When arriving to Mexico in terrestrial means of transportation such amount shall not exceed USD 300 on regular season and USD 500 on high holiday season.		500	Foreign tourists leaving the country by airplane or ship may claim a refund on the VAT paid on the acquisition of goods in Mexico when, among other requirements, the amount paid for the goods in one single store is at least 1 200 MXN.	MXN 1 200	145
Netherlands	EU Scheme[1] In air and sea traffic In land traffic	 EUR 430 EUR 300	 520 363	Refund to individuals exporting goods in their personal luggage to a destination outside the EU Minimum invoice EUR 50.	EUR 50	60

Table 1.A1.13. **Import/export of goods by individual travellers** *(cont.)*

	Thresholds for tax-free import of goods by individual travellers			Refund for individuals upon export		
	Scheme	Max threshold		Scheme	Min Value	
		Nat.Curr.	USD[3]		Nat.Curr.	USD[3]
New Zealand	When entering New Zealand, people are entitled to a personal goods concession which allows them to bring goods up to a total combined value of NZD 700 into the country, free of duty and GST. The personal goods concession applies to goods which accompany that person through Customs, are for that person's personal use or are intended as gifts, are not intended for sale of exchange, are not for use in their businesses or profession and are not imported for other persons at their request. On entering New Zealand a person is entitled to bring, free of duty and GST, the following quantities: Tobacco: 200 cigarettes, or 250 grams of tobacco, or 50 cigars, or a mixture of all three weighing not more than 250gr. Alcoholic Beverages: 4.5 litres of wine or 4.5 litres of beer – 3 bottles containing not more than 1.125ml of spirits, liquor, or other spirituous beverages. Other concessions: Personal effects: wearing apparel, footwear purchased while outside New Zealand for the intended use or wear of the traveller. Goods need to accompany the traveller when arriving in New Zealand. Gifts: if value is less than NZD 110 – free entry, if more than NZD 110 – GST and duty applies on the value in excess of NZD 110. Multiple gift allowances are permitted provide that the separate identity of each recipient can be established. Heirlooms: Items bequeathed to a person in New Zealand may be imported free of all Customs charges.	NZD 700	477	No refund scheme	-	-
Norway	The threshold is NOK 6 000 for travel abroad for more than 24 hours. For travel abroad of less than 24 hours, the threshold is NOK 3 000. For alcohol and tobacco, special quantitative limits apply.	NOK 6 000	612	VAT refunds are available for tourists. For Nordic countries a higher value applies.	NOK 250	26
Poland	EU Scheme[1] In air and sea traffic In land traffic	 EUR 430 (PLN 1894) EUR 300 (PLN 1322)	 1053 734	Refund to individuals exporting goods (excluding fuels) in their personal luggage to a destination outside the EU. Minimum invoice PLN 200 (from 1 June 2016 PLN 300).	PLN 200	489
Portugal	EU Scheme[1] In air and sea traffic In land traffic Travellers under 15 years old	 EUR 430 EUR 300 EUR 150	 725 506 253	Refund to individuals exporting goods (except equipment, fuelling and provisioning of private means of transport) in their personal luggage to a destination outside the EU. Minimum invoice EUR 50.	EUR 50	84
Slovak Republic	EU Scheme[1] In air and sea traffic In land traffic Travellers under 15 years old, regardless their means of transport	 EUR 430 EUR 300 EUR 150	 863 602 301	For travellers without permanent or temporary address within the EU. The total amount including VAT of exported goods to one taxpayer in one day should exceed EUR 175 and goods should be exported within 3 months after the last day of the month where goods were purchased.	EUR 175	351
Slovenia	EU Scheme[1] In air and sea traffic In land traffic Travellers under 15 years old, regardless their means of transport	 EUR 430 EUR 300 EUR 150	 717 500 250	Refund to individuals exporting goods (except mineral oils, alcohol and alcoholic beverages and tobacco products) in their personal luggage to a destination outside the EU. Minimum invoice EUR 50.	EUR 50	83

Table 1.A1.13. **Import/export of goods by individual travellers** *(cont.)*

	Thresholds for tax-free import of goods by individual travellers			Refund for individuals upon export		
	Scheme	Max threshold		Scheme	Min Value	
		Nat.Curr.	USD[3]		Nat.Curr.	USD[3]
Spain	EU Scheme[1] In air and sea traffic In land traffic	 EUR 430 EUR 300	 637 445	Refund to individuals exporting goods in their personal luggage to a destination outside the EU Minimum invoice EUR 90.	EUR 90	133
Sweden	EU Scheme[1] In air and sea traffic In land traffic	 EUR 430 (SEK 3 841) EUR 300 (SEK 2 680)	 440 307	Refund to individuals exporting goods in their personal luggage to a destination outside the EU Minimum invoice SEK 200. Higher value for Norway and the Åland island.	SEK 200	22
Switzerland	Personal belongings; food and non-alcoholic beverages for the day of travel; meat and meat products: 1kg; butter and cream: 1l. or 1kg; oil, grease, margarine for eating purposes 5 litres or 5kg; alcoholic beverages: 5 litres. up to 18°alc. plus 1litre over 18° alc.; tobacco: 250 cigarettes or cigars or 250 grams of other tobacco product; fuel imported in a spare canister of max. 25 litres. Personal belongings means what residents take with them when leaving the country and what non-residents will use during their stay and re-export when going home (clothing, personal-care products, sports equipment, personal computer, audio and video equipment, musical instruments, etc).	CHF 300	235	There is no refund of VAT to any individuals by the Tax Administration. Goods for personal use or for gift purposes are tax free if they are exported by the non-resident purchaser within 30 days after delivery to the latter and if the export is confirmed. Minimum invoice: CHF 300. Selling goods by authorised stores to members of escorted tourist groups directly without VAT within Switzerland.	CHF 300	235
Turkey	–	-	-	VAT refund to passengers who do not reside in Turkey for the purchasing goods taken to abroad. Minimum invoice: TRY 100.	TRY 100	79
United Kingdom	EU Scheme[1] For imports from outside the EU – up to GBP 390 unless passengers arrive by private plane or boat in which case it is up to GBP 270	GBP 390	563	Refund to individuals exporting goods in their personal luggage to a destination outside the EU. Threshold on refunds set by retailer.	-	-
United States	The allowance is USD 800 per person for absences over 48 hours, every 30 days, including up to 1 litre of alcoholic beverages, 200 cigarettes and 100 cigars. The goods must be for personal or household use only, or bona fide gifts, and not for the account of any other person, nor may they be re-sold. The amount may be pooled with family members. A traveller who has already used the USD 800 monthly allowance still has available a USD 200 exemption per crossing. This amount may not be pooled with family members, and if the value of the goods exceeds USD 200 the exemption does not apply and duties are levied on the total value of the goods imported.	USD 800	800	No refund scheme	-	-

1. **European Union:** EU rules allow tax-free import of goods from outside the EU by individuals for non-commercial purposes in their personal luggage to the extent that the global value of the imported goods does not exceed EUR 430 for air and sea travellers and to EUR 300 for land and inland waterways travellers. Nevertheless, special quantitative limits by traveller may apply for the following high-duty goods: tobacco, cigarettes, cigars and alcoholic beverages. The supply of goods exported outside the EU in the personal luggage of non-EU travellers is exempted from VAT if their total value is more than EUR 175 including VAT. Member States can exempt a supply with a total value of less than EUR 175.
2. **Israel:** the statistical data for Israel are supplied by and under the responsibility of the relevant Israeli authorities. The use of such data by the OECD is without prejudice to the status of the Golan Heights, East Jerusalem and Israeli settlements in the West Bank under the terms of international law.
3. Amounts are converted into USD at Purchase Parity Rates (PPPs). PPPs are the rates of currency conversion that equalise the purchasing power of different countries by eliminating differences in price levels between countries. They show the specified number of monetary units needed in each country to buy the same representative basket of consumer goods and services, which costs USD 1 in the United States. The currency conversion rates used in Consumption Tax Trends are the PPP rates for GDP. The PPPs are given in national currency unit per US dollar (see Annex A). For Member States of the European Union, the threshold is mentioned in Euro (EUR) even for those that do not have the Euro as national currency (i.e. Czech Republic, Denmark, Hungary, Poland and Sweden), with the exception of the United Kingdom since the threshold is determined in EUR by common EU legislation (Directive 2007/74/EC). The amount in EUR is converted into USD as follows: it is first converted into local currency at market exchange rate (Eurostat average 2015) and then into USD at PPP exchange rate.

Consumption Tax Trends 2016

Chapter 2

Value added taxes: Rates and structure

This chapter describes a selection of key features of VAT regimes in OECD countries, i.e. tax rates, exemptions, specific restrictions to input tax credit, registration and collection thresholds and the application of margin schemes. It is complemented with a technical discussion of the rationale and impact of reduced VAT rates.

The statistical data for Israel are supplied by and under the responsibility of the relevant Israeli authorities. The use of such data by the OECD is without prejudice to the status of the Golan Heights, East Jerusalem and Israeli settlements in the West Bank under the terms of international law.

2.1. Introduction

Although most VAT systems are built on the same core VAT principles (see Chapter 1), there is considerable diversity in the structure of VAT systems in OECD countries. This is notably illustrated by the variety of reduced rates, exemptions and other preferential treatments and special regimes that are widely used in OECD countries, often for equity or social objectives or for practical or historical reasons.

This chapter presents an overview of the VAT rate structures in OECD countries and their evolution between 1975 and 2016 (Section 2.2) and looks in some detail at the VAT exemptions that exist in these countries (Section 2.3). This is followed by an overview and analysis of the wide variety of special regimes used in OECD countries in the following areas: specific restrictions on the right to deduct VAT on specific inputs (Section 2.4), registration and collection thresholds (Section 2.5), and the application of margin schemes (Section 2.6). The last section (Section 2.7) presents a further detailed technical discussion of the rationale and impact of reduced VAT rates based on OECD research.

2.2. The evolution of standard rates and reduced rates

The evolution of VAT rates can be divided into four periods. During the first period between 1975 and 2000, when many countries first implemented their VAT system, many countries progressively raised their standard rates. Out of the 31 OECD countries that had a VAT in 1995, 20 had raised their standard rate at least once since implementation. Between 1975 and 2000, the OECD average standard rate rose from 15.6% to 18%.

During a second period, between 2000 and 2009, the standard rate of VAT remained stable in most countries, with 23 out of 34 countries maintaining a rate between 15% and 22%. As of 1 January 2009, only 5 countries had a standard rate above 22% (Denmark, Finland, Iceland, Norway and Sweden). Between 2000 and 2009, the OECD average standard rate declined slightly from 18% to 17.7% (see Table 2.A2.1).

The third period, between 2009 and 2014, was marked by a considerable increase in the standard VAT rate in many countries, often in response to financial consolidation pressures caused by the economic and financial crisis. VAT standard rate increases have played a key role in many countries' consolidation strategies, since raising additional revenue from VAT rather than from other taxes (such as income taxes) is often considered more effective (it generates immediate additional revenue) and less detrimental to economic growth and competitiveness than income taxes (OECD, 2010). Between 2009 and 2014, 22 countries raised their standard VAT rate at least once. These changes occurred principally in European Union (EU) countries (Czech Republic, Estonia, Finland, France, Greece, Hungary, Ireland, Italy, Latvia, the Netherlands, Poland, Portugal, Slovak Republic, Slovenia, Spain and United Kingdom) but also in some non-EU countries (Iceland, Israel, Japan, Mexico, New Zealand, and Switzerland). Two OECD countries lowered their standard VAT rate temporarily and then raised it again (Ireland and the United Kingdom). This evolution resulted in a hike of the unweighted OECD average standard VAT rate from 17.7%

in January 2009 to an all-time record level of 19.2% on 1 January 2015. Ten OECD countries now operate a standard rate above 22% against only four in 2009.

The increases in standard VAT rates observed until the end of 2014 have not continued into 2015 and it would appear that OECD countries have entered a new period of relatively stable standard VAT rates. Only two OECD countries increased their standard VAT rate between 2014 and 2016, i.e. Japan (from 5% to 8% as of 1 April 2014) and Luxemburg (15% to 17% as of 1 January 2015). Two OECD countries reduced their standard VAT rate, i.e. Iceland (from 25.5% to 24% as of as of 1 January 2015) and Israel (from 18% to 17% as of 1 October 2015). The unweighted OECD average standard VAT rate has remained stable at 19.2% since 1 January 2015.

Figure 2.1. **Evolution of standard VAT rates – OECD average 1976-2016**

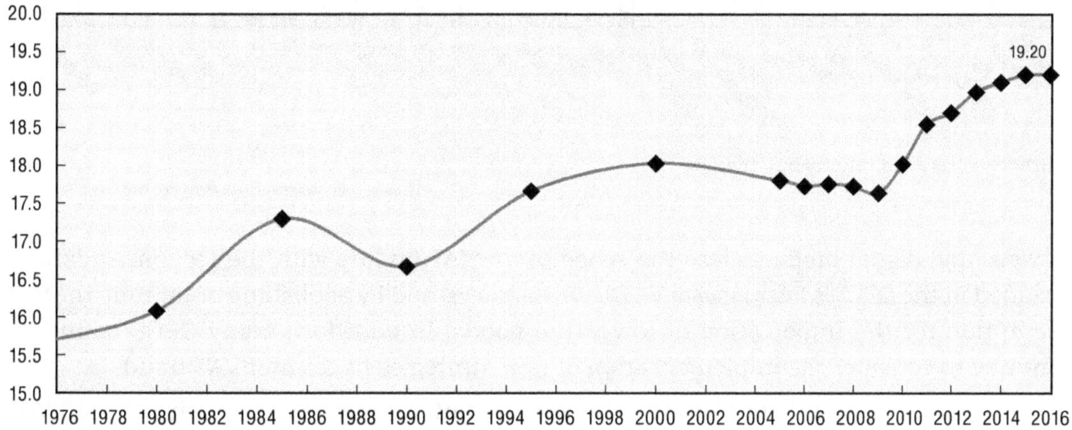

Source: Author's work based on country information.

StatLink http://dx.doi.org/10.1787/888933419952

Major differences in standard rates can still be observed among the OECD countries, with rates ranging from 5% in Canada (although most Canadian provinces levy sales taxes or Harmonised Sales Taxes alongside the Federal 5%) and 8% in Japan and Switzerland to 25% in Denmark, Norway and Sweden and 27% in Hungary (see Figure 2.1).

The average standard rate of the 22 OECD countries that are members of the EU (21.7%) is significantly above the OECD average (19.2%). EU Member States are bound by common rules regarding VAT rates (VAT Directive 2006/112/EC), which set the minimum level of the standard rate at 15%. Two reduced rates of not less than 5% may be applied to a restricted list of goods and services as well as to certain labour intensive services, and no rate can be higher than the standard rate. A multitude of derogations have however been granted to many EU countries, which has resulted in more than 40 different standard and reduced VAT rates being applied in the EU.

OECD countries have relied primarily on increases of the standard rate to raise additional VAT revenue, rather than on reform to broaden the tax base by removing or limiting the scope of reduced VAT rates or VAT exemptions. Most OECD countries continue to apply a wide variety of reduced VAT rates and exemptions (see Tables 2.A2.2 and 2.A2.4). A recent OECD survey (Brys et al. 2016a) suggests, however, that countries may increasingly look at base broadening measures to raise additional revenue from VAT, notably by increasing reduced VAT rates and/or narrowing their scope, by bringing inbound supplies of

Figure 2.2. **Standard rates of VAT in OECD countries, 2016**

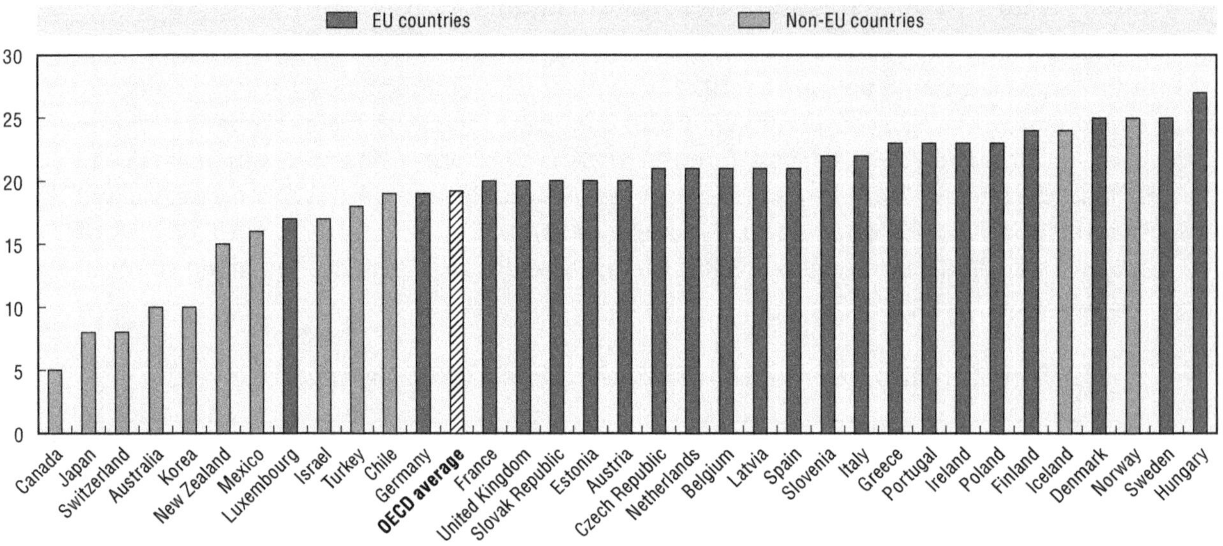

Source: Author's work based on country information.

StatLink http://dx.doi.org/10.1787/888933419966

services and digital products into the scope of the VAT (in line with the recommendations included in the OECD's *International VAT/GST Guidelines*) and by abolishing or limiting the VAT exemption for the importation of low-value goods. In addition, many OECD countries continue to consider the implementation of new strategies to counter VAT fraud.

Since 2014, a significant number of OECD countries have raised their reduced VAT rates and/or have reduced their scope, as is outlined below. These reforms were often in line with the findings and recommendations of the OECD study on the distributional effects of consumption taxes (OECD/KIPF, 2014 – see also Section 2.7 of this Chapter) as they focused on scaling back reduced rates that are inefficient and, in some cases, regressive in the sense that they provide greater benefits to richer households in both aggregate and relative terms. Austria increased its reduced VAT rate for notably hotel accommodation, entrance to cultural and sporting events and to cinemas, and pet food from 10% to 13%. Belgium narrowed the scope of its 6% reduced rate for renovation of private homes (by increasing the age requirement of the private homes from 5 to 10 years), shifted supplies of electricity for household use from the 6% reduced rate to the 21% standard rate, and abolished the VAT exemption for plastic surgery. Estonia will increase its reduced rate for accommodation services from 9% to 14% as of 1 January 2017. Iceland increased its reduced rate from 7 to 11% and narrowed the scope of the exemption for passenger transport to public transport services. France made tickets for admission to sporting events subject to VAT at a reduced rate of 5.5% (no VAT was applied previously), and excluded certain agricultural products from the scope of the 10% reduced rate. In addition to increasing it standard rate (from 15% to 17% – see above), Luxemburg increased its reduced rate from 12% to 14%; and its super reduced rate from 6% to 8%; it also excluded e-books from the scope of the super reduced rate. The Netherlands abolished the application of the reduced VAT rate of 6% for rebuilding, renovation and repair of dwellings older than 2 years. In Norway, the reduced VAT rate for transport services and entertainment was raised from 8% to 10%. In Greece, scope of the 13% reduced VAT rate was significantly narrowed: many types of goods including sugar, coffee, spices, oil for cooking (except olive oil) and salt, became subject to the standard rate of 23% (24% as of 1 June 2016). The standard rate also became applicable to almost all types of services, except admission to theatres (6%), hotel and similar accommodation services (shifted from the super-reduced rate to the reduced rate), and home care services (13%). The VAT increase also included a gradual withdrawal of the scheme granting reduced rates on the Aegean Islands.

On the other hand, a number of OECD countries lowered their reduced VAT rates or increased their scope, mostly for distributional reasons. The justification for lowering reduced rates or expanding their scope was primarily to help the poor (e.g. lower VAT rates on selected foodstuffs in the Slovak Republic and Hungary) and to support families (e.g. lower VAT rates on newly-built homes in Hungary). France shifted sanitary products form the 20% standard rate to the 5.5% reduced rate making their tax treatment equivalent to that of essential items. Canada zero-rated feminine hygiene products. Lowering VAT on sanitary products was also discussed in other OECD countries, such as Australia and the United Kingdom. In other cases, the expansion of reduced VAT rates was motivated by non-distributional objectives. For instance, the Czech Republic announced a VAT rate cut form 21% to 15% for catering services effective 1 December 2016, indirectly providing support to this sector.

While VAT reduced rates are often implemented for equity and social objectives (basic essentials, health, education, etc.), evidence suggests that they are not an effective way of achieving such distributional objectives (OECD/KIPF, 2014). Better-off households tend to benefit more in absolute terms from VAT reduced rates as their consumption of the tax-favoured goods and services is generally greater than that of poorer households. In addition, reduced rates (and exemptions; see next section) create economic distortions, give rise to administrative and compliance costs and trigger tax cascading effects. A more effective policy to achieve distributional objectives may be to remove reduced VAT rates and use measures that are directly targeted at increasing the real incomes of poorer households. However, the obstacles to implementing such a reform (in particular regarding its perceived distributional impact) may be considerable and many countries appear to have found it politically easier to increase their standard VAT rate than to broaden the tax base. The rationale for reduced VAT rates and their effectiveness as a policy measure are discussed in further detail in Section 2.7.

2.3. Exemptions

In addition to reduced rates, countries extensively use exemptions (see Table 2.A2.4). When a supply is VAT-exempt, this means that the supplier may not charge VAT and is unable to recover the related input tax. In some jurisdictions, exemption is referred to as "input taxation" to make it clear that the supply is not free of VAT but that there is a "hidden VAT" in the price of the exempt supply. Exemptions should therefore not be confused with the absence of taxation.

Although it is a significant departure from the basic concept of VAT, all OECD countries (with the exception of Turkey) apply a number of exemptions. Exemptions are often justified on practical ground – where the output is hard to define and therefore to tax (such as financial and insurance services) – and/or to pursue distributional objectives (such as agricultural and fuel exemptions and exemptions for basic health and education). A number of exemptions have their roots in tradition (letting of immovable property, supply of land and buildings) or relate to activities considered as public service (education, postal services). Certain sectors that are exempt from VAT may also be subject to other specific taxes (e.g. property, insurance, financial services).

Exemptions beyond these core items are numerous and cover a wide diversity of sectors such as culture, legal aid, passenger transport, public cemeteries, waste and recyclable material, water supply, precious metals and agriculture (see Table 2.A2.4).

The standard advice in VAT design is to have a short list of exemptions, limited to basic health, education and perhaps financial services (OECD, 2013). By not allowing the deduction of input tax, VAT exemptions create an important exception to the neutrality of VAT (see Chapter 1). The following paragraphs provide an overview of the main consequences of exemptions, which are complex and often adverse.

VAT exemptions introduce a cascading effect when applied in a B2B context. The business making an exempt supply can be expected to pass on the uncreditable input tax in the price of this supply, while this "hidden tax" cannot subsequently be credited by the recipient business. If the outputs of this recipient business are not also exempt, this hidden VAT will presumably be part of the price for the supplies on which it will charge output VAT. The result is a hidden tax at a variable rate depending on the number of production stages that are subject to the tax. This distorts businesses' production decisions and choices of organisational form. The size of this cascading effect depends on where the exemption is applied in the supply chain. If the exemption is applied immediately prior to the final sale, there is no cascading effect and the consequence is simply a loss of tax revenue since the value added at the final stage escapes tax. If the exemption occurs at some intermediate stage, the consequence of the cascading effect may be an increase of net revenues in a non-transparent manner.

Exemptions create incentives for reducing tax liability by vertical integration ("self-supply") and disincentives for outsourcing as firms have an incentive to produce their inputs internally rather than to purchase externally and incur irrecoverable VAT. This may lead to economic inefficiencies as from the resulting distortion of the structure of the supply chain. It can also initiate a dynamic whereby exemptions feed on each other resulting in "exemption creep": once a sector receives an exemption, it has an incentive to lobby for exemptions for those from whom it buys its inputs in order to avoid paying hidden VAT on its inputs.

Exemptions generally lead to the under-taxation of supplies to consumers, who face a tax burden equal to the tax on inputs used by the businesses without its value-added, and an over-taxation of businesses who are unable to deduct the "hidden" tax embedded in their inputs. It also leads to the taxation of investments rather than consumption, which is in contradiction with the main purpose of the tax.

In the international context, exemptions compromise the destination principle for taxation of internationally traded goods and services. When an exporter uses exempt inputs, it is not possible to remove the irrecoverable VAT resulting from the exemption applied at an earlier stage in the production chain. On the other hand, businesses that use exempt inputs have an incentive to import from countries where they are zero rated for export instead of purchasing them from exempt domestic providers. It has been suggested that managing exemptions also imposes increased administrative and compliance costs. As is the case for differentiated rate structures, it may often be difficult for businesses and tax administrations to distinguish between exempt and taxable supplies, in particular in complex areas such as financial services. Businesses that make both taxable and exempt supplies are often faced with complex allocation rules to determine the share which is attributable to taxed outputs and for which it is thus entitled to an input tax credit. However, there is little evidence on the quantitative extent to which exemptions increase administration and compliance costs (Bird and Gendron, 2007).

Some consideration was given recently to the theoretical and practical justification of exemptions (de la Feria, 2013) and to the widening of the tax base by reducing the scope of exemptions as a valid alternative to increasing VAT rates (European Commission, 2010).

2.4. Restrictions to the right to deduct VAT on specific inputs

Although the burden of VAT should not fall on businesses, the right to deduct input taxes is limited to the extent that those inputs are used for businesses' taxable purposes. The right of deduction is legitimately denied in cases where inputs are used to make onward supplies that are not taxable i.e. exempt without refund (e.g. health care, financial services) or outside the scope of VAT (e.g. supplies for no consideration). Input tax credit is also denied when purchases are not (wholly) used for the furtherance of taxable business activity, for example, when they are used for the private needs of the business owner or its employees (i.e. final consumption). All these limitations to the right of deduction are justified by the use businesses make of the related inputs and are perfectly consistent with the VAT principle.

In addition to the rules described above, most OECD countries have legislation in place that provides for restrictions to input tax deduction on a number of goods and services because of their nature rather than because of their use by businesses, generally with a view to ensure (input) taxation of their deemed final consumption (see Table 2.A2.5). Examples include entertainment, restaurant meals and gifts offered to clients as part of the business activity. Only four OECD countries (Israel, Japan, Sweden and Switzerland) have not implemented any such limitations to the right of deduction.

Amongst the other 30 OECD countries, input tax restrictions for VAT incurred on entertainment is the most widespread, although the items included in that category may vary widely. These restrictions may include VAT incurred on restaurant meals; on (alcoholic) beverages; reception costs; hotel accommodation; attendance at sporting or cultural events; and on gifts and transport services. In addition, the VAT connected with the use of cars is also often non-deductible.

In a number of countries, the input VAT restriction is limited to a portion of the VAT incurred. For example, the right of deduction for the VAT incurred on the use of cars by the employees of a business is limited to a fixed percentage. In some countries for example, only 50% of the VAT incurred is deductible, even if the car is fully used for business purposes.

The key rationale behind those limitations is threefold: first, it avoids the administrative burden associated with the need to control the actual use of such goods and services, which may be easily used for dual business/private purposes due to their very nature; second it is a way of reducing the risks of fraud; third such commodities often contain an element of "consumption". This is the case of restaurant meals for example. However, the third justification may be considered inconsistent with the main features of the VAT system. Indeed, businesses (or their employees) never "consume" goods and services within the meaning of the VAT when they are used in the furtherance of a taxable activity.

2.5. Registration and collection thresholds

All taxes impose compliance costs on businesses and administrative costs on tax authorities, but VAT is often considered as particularly burdensome for small and medium size businesses (SMEs) to comply with (European Commission 2012). As a result, many countries have introduced simplified regimes for SMEs as an efficient way to promote compliance. These regimes can be grouped into three main categories: those that provide for an exemption from the VAT regime (exemption thresholds); those that facilitate the calculation of the VAT liability; and those that simplify accounting, filing or payment obligations (OECD, 2015).

Most OECD countries (except Chile, Mexico, Spain, Sweden and Turkey) apply exemption thresholds below which small businesses are not required to charge and collect the tax. Under these thresholds, small businesses do not account for output VAT and consequently are not entitled to deduct input tax incurred on their purchases of goods and services. The consequences of such exemptions are equivalent to treating small businesses as non-taxable businesses. There are two kinds of exemption thresholds: registration thresholds that relieve suppliers from both the requirement to register for VAT and to collect the tax; and collection thresholds for which taxpayers, even those below the threshold, are required to register for VAT, but are relieved from collecting the tax until they exceed the threshold. Different types of activities (e.g. supply of services vs supply of goods) or sectors (e.g. the non-profit sector) may be subject to different thresholds or even be excluded from their application (e.g. the construction sector). In most cases registration thresholds do not apply to foreign businesses and in some cases collection thresholds apply only to individuals or to businesses for which commercial accounting is not compulsory.

Table 2.A2.3 provides an overview of applicable collection and registration thresholds in OECD countries. In principle, the calculation of thresholds is based on annual turnover. In the Netherlands, however, the basis for calculation is the net annual VAT due. In Japan businesses (companies and individuals) are not required to register and account for VAT during the first two years of establishment during which a threshold based on their capital (etc.) applies; a threshold based on an annual taxable turnover applies only after the first two years (if turnover exceeds a certain amount in the first half of the previous year, it applies after the first one year.). It should be noted however that even in countries where the threshold is based on an annual turnover its application may be subject to additional requirements. The levels of these thresholds vary significantly across OECD countries and may be split into three broad groups:

- Sixteen countries have a relatively high threshold (more than USD 30 000): Australia, Austria, Belgium, Czech Republic, France, Hungary, Ireland, Italy, Japan, Latvia, New Zealand, Poland, Slovak Republic, Slovenia, Switzerland and the United Kingdom. Of these France, Japan and the United Kingdom have a particularly higher threshold (above USD 90 000).
- Thirteen countries have a relatively low threshold (between USD 1 500 and 30 000): Canada, Denmark, Estonia, Finland, Germany, Greece, Iceland, Israel, Korea, Luxembourg, Netherlands, Norway and Portugal.

- Five countries have no general exemption threshold: Chile, Mexico, Spain, Sweden and Turkey.

Since 2014, four countries have raised their threshold: Belgium, Finland, Greece, Italy and the United Kingdom while none has reduced its threshold. Only Sweden has removed several years ago its threshold of SEK 30 000 (USD 3 400).

There are no definitive arguments on the need for, or the level of, thresholds. The main reasons for excluding "small" businesses (and this notion may vary considerably across countries) are that the costs for the tax administration are disproportionate to the VAT revenues from their activity and, similarly, the VAT compliance costs would be disproportionate for many small businesses compared to their turnover. It is also assumed that smaller businesses may be less compliant. A relatively high threshold may give an advantage to small businesses, distorting competition with larger companies while a relatively low threshold may be seen by businesses as a disincentive to grow or as an incentive to avoid VAT by splitting activities artificially. It can also frustrate policy efforts to have all businesses actively participate in the formal economy. However, the latter may be at least partly addressed if firms below the VAT threshold are subject to another, simpler, tax and thus be part of the "formal" economy. The level of the threshold is often the result of a trade-off between minimising compliance and administration costs and the need to avoid jeopardising revenue or distorting competition.

Most OECD countries that have a registration or collection threshold give the option to businesses below the threshold to register and account voluntarily for VAT, except Israel, Korea and the Netherlands. Voluntary registration is often intended to circumvent the disadvantages of non-registration for small businesses but they increase tax administration costs and impose compliance costs on entities that elect to be in the system. Additionally, caution needs to be exercised to avoid VAT fraud by "fly-by-night" traders who may register and ask for refund claims on an ad hoc basis. For this reason, several countries impose a minimum period of time during which taxpayers that have registered voluntarily must remain registered. This period varies from one year (Australia, Canada, Czech Republic, Greece, Hungary, Slovak Republic and Switzerland) to two years (Denmark, France, Japan and Norway) or in some cases, up to five years (Austria, Germany, Slovenia).

Another issue related to the adoption of a threshold is how to encourage borderline businesses to increase their turnover or at least to discourage them from underreporting turnover to remain below the exemption threshold. The adoption of a flexible threshold is one option. In this case small businesses that reach the regular threshold are not obliged to register immediately but are allowed to continue to benefit from the exemption as long as their annual turnover does not exceed the threshold by a significant percentage. For example in France, when businesses exceed the regular thresholds of EUR 82 200 (for goods) and EUR 32 900 (for most services) they may continue to benefit from the exemption if their turnover does not exceed EUR 90 300 and EUR 34 900 respectively for more than a year. Another example of a flexible threshold is used in the Netherlands, which provides a flexible collection threshold based on the net annual VAT due. If the net annual VAT due is less than EUR 1345, no VAT is remitted to the tax authorities. If the net annual VAT due is between EUR 1 345 and EUR 1 883 the taxpayer gets a gradual tax reduction which ensures its smooth entry into a taxpaying position.

Other ways exist to reduce compliance costs for SMEs while avoiding the disadvantages of the exemption. One way used in many countries is to apply simplified presumptive schemes to facilitate the calculation of the VAT liability. For example, certain SMEs may be allowed to apply a single flat rate to turnover for determining the amount of VAT to be remitted to tax authorities instead of requiring a detailed VAT calculation of input and output VATs. An alternative simplification scheme for calculating VAT liability relies on simplified input tax credit calculations. A more detailed description of such regime is given in a recent OECD study on SME taxation (OECD, 2015).

2.6. Application of margin schemes

Most countries allow or utilise specific VAT collection methods in special circumstances. The purpose of these methods is usually to simplify the collection process in order to reduce the administrative and compliance burden or take specific situations into account. In this context, margin schemes are often used when the deduction of input tax would be difficult or impossible such as the resale of second-hand goods bought from private individuals or travel agencies. Under the margin scheme, the tax base is calculated on the difference between the price paid by the taxpayer for an item and the price of resale rather than on the full selling price. The reseller is not allowed to deduct the input VAT embedded in the buying price of the items resold under the margin scheme. Table 2.A2.6 shows that all the EU countries employ a margin scheme for travel agencies, second-hand goods, works of art, collector's items and antiques since they share the same legislative root. Beyond the EU, five other OECD countries employ margin schemes i.e. Australia (on new residential property, gambling and second hand goods); Israel (on coins and postal stamps, furniture, dwellings, used vehicles and foreign currency exchange); Norway (on second hand goods, works of art, collectors' items and antiques) and Turkey (on travel agencies).

2.7. Technical note – Rationale and impact of reduced VAT rates

With the exceptions of Chile and Japan, all OECD countries have one or more reduced rates (including domestic zero rates, also called "GST-free supplies" or "exempt with right to deduct input tax" that should not be confused with the zero-rating of exports). Derogations from the application of the standard rate broadly fall within the following categories (see Table 2.A2.2):

- Basic essentials such as medical and hospital care, food, energy products and water supplies.
- Certain activities considered traditionally to be utilities (public transport, postal services, public television).
- Activities that are considered socially desirable (charitable services, culture and sport) or supporting employment (e.g. locally supplied labour intensive services).
- Geographic areas that are considered as deserving preferential treatment (islands, territories far away from metropolitan areas, border areas).

The reasons for the existence of reduced rates may be rooted in a country's socio-economic history and address issues that are considered as priority matters for a given society at a point in time. One of the reasons for the introduction of a differentiated rate structure is the promotion of equity (ensuring a fairer distribution of aggregate income). Countries have generally considered it desirable to alleviate the tax burden on goods and services that form a larger share of expenditure of the poorest households (e.g. basic food, water). Countries have also tended not to want to tax medicine, health services and housing at high rates.

Reduced VAT rates are also used for stimulating consumption of "merit goods" (e.g. cultural products and education) and goods with positive externalities (e.g. energy-saving appliances). However, other reduced rates seem less targeted. Amongst these are admissions to cultural events, including circuses and cinemas, hotel accommodation and cut flowers.

To decide whether to implement or maintain a reduced VAT rate, the cost of the given reduced rate both in terms of revenue foregone (the tax expenditure) and compliance should be compared with its ability to produce the desired outcome at the lowest cost. In this regard, alternative measures, such as direct subsidies to certain activities or population sub-groups should be considered where possible. The rationale for a number of reduced rates is discussed in more detail below.

Equity objectives

Most countries implement reduced VAT rates on necessities such as food and water in order to alleviate the tax burden on low-income households. The question is whether such reduced rates are an effective way of achieving distributional objectives. An OECD study (OECD/KIPF, 2014 – hereafter "the study") discusses the issue in detail. The study shows that most of the reduced rates that are introduced for the distinct purpose of supporting the poor, such as reduced rates on food, water, and on energy products, do have a progressive effect (when measured as a percentage of income or expenditure). However, it also shows that reduced rates are a poor tool for targeting support to those poor households. At best, rich households receive roughly as much benefit – in absolute value – from a reduced rate as do poor households. At worst, rich households benefit vastly more than poor households. This result is unsurprising as better off households can be expected to consume more, and often more expensive, products than poorer households. Thus, while poorer households may benefit from reduced VAT rates on "necessities" the wealthier gain even more. As a result, a disproportionate part of the tax expenditure (i.e. the difference between the tax actually collected and the tax that would have been collected if the tax base was subject to the standard rate) benefits those who are not targeted by the measure.

The situation will of course depend on the type of good or service considered. For example, in the countries surveyed that have a reduced rate on food, the reduced rate tends to provide a far more similar level of support to poor and rich households than was the case for all reduced rates. This is because poorer households spend a significantly greater proportion of their total expenditure on food than rich households do. The vast majority of the total level of support provided to the poor through reduced VAT rates comes from the reduced rate on food. However, as rich households still tend to spend more on food in absolute terms, the reduced rate on food can still be seen as a badly targeted means of supporting the poor.

In terms of targeting the poor, the performance of reduced VAT rates on pharmaceuticals is much worse. In the 15 countries surveyed that have a reduced rate on pharmaceuticals, higher income households tend to gain substantially more than lower income households in absolute terms, even if, as a proportion of expenditure, the reduced rates on pharmaceuticals still tend to benefit lower more than higher income households. In absolute value, the 20% highest income households get 1.6 times as much tax relief as the 20% lowest income households

This raises the question of whether removing reduced VAT rates and using direct transfers to poorer households to achieve distributional objectives would be a more effective policy. Economic literature generally considers that direct lump-sum payments to households related only to their socio-economic characteristics are better in terms of both equity and efficiency. Transfers directly targeted to low-income households (including increased personal income tax allowances and state benefits) may also be more effective in enhancing equity than "scatter-gun" VAT provisions (OECD, 2010).

In addition, it may well be difficult to define "necessities" in practice. For instance, a reduced rate may apply to all food including "luxury" items. Drawing distinctions tends to raise administrative costs (defining and monitoring) and compliance costs (identifying and understanding); and it encourages litigation to secure a reduced rate category for a wide selection of products. For example, how would the line be drawn between different types of potato products and between biscuits and cakes?

Finally, low income observed at a single point in time may often be temporary and need not reflect low living standards across a lifetime. While it is true that some people are persistently poor, many have variable earnings – and expenses – over their lifetime. Looking at the effect of taxes on lifetime income inequality may consequently produce a different picture to an analysis based on current income.

Distributional arguments in favour of VAT rate differentiation may be more persuasive where countries do not have the administrative capacity to provide more direct transfers to poorer households (Heady and Smith, 1995). In low-income countries, significant and stable differences in consumption patterns between high- and low-income groups allow for an easier and more efficient alleviation of poverty through exemptions from consumption taxes or low rates. In these countries, low-income families purchase most of their goods from local small-scale producers whose output either may be exempted or escape taxation, while high-income families are likely to buy more factory-made or imported goods that can be taxed more effectively (Copenhagen Economics, 2007).

Other policy objectives

Supporting cultural objectives

A number of reduced VAT rates are not introduced specifically to support poor households. For example, reduced rates may be aimed at supporting cultural activities and social goods. However, these concessions may still have a significant impact on the income distribution if they favour some groups over others. In order to develop coherent economic policy, it is important to be able to quantify the distributional effects of such concessions so that the impact on distributional goals can be weighed against the merits of supporting such cultural objectives or encouraging consumption of social goods.

The above-mentioned study presents results for the four most common categories of expenditure that are supported for broader social and cultural reasons (books; newspapers and periodicals; cinema, theatre and concerts; and museums and zoos). Reduced rates

See OECD (2014) for further discussion of analysis on the basis of current versus lifetime income in the VAT context.

might have the unintended effect of subsidising the consumption of these goods and services by high-income households, who tend to consume more merit goods, rather than leading to an effective increase in consumption by lower-income households. For example, the study shows that reduced VAT rates on cinema, theatre and concerts provide substantially more benefit to high-income households than low-income ones. In absolute value, from a total annual tax expenditure of EUR 67 per household on average, only EUR 6 a year go to the 20% lowest income and EUR 25 to the 20% higher income households. As mentioned above, such reduced rates may not have a distributional objective, but one should be conscious of the distributional impact of the choice of the VAT instrument to support the production of such merit services.

Promoting locally supplied labour-intensive activities

Efficiency considerations may also justify reduced VAT rates for specific labour-intensive activities. The low taxation of commodities that are close substitutes with self-supply or underground economy work (e.g. home improvement and repair services, gardening and hairdressing) may mitigate the disincentive to work in and purchase from the formal economy created by the tax system. The argument is that high tax wedges (high income tax, social security contributions and VAT rates) make it expensive to buy these services on the market and more attractive to self-supply or to buy these services in the informal sector (black economy). This may lead to inefficiencies for instance if high-skilled professionals end up spending time on low-skilled work at home.

On the other hand, this result may change (and administration costs will be reduced) when a broad-based single rate VAT (set at a reasonable rate) is combined with an appropriate VAT threshold and a well-targeted audit programme. In addition, if the theoretical motivation for these reduced rates is to raise demand for low-skilled labour by boosting the demand for such services or increasing the profit margin in the sector to encourage social reform, other policy instruments such as labour market reforms (flexibility, administrative simplifications, etc.) could be more efficient in achieving this objective (Copenhagen Economics, 2007).

Correcting externalities

Finally, it is sometimes argued that correcting externalities might justify VAT rate differentiation; for example, higher rates on goods that generate pollution or reduced rates on energy-saving appliances. In these cases, rate differentiation may improve efficiency if it means that the private marginal costs of an activity are brought closer to the marginal costs for society. However, VAT is a blunt instrument for correcting environmental externalities, as it may be hard to target the actual source of pollution. For example, reduced rates on energy-saving appliances, by reducing the private marginal cost of these goods, may boost demand for them and, therefore, stimulate consumption of these goods. The reduced VAT rate may give incentives to shift from more to less energy-consuming items (consumers might replace their old refrigerator with a new one, for instance). However, this may also lead to an increase in the purchase of energy-intensive products (i.e. consumers may replace their old refrigerator with a new refrigerator and a freezer) (Copenhagen Economics, 2007).

The application of reduced rates as part of wider tax policy

The OECD study confirms and provides evidence that most, if not all, of the reduced rates that are introduced for the purpose of supporting the poor, such as reduced rates on food and on energy products, do have the desired progressive effect. Nevertheless, it clearly shows that, despite this progressive effect, reduced VAT rates are a poor tool for targeting support to poor households. At best, rich households receive as much benefit from a reduced rate as do poor households. At worst, rich households benefit vastly more than poor households. In some cases, the benefit to rich households may be so large that the reduced VAT rate actually has a regressive effect – benefiting the rich more both in absolute terms, and as a proportion of expenditure. This is generally the case for most reduced rates introduced to address social, cultural and other non-distributional goals (OECD/KIPF, 2014).

In contrast to its perceived regressivity, the study concludes that the VAT is generally either proportional or slightly progressive of a percentage of expenditure. Of course this does not necessarily mean that the VAT, when considered in isolation, is a fair tax. A proportional VAT will still have a greater negative impact on the welfare of the poor than the rich. A proportional VAT may also have a greater welfare cost on credit constrained households than on those with full access to finance. However, these are not reasons to consider the VAT regressive. Rather, they are reasons to consider increasing the progressivity of the tax/benefit system as a whole Effective redistribution policy is not implemented on a tax by tax basis but by considering the entire tax and benefit systems. Addressing equity issues should be done by an appropriate mix of measures. In order to offset the regressive equity impact of VAT base broadening, part of the revenue raised from broadening the VAT base could be used to compensate low-income households through income-tested tax credit or benefit payments (Brys et al. 2016b).

However, there are still arguments for reduced rates in some circumstances. First, alternative ways for addressing equity issues may not be readily available, in particular in countries where the social or fiscal system is not developed enough for providing appropriate support to lower-income households. Second, it may not be socially and politically feasible to remove reduced VAT rates, especially when they have existed for a long time. Third, a sudden increase of VAT from a low, or zero, rate to the standard rate (especially if it is quite high) would involve higher prices that would hit poorer households harder and immediately, while appropriate compensating measures may have a delayed effect and may not be able to cover all these households. It is also true that in sectors where the elasticity of demand is high, the producers would not be able to reflect a significant and sudden increase in the VAT rate in their price, and this would therefore threaten the viability of the businesses. Nevertheless, the study does suggest the need for a careful, case-by-case reassessment of the relative merits of various reduced VAT rates in many countries.

References

Benedek, D., De Mooij, R., Keen, M., Wingender, P. (2015), *Estimating VAT Pass Through*, IMF Working Paper WP/15/214.

Bird, R.M. and P.P. Gendron (2007), *The VAT in Developing and Transitional Countries*, Cambridge University Press, New York.

Bodin, J.-P., Ebrill, L., Keen, M. and Summers, V. (2001), *The Modern VAT*, International Monetary Fund, Washington DC.

Brys, B., Perret, S., Thomas, A., O'Reilly, P. (2016a), *Tax Policy Reforms in the OECD 2016*, OECD Taxation Working Papers, OECD Publishing, Paris. *http://dx.doi.org/10.1787/9789264260399-en.*

Brys, B., Perret, S., Thomas, A., O'Reilly, P. (2016b), *Tax Design for Inclusive Economic Growth*, Taxation Working Papers, OECD Publishing, Paris *http://dx.doi.org/10.1787/5jlv74ggk0g7-en.*

Charlet, A. and Owens, J. (2010), *"An International Perspective on VAT"*, Tax Notes International, Volume 59, Number 12, September 20, 2010, p. 943.

Copenhagen Economics (2007), *Study on reduced VAT applied to goods and services in Member States in the European Union*, Copenhagen, 2007.

de la Feria, R. (2013), *VAT exemptions, consequences and design alternatives*, Wolter Kluwers, Alphen in the Rijn.

European Commission (2010), *Green Paper on the future of VAT, Towards a simpler, more robust and efficient VAT system*, COM(2010)695/4, Brussels.

European Commission (2012), *Top 10 most burdensome legislative acts for SMEs*, *http://ec.europa.eu/enterprise/policies/sme/files/smes/top10report-final_en.pdf.*

European Commission (2016), *Tax Reforms in EU Member States 2015*, Institutional Paper 008, September 2015.

Heady, C. and S. Smith (1995), "Tax and Benefit Reform in the Czech and Slovak Republics", in D. Newbery (ed.), *Tax and Benefit Reform in Central and Eastern Europe*, London, Centre for Economic Policy Research.

OECD (2015), Taxation of SMEs in OECD and G20 Countries, OECD Publishing, Paris. DOI: *http://dx.doi.org/10.1787/9789264243507-en.*

OECD/KIPF (2014), The Distributional Effects of Consumption Taxes in OECD Countries, OECD Publishing, Paris. DOI: *http://dx.doi.org/10.1787/9789264224520-en.*

OECD (2013), *Key issues and debates in VAT, SME taxation and the tax treatment of the financial sector*, International Tax Dialogue, OECD, Paris, *www.itdweb.org/documents/ITD_VAT_SME_Financial_Sector_Taxation2013.pdf.*

OECD (2010), *Tax Policy Reform and Economic Growth*, OECD Publishing, Paris. DOI: *http://dx.doi.org/10.1787/9789264091085-en.*

VAT Directive 2006/112/EC of 28 November 2006, Official Journal of the European Union L 347, 11 December 2006, p. 1, Brussels.

ANNEX 2.A2

Data on VAT rates and structures

Table 2.A2.1. VAT rates[1]

	Implemented	Standard rate																	Reduced rates[2]	Specific regional rates
		1975	1980	1985	1990	1995	2000	2005	2007	2008	2009	2010	2011	2012	2013	2014	2015	2016		
Australia	2000	-	-	-	-	-	-	10.0	10.0	10.0	10.0	10.0	10.0	10.0	10.0	10.0	10.0	10.0	0.0	-
Austria*	1973	16.0	18.0	20.0	20.0	20.0	20.0	20.0	20.0	20.0	20.0	20.0	20.0	20.0	20.0	20.0	20.0	20.0	10.0/13.0	19.00
Belgium	1971	18.0	16.0	19.0	19.0	20.5	21.0	21.0	21.0	21.0	21.0	21.0	21.0	21.0	21.0	21.0	21.0	21.0	0.0/6.0/12.0	-
Canada*	1991	-	-	-	-	7.0	7.0	7.0	6.0	5.0	5.0	5.0	5.0	5.0	5.0	5.0	5.0	5.0	0.0	13.0/14.0/15.0
Chile	1975	20.0	20.0	20.0	16.0	18.0	18.0	19.0	19.0	19.0	19.0	19.0	19.0	19.0	19.0	19.0	19.0	19.0	-	-
Czech Republic	1993	-	-	-	-	22.0	22.0	19.0	19.0	19.0	19.0	20.0	20.0	20.0	21.0	21.0	21.0	21.0	10.0/15.0	-
Denmark	1967	15.0	20.25	22.0	22.0	25.0	25.0	25.0	25.0	25.0	25.0	25.0	25.0	25.0	25.0	25.0	25.0	25.0	0.0	-
Estonia	1991	-	-	-	-	18.0	18.0	18.0	18.0	18.0	18.0	20.0	20.0	20.0	20.0	20.0	20.0	20.0	0.0/9.0	-
Finland	1994	-	-	-	-	22.0	22.0	22.0	22.0	22.0	22.0	22.0	23.0	23.0	24.0	24.0	24.0	24.0	0.0/10.0/14.0	-
France*	1968	20.0	17.6	18.6	18.6	20.6	20.6	19.6	19.6	19.6	19.6	19.6	19.6	19.6	19.6	20.0	20.0	20.0	2.1/5.5/10.0	0.9/2.1/10.0/13.0 & 1.05/1.75/2.1/8.5
Germany	1968	11.0	13.0	14.0	14.0	15.0	16.0	16.0	19.0	19.0	19.0	19.0	19.0	19.0	19.0	19.0	19.0	19.0	7.0	-
Greece*	1987	-	-	-	18.0	18.0	18.0	18.0	19.0	19.0	19.0	19.0	23.0	23.0	23.0	23.0	23.0	23.0	6.0/13.0	4.0/9.0/16.0
Hungary	1988	-	-	-	25.0	25.0	25.0	25.0	20.0	20.0	20.0	25.0	25.0	27.0	27.0	27.0	27.0	27.0	5.0/18.0	-
Iceland	1990	-	-	-	22.0	24.5	24.5	24.5	24.5	24.5	24.5	25.5	25.5	25.5	25.5	25.5	24.0	24.0	0.0/11.0	-
Ireland	1972	19.5	20.0	23.0	23.0	21.0	21.0	21.0	21.0	21.0	21.5	21.0	21.0	23.0	23.0	23.0	23.0	23.0	0.0/4.8/9.0/13.5	-
Israel*	1976	-	12.0	15.0	15.0	17.0	17.0	17.0	15.5	15.5	15.5	16.0	16.0	16.0	17.0	18.0	18.0	17.0	0.0	0.0
Italy	1973	12.0	14.0	18.0	19.0	19.0	20.0	20.0	20.0	20.0	20.0	20.0	20.0	21.0	21.0	22.0	22.0	22.0	4.0/5.0/10.0	-
Japan	1989	-	-	-	3.0	3.0	5.0	5.0	5.0	5.0	5.0	5.0	5.0	5.0	5.0	5.0	8.0	8.0	-	-
Korea	1977	-	10.0	10.0	10.0	10.0	10.0	10.0	10.0	10.0	10.0	10.0	10.0	10.0	10.0	10.0	10.0	10.0	0.0	-
Latvia	1995	-	-	-	-	-	18.0	18.0	18.0	18.0	21.0	21.0	22.0	22.0	21.0	21.0	21.0	21.0	0.0/12.0	-
Luxembourg	1970	10.0	10.0	12.0	12.0	15.0	15.0	15.0	15.0	15.0	15.0	15.0	15.0	15.0	15.0	15.0	17.0	17.0	3.0/8.0/14.0	-
Mexico	1980	-	10.0	15.0	15.0	10.0	15.0	15.0	15.0	15.0	15.0	16.0	16.0	16.0	16.0	16.0	16.0	16.0	0.0	-
Netherlands	1969	16.0	18.0	19.0	18.5	17.5	17.5	19.0	19.0	19.0	19.0	19.0	19.0	19.0	21.0	21.0	21.0	21.0	6.0	-
New Zealand	1986	-	-	-	12.5	12.5	12.5	12.5	12.5	12.5	12.5	12.5	15.0	15.0	15.0	15.0	15.0	15.0	0.0	-
Norway	1970	20.0	20.0	20.0	20.0	23.0	23.0	25.0	25.0	25.0	25.0	25.0	25.0	25.0	25.0	25.0	25.0	25.0	0.0/10.0/15.0	-
Poland	1993	-	-	-	-	22.0	22.0	22.0	22.0	22.0	22.0	22.0	23.0	23.0	23.0	23.0	23.0	23.0	5.0/8.0	-
Portugal*	1986	-	-	-	17.0	17.0	17.0	19.0	21.0	21.0	20.0	20.0	23.0	23.0	23.0	23.0	23.0	23.0	6.0/13.0	4.0/9.0/18.0 & 5.0/12.0/22.0
Slovak Republic	1993	-	-	-	-	25.0	23.0	19.0	19.0	19.0	19.0	19.0	20.0	20.0	20.0	20.0	20.0	20.0	10.0	-
Slovenia	1999	-	-	-	-	-	19.0	20.0	20.0	20.0	20.0	20.0	20.0	20.0	20.0	22.0	22.0	22.0	9.5	-
Spain*	1986	-	-	-	12.0	16.0	16.0	16.0	16.0	16.0	16.0	16.0	18.0	18.0	21.0	21.0	21.0	21.0	4.0/10.0	0.0/2.75/3.0/7.0/9.5/13.5/20.0 & 0.5/10.0
Sweden	1969	17.7	23.5	23.5	23.5	25.0	25.0	25.0	25.0	25.0	25.0	25.0	25.0	25.0	25.0	25.0	25.0	25.0	0.0/6.0/12.0	-
Switzerland	1995	-	-	-	-	6.5	7.5	7.6	7.6	7.6	7.6	7.6	8.0	8.0	8.0	8.0	8.0	8.0	0.0/2.5/3.8	-
Turkey	1985	-	-	10.0	10.0	15.0	17.0	18.0	18.0	18.0	18.0	18.0	18.0	18.0	18.0	18.0	18.0	18.0	1.0/8.0	-
United Kingdom	1973	8.0	15	15	15	17.5	17.5	17.5	17.5	17.5	15.0	17.5	20.0	20.0	20.0	20.0	20.0	20.0	0.0/5.0	-
Unweighted average		15.6	16.1	17.3	16.7	17.7	18.0	17.8	17.8	17.7	17.7	18.1	18.7	18.8	19.0	19.1	19.2	19.2		

* See country notes in Box 2.A2.1.

1. **Yearly data:** The rates shown in the table are rates applicable on 1 January of each year. Reduced rates and specific rates applicable in specific regions are those applicable as at 1 January 2016
2. **Reduced rates:** Reduced rates include zero-rates applicable to domestic supplies (i.e. an exemption with right to deduct input tax). This does not include zero-rated exports.

Source: National delegates – position as at 1 January 2016.

StatLink http://dx.doi.org/10.1787/888933420089

Box 2.A2.1. **Country notes**

Austria: A standard rate of 19% applies in Jungholz and Mittelberg.

Canada: The following provinces have harmonised their provincial sales taxes with the federal Goods and Services Tax and therefore levy a rate of GST/HST of: New Brunswick, Newfoundland and Labrador, Ontario: 13%; Prince Edward Island: 14%; Nova Scotia 15%. During 2016, the provinces of New Brunswick, Newfoundland and Labrador and Prince Edward Island will raise their provincial rates resulting in a combined GST/HST rate of 15%. Québec applies GST at a rate of 5% and Québec Sales Tax at a rate of 9.975% (applied on the same tax base as the GST). Other Canadian provinces, with the exception of Alberta, apply a provincial sales tax to certain goods and services.

France: Rates of 0.9%; 2.1%; 10.0%; 13.0% and 20.0% apply in Corsica; rates of 1.05%; 1.75%; 2.1% and 8.5% apply to overseas departments (DOM) excluding French Guyana and Mayotte.

Greece: Specific regional rates of 4.0%; 9.0% and 16.0% apply in the islands of Lesbos, Chios, Samos, Dodecanese (with the exception of Rhodos since 1 October 2015), Cyclades (with the exception of Mykonos, Naxos, Paros, Santorini since 1 October 2015), Thassos, Northern Sporades (with the exception of Skathos since October 2015), Samothrace and Skiros. According to current planning, the reduced rates on the rest of the Aegean Islands will apply only until 31 December 2016. Since July 2015 the super-reduced rate of 6.5% was decreased to 6%. The standard VAT rate was increased form 23% to 24% on 1 June 2016.

Israel: The rate of 0% applies when an Eilat resident dealer buys foods from Eilat non-residents. Supplies made by an Eilat resident supplier (to be consumed in Eilat) are exempt from VAT. The statistical data for Israel are supplied by and under the responsibility of the relevant Israeli authorities. The use of such data by the OECD is without prejudice to the status of the Golan Heights, East Jerusalem and Israeli settlements in the West Bank under the terms of international law.

Portugal: In the Islands of Azores, the standard VAT rate is 18% and the reduced rates are 4% and 9%. In the Islands of Madeira the standard rate is 22% and reduced rates are 5% and 12%.

Spain: Rates of 0.0%, 2.75%; 3.0%; 7.0%, 9.50%; 13.50%, 20% apply in the Canary Islands. Rates of 0.5% and 10% apply in Ceuta and Melilla.

Table 2.A2.2. **Application of lower VAT rates**

Country	Lower VAT rates, including domestic zero rate – 0%[1]
Australia	0%: most food and beverages for human consumption (excl. prepared food); most health and medical supplies; some education courses and students accommodation; some child care services; some religious services; some activities of charitable institutions; water (except supplied in, or transferred to, a container less than 100L); sewerage and drainage; sales of businesses as going concerns; precious metals (first supply after refinement); grants of freehold and similar interests by governments; farm land; cars for use by disabled people subject to a (general) threshold of AUD 57 466; supplies of accommodation and meals to residents of retirement villages by certain operators; certain government services; some telecommunication supplies made under arrangements for global roaming in Australia; international mail.
Austria	10%: food; water supply; pharmaceuticals; passenger transport (except domestic flights); books; newspapers and periodicals; pay television; some supplies of artists, writers and composers; forestry; restaurants (except beverages); collection of domestic waste and street cleaning; sewage.
	13%: hotel accommodation, supply of wine by producing farmers; agricultural supplies; admission to cultural, sporting events and cinemas; domestic flights.
Belgium	0%: cars for disabled persons; certain newspapers and periodicals, certain recovered materials and by products.
	6%: food; some beverages; water supply; pharmaceuticals; equipment for the disabled; passenger transport; books; newspapers and periodicals; culture; sport; works of art, collectors' items and antiques; works of art delivered by their authors/creators; agriculture; hotel accommodation and camping sites; renovation of dwellings over 5 years old (over 10 years old as of 12 February 2016); private homes and establishments for disabled; subsidised social housing; some labour intensive services (small repair services); reconstruction subsequent to demolition works leading to the construction of new private housing (under strict conditions and specific limitations as to the amount); funeral services; cut flowers and plants.
	12%: restaurants (except beverages); certain energy products (coal, coke; lignite); certain social housing.
Canada	0%: prescription medicine, basic groceries; certain financial services provided by financial institutions (usually to non-residents); certain agricultural and fishing products; certain medical devices; international bridge or tunnel authorities (on certain purchases only); precious metals; sales of 25 cents or less made through mechanical coin-operated devices.
Chile	-
Czech Republic	10%: essential child nutrition; gluten-free products; certain pharmaceutical products; certain printed books.
	15%: food; pharmaceutical products and printed books (when not subject to the lower rate of 10%) some beverages; water supply; medical services (if not exempt); equipment and repair for the disabled; passenger transport; art; cultural services; newspapers and periodicals; construction of private dwellings and social housing; renovation and repair of private dwellings; collection and treatment of waste and waste water; hotel accommodation; health care and domestic care services; cleaning in households; funeral services; sport activities; agricultural products; cut flowers and plants; heating.
Denmark	0%: newspapers and periodicals.
	5%: first time sale of products of artistic work valued over DKK 300 000 (the standard rate of 25% applies to 20% of the tax base resulting in an effective rate of 5%).
Estonia	0%: certain commercial aircraft and see-going vessels and certain supplies of goods and services related to them; international transport of passengers.
	9%: pharmaceuticals; medical equipment or devices for disabled; books; newspapers and periodicals; hotel accommodation.
Finland	0%: printing services for certain membership publications; certain vessels.
	10%: pharmaceuticals; passenger transport; books, subscribed newspapers and periodicals; hotel accommodation; admission to cultural, entertainment and sporting events and cinema performances; use of sports facilities; works of art supplied by their creators or imported; copyrights to literary and artistic works; TV licence fees.
	14%: food; non-alcoholic drinks; animal food; restaurants (except alcoholic beverages).
France	2.1%: newspapers and periodicals; pharmaceuticals.
	5.5%: most food products and beverages (except alcoholic beverages); water supply; equipment for the disabled; books; admission to cultural services; work on dwellings over 2 years old under certain conditions; social housing; domestic care services; subscription fees to natural gas and electricity networks; district heating; supplies of works of art by their creators; women's sanitary products.
	10%: passenger transport; admission to amusement parks; pay TV; domestic care services; restaurant services and catering (except alcoholic beverages); hotel accommodation; farm products; gardens, plants and flowers; treatment of waste; sewage; passenger transport; author's rights.
Germany	7%: food; water supply; equipment for the disabled; medical services (if not exempt); books and newspapers; plants; flowers; certain cultural events; museums; zoos; circuses; charitable work (if not exempt); author's rights; local public passenger transport within a municipality or if the distance covered is not more than 50 km; hotel accommodation; cut flowers and plants; works of art supplied by their creator or successors in title and importation of collector's items.

Table 2.A2.2. **Application of lower VAT rates** *(cont.)*

Country	Lower VAT rates, including domestic zero rate – 0%[1]
Greece	6%: pharmaceutical drugs and vaccines for human medicine; books; newspapers, journals and periodicals; admission to the theatre (theatrical plays).
	13%: water, basic food goods (meat and abattoir by-products; meat preparations; fish,squid, octopus and cuttlefish excluding livers, eggs and semen; milk and dairy products; birds' eggs; natural honey; vegetables, plants, some types of roots and tubers; fruit and nuts; cereal; flour and flour products; olive oil; preparations for infant use, put up for retail sale; pasta not baked or stuffed or otherwise processed; bread; excluding the undermentioned subject to the standard rate:most types of processed food, beverages, alcoholic products, fruit and vegetable juices, aerated waters); live plants and their roots, cuttings and slips; pharmaceutical products (besides those subject to 6%); medical equipment and other appliances for the disabled persons; intrauterine contraceptives; catheters; feeding syringes; "talking" sphygmomanometers; needles for insulin pens and dialysis needles; water supply; electricity; natural gas; district heating; hotel and similar accommodation; home care services.
Hungary	5%: pharmaceuticals for humans; certain equipment for the blind; books, newspapers and sheet music; live pigs and carcasses of pig; certain live cattle, sheep, lamb, goat, and their meat in bulk; district heating; services supplied by performing artists.
	18%: milk and dairy products; products containing cereals, flour, starch or milk; provision of accommodation; certain open-air concerts.
Iceland	0%: ship-building and maintenance of ships and aircraft; services to foreign fishing vessels related to landing and sale of fish in Iceland; direct payments to farmers.
	11%: food and beverages; passenger transport (if not exempted); services of travel agencies, travel organizers and touring associations; travel guidance; books including music books; audio recordings of books. CD's and similar media with text as well as electronic version of such books; magazines, newspapers and countryside- and district newspapers; periodicals; subscriptions to radio and TV; rental of hotels, guestrooms and other guest services; hot water, electricity and fuel oil used for the heating of houses and swimming pools; admission tolls to land transportation projects; CD disks, records, magnetic tapes and other similar means of music recordings, other than visual records. Electronic version of music other than visual; condoms; diapers for children; admission fees to bathhouses, bathings, saunas and spas (if not exempted).
Ireland	0%: books; children's clothing and footwear; oral medicine; certain medical equipment; food products; seeds; fertilisers; certain aircraft and sea-going vessels.
	4.8%: livestock and horses for food or agricultural production.
	9%: newspapers and certain periodicals; admission to cinemas/certain musical performances and sporting facilities; recreational and sport services; certain nursery and garden centre; holiday accommodation; restaurant/hotel meals; agricultural services.
	13.5%: waste disposal; energy for heating and light; fuel for certain purposes; gas; electricity; building services; immovable goods; repair services; tour guide services; photographic prints; works of art; short-term car and boat hire; driving instruction; veterinary services; plants and flowers; medical services (if not exempt).
Israel[2]	0%: hotel accommodation for foreign tourists and another hotel services (serving food and beverage, laundry, pool, gym, etc.); sale of, to a foreign tourist, tickets for an international conference in which more than 50 foreign tourists are in attendance; rental of a private motor vehicle to a tourist to drive himself; transportation of tourists in a private motor vehicle, a bus or an airplane; hospitalization of a foreign tourist; sale of fruits and vegetables; sale of dealer's/dealers' assets to a company in exchange for the company's stock only, provided that the dealer/dealers owns 90%, or more, of the voting power immediately after the assets transfer; sale of all of the company's assets to its shareholders in a liquidation process, in which, the assets are divided amongst the said shareholders in proportion to the shares respectively held by them; supplies of goods to who would be exempted from sales tax due to entry to Israel (supplies of certain goods to new immigrants and to students returning from study abroad); sale of a real estate by a non-profit organization or by a financial institution to a non-profit organization or to a financial institution as part of restructuring; renting exhibition space by non-resident; services given by an Israeli production company to a non-resident for film production in Israel; services given to a non-resident in respect of human clinical trials; an Eilat resident dealer buys goods from an Eilat non-resident.
Italy	4%: certain food; medications and health products/services for the disabled; supply of construction for residential housing; books; newspapers; weekly magazines.
	5%: social and health service for the elderly, drug addicts, migrants, prisoners, handicapped, AIDS patients.
	10%: water supply; pharmaceutical products; medical services (if not exempt); passenger transport; combustible gas for cooking; electricity; gas; urban waste; purification stations; livestock meat and fish; renewable-source energy; works of art; admission to shows and cultural events; letting of immovable property by building enterprises; renovation and maintenance work for residential housing; restaurants.
Japan	–
Korea	0%: supply of certain machinery and materials for agriculture; fishery; livestock and forestry; supply of mineral oil used for certain purposes in agriculture, fishery and forestry; certain equipment for the disabled.
Latvia	12%: medicinal products; medical devices; food for infants; pharmaceutical products; inland passenger transport services; books, newspapers and periodicals; hotel accommodation; district heating.
	0% – transport of passengers.
Luxembourg	3%: food for human and animal consumption; water supply; pharmaceutical products; certain medical equipment; certain aids and other appliances normally intended to alleviate or treat disability; passenger transport; accommodation; books, newspapers and periodicals, but excluding material with predominantly adult content; admission to cultural and sporting events; use of sporting facilities; restaurant services but excluding alcoholic beverages; author's rights; goods and services of a kind normally intended for use in agricultural production; services supplied in connection with waste collection and treatment; children's clothing and footwear; housing used by the owner, for his own use, as principal dwelling; substantial works on housing used as principal dwelling and (i) constructed more than 20 years prior to the start of the works (ii) newly acquired, the works to be completed in the five years following the acquisition; funeral services; reception of radio and television broadcasting services but excluding exclusively adult content services.
	8%: certain labour intensive services; works of art delivered by their authors/creators or by their heirs or imported; gas; electricity; firewood; district heating; flowers and ornamental plants.
	14%: certain wines; certain fuels; washing and cleaning products; printed advertising; heat and air conditioning; certain financial services.

Table 2.A2.2. **Application of lower VAT rates** *(cont.)*

Country	Lower VAT rates, including domestic zero rate – 0%[1]
Mexico	0%: sale of non-industrialised animals (except dogs, cats and small species used as home pets) and vegetables (except rubber); patent medicines; milk; bottled water; juices, nectar and concentrated fruits and vegetables; ice; food (except sale of processed food in restaurants and food establishments, chewing gum, caviar, smoked salmon, foie gras, pet food and soft drinks); agricultural equipment; machinery and fishing boats; wholesale of gold; gold bullion (with a content of at least 80% of gold) and jewellery; some agricultural and fishing services; magazines, books and newspapers printed by the taxpayer himself; domestic water supply; hotel services provided to foreign tourists participating in congresses, conventions and trade shows; use of convention centres by event organisers who are residents abroad; call centre services for telephone calls originated abroad, as long as the services are contracted and paid a foreign resident without a permanent establishment in Mexico.
Netherlands	6%: food; catering; goods and services for the disabled; medicine; accommodation; agricultural inputs; books; lending of books; newspapers; magazines; passenger transport (except passenger transport by air); water supply; entrance fees for sports events; amusement; parks; museums; cinemas; zoos and circuses; cut flowers and plants; restaurant and hotel meals; aids for the visually disabled; use of sports accommodation; art and antiques; hotel and holiday accommodation; certain labour intensive services like some specific services for the maintenance and isolation of dwellings; cleaning of dwellings and hairdressing.
New Zealand	0%: supply of taxable activity (business) as a going concern; supply of fine metal (gold, silver or platinum) from a refiner in fine metal to a dealer in fine metal; supply by local authorities of the local authorities petroleum tax; supply of financial services to registered GST businesses. Supply of land by and to a GST registered person when the recipient intends to use it to make taxable supplies and it is not intended to be used as a principal place of residence (this zero-rating between GST-registered persons is equivalent to the domestic reverse charge).
	Long-term stay in a commercial dwelling; certain services provided as part of the right to occupancy (taxed at the standard rate on 60% of the value of the supply).
Norway	0%: books; newspapers; certain periodicals and publications; electricity and energy supplied from alternative energy sources for household use in the counties of Finnmark, Troms and Nordland; the purchase and leasing/hiring of electric motor vehicles and batteries; second-hand vehicles covered by re-registration tax; supply of certain ships, aircrafts and drilling platforms and hiring out such vessels; services that are directly related to the construction of embassy buildings (to final consumer); goods and services to specific international military forces and command units; supply of taxable activity (business) as a going concern; supply of human organs, blood; supply by funeral directors of services relating to the transportation of deceased persons.
	10%: accommodation, passenger transport and transport of vehicles by ferries or other vessels in connection with the domestic road network; public broadcasting; admission to sporting events, museums, cinemas and amusement parks.
	15%: food and non-alcoholic beverages.
Poland	5%: Certain food; certain beverages; certain books and periodicals.
	8%: water supply; pharmaceutical products; certain goods for disabled; medical services (if not exempt); passenger transport; newspapers; reception of broadcasting services; admission to cultural and sporting events; author's rights; certain construction services; supply of housing; hotel accommodation; restaurant services; cemetery services; collection and treatment of waste; some labour intensive services; children footwear; animals; fodder and; basic agricultural means of production; certain agriculture services.
Portugal	6%: essential food; water supply; pharmaceutical products; devices for the disabled; medical services (if not exempt); books, newspapers and periodicals; passenger transport; hotels and similar services; social housing; some goods used in agriculture; certain agriculture products and certain agriculture services.
	13%: some other food; still wine; diesel fuel for agriculture; machinery mainly used in agricultural production; admission to cultural events.
Slovak Republic	10%: certain food; radioactive elements and isotopes and compounds for health service; pharmaceutical products; diagnostic or laboratory reagents; certain medical and sanitarian means; printed books, brochures, leaflets and similar printed matter; music; orthopaedic appliances; contact and spectacle lenses; certain means for blind and partly blind persons, hard-of-hearing persons and hard health-disabled persons.
Slovenia	9.5%: foodstuff (for human and animal consumption); preparation of food; water supply; medicine, devices for the disabled; passenger transport; books on all physical means of support, newspapers and periodicals; admission to cultural and sporting events; author's rights; import and supply of certain works of art, collectors' items or antiques; social housing; renovation and maintenance work of residential housing not provided as part of a social policy; livestock and certain supplies in connection with agricultural production; hotel accommodation; restaurant (except beverages); use of sporting facilities; supplies by undertakers and cremation services; public hygiene services; window-cleaning and cleaning in private households; minor repairing of bicycles, shoes and leather goods; domestic care services; hairdressing; cut flowers and plants.
Spain	4%: food (for human and animal consumption); social accommodation; medicines and other medical devices (e.g. lenses); books, newspapers and periodicals; supply of new buildings for private and social housing.
	10%: water supply; supplies to the disabled; passengers transport; minor work on private housing; cleaning; restaurants and catering; certain cultural and entertainment services; hotels; public amenities; agriculture and forestry products used as food; goods used in agricultural and forestry undertakings, including flowers and plants; waste treatment; cleaning of public sewage; burial services; cleaning and maintenance services.
Sweden	0%: commercial aircraft and ships and certain services related to these; aircraft fuel; prescribed medicine; printing of certain membership publications.
	6%: passenger transport; books, newspapers and magazines; culture (theatre, cinema, etc.); author's rights; zoos; commercial sports events; commercial museums.
	12%: food and restaurants services; accommodation; works of art owned by the originator; import of antiques, collector's items and works of art.

Table 2.A2.2. **Application of lower VAT rates** *(cont.)*

Country	Lower VAT rates, including domestic zero rate – 0%[1]
Switzerland	0%: Supply of services by travel agents and organisers of events, if they make use of supplies of goods and services by third parties that are provided abroad; certain supplies of goods and services to international airlines; state minted gold coins, fine gold for investment purposes and gold destined for refining or recovery. 2.5%: water supply, food, cattle, poultry, fish, grains, seeds, planting roots and bulbs, living plants, cuttings, scions and cut flowers and branches, animal feed, silage acids, scatterings for animals, fertilisers, pesticides, mulch, medication, books, newspapers, magazines, non-commercial services of radio and television companies, certain supplies in connection with agricultural production. The 2.5% rate also applies to certain cultural services supplied directly to the public, considerations demanded for sporting events, cultural services and the supply of works by their creators when the suppliers have opted for taxation (otherwise those supplies are exempt without right of deduction). 3.8%, accommodation services.
Turkey	0%: supply of ships, aircraft, and rail transportation vehicles; supply of services related to the manufacture, repair, maintenance of such vehicles; supply of services to ships and aircraft at harbours or airports; supply of goods and services for the exploration, management and refining of gold, silver, platinum, and oil; supply of machinery and equipment to persons who have an investment incentive document; goods and construction works for the construction, restoration and enlargement of seaports and airports; some goods and services related to national security; international roaming services supplied in Turkey according to the reciprocity principle; supply of goods that are listed in the second list of excise duty tax law to the prime ministry central organisation; the first supply of product certificate that are drawn up according to agricultural product license warehousing law via commodity exchange market; exemption for delivery of equipment produced for the disabled. 1%: some agricultural products; second-hand cars; newspapers and periodicals; blood and blood component; funeral services; supply of residential housing under 150 m^2 in cities other than metropolitan ones and in metropolitan cities if land value per m^2 lower than TRY 500; lease of specified machinery and equipment; seeds. 8%: basic food; books; e-books and e-newspapers; cinema; theatre; opera and ballet tickets; private educational service; vaccines; some medical products and services; ambulance services; medicine; medical equipment; textile and confection products and custom manufacturing of them; accommodation services; meal services at non-luxury restaurants (excluding alcoholic beverages); services provided by orphanage and nursing homes; some constructional and agricultural machines; clothing; stationery goods; waste water services; supply of residential housing under 150 m^2 in metropolitan cities and with land value per m^2 is between TRY 500 and TRY 999.
United Kingdom	0%: food; certain services and goods supplied to charities; children's clothing; passenger transport; books; newspapers; domestic sewage and water; prescribed drugs; medicine; certain aids and services for disabled people; new housing, including the construction of new houses; residential and some charitable buildings. 5%: fuel and power for domestic and charity use; certain energy saving materials supplied together with fitting services to recipient of benefits; certain grant-funded installations of heating equipment; children car seats; certain pharmaceutical products.

1. In this context, "domestic zero rate" means situations where VAT/GST is not charged by the supplier on domestic supplies but where deduction of input tax is allowed. In some countries these supplies are called "exempt with right of deduction" and in others "GST Free Supplies". For the purpose of this table, are not considered as "domestic zero rate" the zero-rating of exports of goods, services or intangibles; the supplies closely connected to exports such as international transport, customs regimes, duty-free shops, etc.; and supplies to diplomatic missions and international organisations.
2. **Israel:** The statistical data for Israel are supplied by and under the responsibility of the relevant Israeli authorities. The use of such data by the OECD is without prejudice to the status of the Golan Heights, East Jerusalem and Israeli settlements in the West Bank under the terms of international law.

Source: National delegates; position as at 1 January 2016.

Table 2.A2.3. **Annual turnover concessions for VAT registration and collection (domestic businesses)**

	National currency	Registration/collection thresholds[1]					Voluntary registration or collection[2]	Minimum registration period[3]	Limitations or specific rules for the application of the thresholds[5]
		Registration or collection threshold[1]	General threshold		Other thresholds				
			Nat. curr.	USD[4]	Nat. curr.	USD[4]			
Australia*	AUD	R	75 000	50 336	150 000	100 671	Yes	1 year	See note
Austria[6]	EUR	R	30 000	36 585			Yes	5 years	
Belgium[6, *]	EUR	C	25 000	30 488			Yes	None	See note
Canada*	CAD	R	30 000	24 000	50 000	40 000	Yes	1 year	See note
Chile*	CLP	None	None						See note
Czech Republic[6]	CZK	R	1 000 000	75 873			Yes	1 year	
Denmark[6,*]	DKK	R	50 000	6 667	170 000 300 000	22 667 40 000	Yes	2 years	See note
Estonia[6]	EUR	R	16 000	28 571			Yes	None	
Finland[6, *]	EUR	R	10 000	10 753	30 000	32 258	Yes	None	See note
France[6, *]	EUR	R	82 200	100 244	32 900 42 600	40 122 51 951	Yes	2 years	See note
Germany[6, *]	EUR	C	17 500	22 152	50 000	63 291	Yes	5 years	See note
Greece[6,*]	EUR	R	10 000	16 393			Yes	1 year	See note
Hungary[6]	HUF	C	6 000 000	44 823			Yes	1 year	
Iceland	ISK	R	1 000 000	7 032			Yes	None	
Ireland[6, *]	EUR	R	75 000	88 339	37 500	44 170	Yes	None	
Israel*	ILS	C	99 006	25 517			No	None	See note
Italy[6*]	EUR	R	30 000	40 000	50 000	66 667	Yes	None	See note
Japan*	JPY	R	10 000 000	94 940			Yes	1 year	See note
Korea	KRW	C	24 000 000	26 928			No	None	
Latvia	EUR	R	50 000	98 619			Yes	None	
Luxembourg[6, *]	EUR	C	25 000	27 778			Yes	None	See note
Mexico	MXN	None	None						
Netherlands[6, *]	EUR	C	1 345	1 620	1 883	2 269	No	None	See note
New Zealand	NZD	R	60 000	40 816			Yes	None	
Norway*	NOK	R	50 000	5 102	3000 000 140 000	306 122 14 286	Yes	2 years	See note
Poland[6]	PLN	R	150 000	83 333			Yes	None	
Portugal[6, *]	EUR	C	10 000	16 949	12 500	21 186	Yes	None	See note
Slovak Republic[6]	EUR	R	49 790	99 580			Yes	1 year	
Slovenia[6]	EUR	R	50 000	83 333			Yes	5 years	
Spain[6]	EUR	None	None						
Sweden[6]	SEK	None	None						
Switzerland*	CHF	R	100 000	78 125	150 000	117 188	Yes	1 year	See note
Turkey	TRY	None	None						
United Kingdom[6]	GBP	R	82 000	118 841			Yes	None	

* See country note in Box 2.A2.3.

1. Registration/collection thresholds identified in this table are general concessions that relieve domestic suppliers from the requirement to register for and/or to collect VAT until such time as they exceed the turnover threshold. Except where specifically identified, registration thresholds also relieve suppliers from the requirement to charge and collect VAT on supplies made within a particular jurisdiction. Relief from collection and/or registration may be available to specific industries or types of traders (for example non-resident suppliers) under more detailed rules, or a specific industry or type of trader may be subject to more stringent registration and collection requirements. The "R" indicates countries where registration threshold applies i.e. where suppliers having a turnover below the threshold should not register for VAT and are relieved from any VAT obligation. The "C" indicates countries where a collection threshold applies i.e. where all suppliers are required to register for VAT, but will not be required to charge and collect VAT until they exceed the collection threshold. Thresholds shown in this table apply to businesses established in the country. In most countries, the registration threshold does not apply to foreign businesses i.e. businesses having no seat, place of business, fixed establishment, domicile or habitual residence within the country.
2. "Yes" means a supplier is allowed to voluntarily register and collect VAT where their total annual turnover is less than the registration threshold.
3. Minimum registration/collection periods apply to general concessions. This period is the minimum term during which the concession is applied to taxpayers which have opted for it.
4. Exchange rates for conversion into USD are Purchase Parity Rates (PPPs) for GDP (see Annex A).
5. Restrictions or conditions to the application of the tax relief for businesses below the threshold.
6. Limitations for Member States of the European Union. Directive 2006/112/EC excludes from the application of the threshold the supply of new buildings or building land, certain supplies of new means of transport and disposals of the assets of the enterprise. The threshold does not apply to non-resident businesses and to supplies taxable under the EU Mini One Stop Shop (MOSS).

Source: National delegates; position as at 1 January 2016.

StatLink http://dx.doi.org/10.1787/888933420098

Box 2.A2.3. **Country Notes**

Australia: for taxi drivers, including chauffeur driven limousines and hire cars, there is no registration threshold. The applicable registration threshold to not-for-profit organisations is AUD 150 000.

Belgium: the registration threshold for Belgium does not apply to several sectors: real estate; hotels and restaurants; sale of used and waste materials. A number of specific supplies are also excluded from the application of the threshold: several supplies of new real estate, supplies of certain products subject to excise duties and undeclared and illicit activities.

Canada: the registration threshold does not apply to certain selected listed financial institutions, non-residents who enter Canada to make taxable supplies of admissions to a place of amusement, a seminar, an activity or an event, and persons who carry on a taxi or limousine business. These persons are required to register for and collect GST/HST. An alternative threshold applies to charities and public institutions. A charity or public institution is not required to register if either its revenue from worldwide taxable supplies is CAD 50 000 or less in a calendar quarter and over the last four consecutive calendar quarters, or its gross revenue in either of its two preceding fiscal years is CAD 250 000 or less.

Chile: all taxpayers are required to register and obtain a taxpayers' identification number that not only serves for VAT purposes but for all types of taxes. However, small businesses, craftsman and small service providers can be subject to a special regime according to which they account for output VAT a monthly fixed amount based on the average level of income for the last 12 months, which cannot exceed 20 Monthly Tax Units (CLP 899 100 – USD 2 178). This simplified tax regime does not apply to legal entities but only to individuals. This system must be adopted for at least for 12 months after which the taxpayer can return back to the ordinary regime.

Czech Republic: a taxable person who is not established in the Czech Republic should register immediately once he starts to provide any taxable supply within the territory of the country, except for supplies being subject to the reverse charge mechanism or to the mini one-stop shop (MOSS).

Denmark: a higher threshold of DKK 170 000 (EUR 22 840) applies to the blind, and a threshold of DKK 300 000 (EUR 40 300) applies to the first sale of works of art by their creator or his successors in title. For the purposes of the latter exemption, the threshold of DKK 300 000 must not have been exceeded in the current or preceding year.

Finland: where a business has exceeded the registration threshold of EUR 10 000, it must register and is subject to VAT, but a graduated relief is available until they reach a second threshold of EUR 30 000.

France: the VAT relief apples to businesses whose annual turnover does not exceed EUR 82 200 or when their turnover does has not exceeded EUR 90 300 the preceding calendar year (when the turnover has not exceeded EUR 82 200 the penultimate year). For supplies of services (except hotel accommodation and food and drink in restaurants), the annual turnover must not exceed EUR 32 900 or EUR 34 900 the preceding calendar year (when the turnover has not exceeded EUR 32 900 the penultimate year). For lawyers (in the furtherance of their regulated business), writers and artists, the turnover must not exceed EUR 42 600 (the threshold is EUR 17 500 for their supplies outside the normal framework of their affairs).

Germany: taxpayers are relieved from VAT obligations if their annual turnover does not exceed EUR 17 500 and their expected turnover for the current calendar year will not exceed EUR 50 000.

Greece: If the annual turnover is less than EUR 10.000, the business can voluntarily enter the Special Scheme for small businesses under which no VAT is collected. Yet each new business has to register and collect VAT during the first administrative period regardless its asset or equity size, legal status etc. In case the first administrative period is less than a year, the annual turnover is calculated on a proportional basis for the purpose of entering the special scheme for the next year. Each small business entering the Special Scheme has to remain there for two years. The VAT collection threshold does not apply to farmers under the special scheme.

Box 2.A2.3. **Country Notes** *(cont.)*

Ireland: while the general turnover threshold for the supply of goods is EUR 75 000, persons supplying goods liable at the reduced or standard rates which they have manufactured or produced from zero-rated materials must register if their turnover is EUR 37 500 or more. While the general turnover threshold for the supply of services is EUR 37 500, for persons supplying both goods and services where 90% or more of the turnover is derived from supplies of goods (other than of the kind referred to in the previous sentence) then the threshold for Goods applies.

Israel: self-employed persons with annual revenue below NIS 99 006 are considered "Exempt Dealers". Some professions are not allowed to be Exempt Dealers: agronomist, architect, technician, private investigator, rabbinical attorney, dental technician, organizational consultant, management consultant, scientific consultant, economist, engineer, surveyor, bookkeeper, translator, insurance agent, lawyer, accountant or appraiser, chemical or medical laboratory owner, artistes, various others in show business, doctor, psychologist, physiotherapist, veterinary surgeon, dentist, driving school owner, school owner, real estate agent or dealer. The statistical data for Israel are supplied by and under the responsibility of the relevant Israeli authorities. The use of such data by the OECD is without prejudice to the status of the Golan Heights, East Jerusalem and Israeli settlements in the West Bank under the terms of international law.

Italy: the micro-sized taxpayers' scheme ("Regime forfetario") applies to some small businesses (depending on activity) that have an income lower than EUR 30 000 or 50 000 (depending on activity too). It notably involves exemption from VAT (excluded taxpayers subject to reverse charge mechanism). The threshold does not apply to persons who are members of partnerships, professional associations or SRLs (limited liability companies) and are subject to the "regime di transparenza" for income tax; persons who carry out sale of buildings or land or intra-EU supplies of new cars and trucks. Are also excluded foreign businesses not established in Italy, except for those who are established in one of the EU Member States, or in a State party of the European Economic Area, and produce in Italy at least 75 percent of their total revenue.

Japan: domestic and foreign businesses (both companies and individuals) whose taxable sales in Japan are less than 10 million yen, as well as new businesses of up to 2 years (except for the subsidiary of a certain large corporation) are exempt from JCT return. Exempted businesses can opt to be liable for Consumption Tax, in which case they shall remain liable for at least two years.

Luxembourg: taxpayers established in Luxembourg are entitled to opt for the special scheme; the exemption only applies to goods and services supplied in Luxembourg. Taxpayers can opt out of the special scheme but have then to apply the normal VAT rules for at least five years.

Netherlands: the VAT relief threshold applies to individuals or associated groups of individuals (e.g. partnerships) but excluding corporate businesses. The threshold is not determined with reference to the turnover but on the net annual VAT due: where the total amount of VAT (output tax less input tax) due for a calendar year on supplies of goods and services does not exceed EUR 1 345, the taxpayer is exempt from VAT (but has still to register as VAT taxpayer). If the annual VAT due is more than EUR 1 345 but less than EUR 1 883, the taxpayer gets a partial VAT rebate.

Norway: the higher threshold of NOK 3 000 000 applies for admission to sporting events

Portugal: the collection threshold does not apply to commercial legal entities. For small retailers that fulfil some specific conditions the collection threshold is EUR 12 500.

Switzerland: the threshold of CHF 100 000 also applies for the registration of non-resident businesses. The higher threshold of CHF 150 000 applies to non-for-profit sport and cultural associations and to public interest institutions.

United Kingdom: the registration threshold will be raised from GBP 82 000 to GBP 83 000 on 1 April 2016.

Table 2.A2.4. VAT Exemptions[1]

Country	Exemptions	Taxation of "common exemptions" in the country[2]
Australia	Financial services; residential rent and residential premises (other than new residential premises); certain supplies of precious metals; school canteens operated by non-profit bodies (optional); certain fund raising events conducted by charitable institutions.	Domestic postal services; sporting services; cultural services excluding religious services (zero rate); insurance and reinsurance excluding health insurance (zero rate); gambling (including lottery tickets and betting); supplies of land and buildings (except certain supplies of farm land and supplies of going concerns– zero rate and existing residential premises – exempt).
Austria	Common exemptions[2]	Letting (private housing)
Belgium	Common exemptions[2]	-
Canada	Common exemptions[2]; legal aid; public transit; ferry, road and bridge tolls; child and personal care services; certain regulatory/administrative supplies by a government or a municipality.	Most betting, lotteries and gambling; supply and leasing of commercial land and buildings; sales of newly constructed or substantially renovated housing; domestic postal services; most cultural and sporting services e.g. adult programmes; services provided by other than public sector bodies; most admissions to a place of amusement (e.g. museums, films, professional performances and sporting events, etc.); human blood and certain biologicals (zero rate).
Chile	Used motor vehicles; goods provided by the employer to dependant employees; domestic raw materials used in the production, processing or manufacture of goods for export; some imports made by the Ministry of Defence, the Army and other related organisms; some imports made by the *Cuerpos de Bomberos* and the *Junta Nacional de Cuerpos de Bomberos;* some imports made by *Casa de Moneda de Chile S.A.* and other persons provided that the import is made in the context of operations with the Central Bank of Chile; capital goods imported and assigned to projects involving investments of USD 5 000 000 or more; income received from tickets to shows and meetings; international freight, passenger transport; premiums and disbursements of reinsurance contracts; commissions earned by the Regional and Metropolitan Housing and Urbanisation Services and Social Security Institutions on mortgages; non-taxable income; income subject to additional income tax; income such as wages, salaries, pensions, income obtained by independent workers and directors fees if taxed with income tax; insertions and notices to be published and disseminated under the right of reply; certain insurance premiums; financial interests; commissions coming from guarantees issued by financial institutions; letting and lease with a purchase option of immovable property; remunerations linked to exports; income obtained from services rendered to persons domiciled or resident abroad and qualified as exportable services by Customs; income obtained by hotels relating to services rendered to foreign tourists; fees paid for managing retirement savings earned by specific authorized institutions; income obtained by independent professionals, where the physical effort is more relevant than the capital or materials used; sale, general construction contracts and finance lease of a house financed with a housing subsidy granted by the Ministry of Housing and Urban Development; broadcasting and television enterprises excluding income from advertisement; news agencies; educational services; health services; health contributions paid to Private Health Insurance Companies; manufacturing of currency by *Casa de Moneda de Chile*; postal services rendered by *Servicio de Correos y Telégrafos de Chile*, interests, premiums, commissions or other forms of remunerations paid by *Polla Chilena de Beneficencia* and *Lotería de Concepción* to individual or legal entities for business services; other minor exemptions.	Income from artistic shows or plays not sponsored by the Ministry of Education; income from certain circus and sports events if certain requirements are not met.
Czech Republic	Common exemptions[2]; public television and radio.	Certain cultural services (e.g. admission to theatres, cinemas, concerts, etc. subject to reduced rates); sporting services provided by others than by non-profit making organisations; supply of construction land; supply of new building and building land (subject for the option to taxation).
Denmark	Hospital and medical care; dental care; social service; education; non-commercial activities of some non-profit making organisations; non-profit sport activities etc.; cultural services (some exceptions); literary and composing activities; creative artist; letting of immovable property; supply of immovable property; insurance and reinsurance; financial services; lotteries and gambling; postal service; stamps; transport of persons; funeral service; certain fund-raising events; charitable work.	Cultural services as radio, television broadcasting, cinema, theatre, concerts etc.; short term letting of immovable property; option to tax commercial letting; supply of new building and building land; some commercial postal service.
Estonia	Common exemptions[2]	Immovable property, except dwellings (optional); financial services (optional); cultural services

Table 2.A2.4. **VAT Exemptions**[1] *(cont.)*

Country	Exemptions	Taxation of "common exemptions" in the country[2]
Finland	Common exemptions[2]; services of performers; copyright to literary and artistic works (excluding payments to or from an organisation representing the copyright holders); certain transactions by blind people; public cemetery services; self-picked natural berries.	Cultural services; letting of commercial buildings in certain cases (optional)
France	Common exemptions[2]; construction, improvement, repair and maintenance work on monuments, cemeteries and graves commemorating war victims undertaken for public authorities and non-profit bodies; commodity futures transactions carried out on a regulated market; services rendered by resource consortia to their members composed of natural or legal persons that are VAT exempt or not subject to VAT.	Letting of immovable property (full taxation for letting of developed immovable property and land for professional use; option to tax for letting of undeveloped immovable property for professional use in certain circumstances and letting of land and buildings for agricultural use); transport services for sick/injured persons in vehicles not specially equipped for this purpose and/or carried out by persons who do not have administrative certification; recreational and sporting services; cinemas, concerts and theatres.
Germany	Common exemptions[2]	
Greece	Common exemptions[2]; Greek Post Office (EL.TA.) services and the supply of goods incidental thereto; national radio and TV broadcasting activities other than those of commercial nature; remunerative contributions imposed by Organizations of Territorial Improvements to their members for the supply of irrigating water and relative supplies directly connected thereto; hospital and medical care supplied by public law organisations or non-profit organisations provided the latter do not create a risk of distortion of competition; medical care provided in the context of medical and paramedical professions; transport of patients by ambulances; services provided by dental technicians and the supply of dental prosthetics; supply of human organs, blood and breast milk; supply of services and goods closely connected to welfare and social security works and the protection of children and youth; services by entities to their members (non-taxable persons or persons involved in exempt activities); education services; sporting services; cultural services and closely related supply of goods; supply of services and closely related supply of goods- for a subscription to their members- by non-profit organizations who pursue collective interests in the field of politics, trade unionism, religion, philosophy, charity or national interests; insurance and reinsurance services; financial services; rental of immovable property; supply of immovable property excluding that of new buildings; legal gambling services; postage and other official stamps not disposed to collectors; supply of goods used until then exclusively in an exempt from (or out of scope of) VAT activity provided the supplier was not allowed to input tax deduction.	Postal services not rendered by the Greek Post Office (ELTA.); cultural services by profit organizations or under conditions which distort competition; hospital and medical care supplied by profit organisations or by non-profit organisations under distortion of competition; charitable work when provided by organisations without state recognition; sporting services supplied by profit organisations or subject to distortion of competition; religion related, philosophy related etc. services subject to distortion of competition; supply of new buildings; letting of immovable property for professional use (optional taxation).
Hungary	Common exemptions[2]; public radio and TV broadcasting (except for commercial activities).	Building land, supply of new buildings (taxation of further supplies and letting of immovable property is optional); certain cultural services (e.g. admission to theatres, cinemas, concerts), certain sporting services (e.g. swimming pool services, entrance tickets to sporting events).
Iceland	Common exemptions[2]; sports, admission fees to athletic events and health facilities; public transportation, organized transportation of disabled, elderlies and school children, taxi services; authors, composers, burials and church-related services; medical and social services; cultural services; operation of schools and educational institutions; rental of real properties and parking spaces; lotteries and betting pools, charities.	
Ireland	Common exemptions[2]; passenger transport; national broadcasting; supply of water by public authorities; admissions to sporting events; funeral undertaking.	Letting of commercial immovable property (subject to the option for taxation by the landlord); supply of undeveloped land and buildings that are not new; recreational and sporting services.
Israel[3]	Rentals for residential purposes for a period of not more than 25 years; the sale of a part of a building which was approved as a rental building; transactions of an exempt dealer, other than transactions that are sales of real estate; the sale of an asset, on which input tax in respect of its acquisition or importation could not be deducted lawfully at the time of its acquisition or importation; deposits in a financial institution or giving a loan to a financial institution; goods whose import is tax exempt in certain cases; supplies made by an Eilat resident supplier(to be consumed in Eilat);	

Table 2.A2.4. **VAT Exemptions**[1] *(cont.)*

Country	Exemptions	Taxation of "common exemptions" in the country[2]
Italy	Common exemptions[2]; taxi; funeral services.	Supply and letting of land; supplies of buildings are taxed in the first five years when sold by building enterprises within five years from their construction or after five years if the latter has opted for non-exemption. This scheme applies in the case of commercial buildings, while for residential housing taxation only applies when let by building enterprises which have opted for non-exemption. Rates are 4% for non-luxury owner-occupied dwelling, 10% for other non-luxury houses and 22% for luxury housing. Medical care is exempt only if earmarked to elderly or poor people, or to people with AIDS.
Japan	Common exemptions[2]; social welfare services; sale of certain kinds of equipment for the disabled people; administrative services; alienation of securities, textbooks, tuition fees.	Postal services; supply of buildings; cultural and sporting services provided by others than non-profit organisations; letting of immovable property by business.
Korea	Common exemptions[2]; certain public transport; supply of water and certain coal; mineral oil used for certain purposes in agriculture and fishery; funeral undertaking; certain personal services similar to labour; books, newspapers and magazines; broadcasting services; supply of farm, marine and forest products.	Rental and supply of commercial buildings; commercial cultural services; gambling in licensed clubs.
Latvia	Common exemptions[2]; royalty received by the author.	Supply of used immovable property (only a registered taxable person has the right to apply tax on the supply thereof).
Luxembourg	Common exemptions[2].	-
Mexico	Common exemptions[2]; gold and silver coins; shares; foreign currency; retailing of gold bullion with a content of at least 99% gold; authors' rights; urban, suburban and metropolitan public transport of passengers by land (including by train); sale of used movable property (with exception of those sold by companies); professional medical services.	Postal services; insurance services (except life and agricultural insurance); transport of sick/injured persons; private hospital and medical care, sports services; financial services for consumer and personal credits; certain kinds of public spectacles like movie tickets; supplies of land and buildings (except housing) and certain fund raising events.
Netherlands	Common exemptions[2]; burials; cremations; public broadcasting; sports clubs; the services of composers, writers and journalists.	Cultural services (mostly lower rate); letting of immovable property other than houses (only at combined request by letter and hirer); supply of immovable property (only at the combined request of supplier and purchaser); the use of sports accommodation; recreational and sporting services; admission to cinemas, concerts and theatres; sporting events; museums and zoological gardens.
New Zealand	Financial services; supply of residential accommodation in a dwelling; fine metal; supply by a non-profit body of donated goods and services.	Postal services; human blood, tissues and organs; hospital and medical care; transport of sick/injured persons; dental care; charitable work; certain fund raising events; education; non-commercial activities of non-profit making organisations (other than unconditional gifts); cultural services; sporting services; insurance and reinsurance (other than life insurance and reinsurance); letting of immovable property (other than residential accommodation); betting, lotteries and gambling; supply of land and buildings (other than land and buildings which have been used for the provision of residential accommodation for five years or more).
Norway	Common exemptions[2]; certain alternative treatments/fringe medicine; burials; stamps and coins for collection purposes; management services by a housing association to an affiliated housing cooperative; services in the form of membership of a board, supervisory board, committee, council or similar if the consideration is included in the employer's National Insurance contributions; services in the form of offsetting emission allowances	Postal services; infrastructural services within the passenger transport sector; admission to sporting events, museums, cinemas and amusement parks; letting of commercial buildings (optional).
Poland	Common exemptions[2]; public radio and television.	Rental or tenancy of the dwelling buildings used for commercial purposes; supply of building land or land for development and buildings.
Portugal	Common exemptions[2], burials and cremations, copyright to the literature and works of art.	-
Slovak Republic	Common exemptions[2]; public television and radio; services supplied to members; sale of postal and fiscal stamps.	Supply of a construction, including the supply of building land, on which the structure is constructed, provided that the supply is made within five years after the first approval of the building or a part thereof based on which the building or a part thereof was approved for use or within five years from the day when the building or a part thereof was put in use for the first time; option to tax supply and letting of immovable property; training, educational, sporting and cultural services provided by others than by non-profit making organisations.
Slovenia	Common exemptions[2]; public television and radio.	Supply of new buildings; admission to cultural and sporting events; educational, sporting and cultural services provided by profit making organisations; option to tax letting of immovable property.

Table 2.A2.4. **VAT Exemptions**[1] *(cont.)*

Country	Exemptions	Taxation of "common exemptions" in the country[2]
Spain	Common exemptions[2]; copyright to literature and works of art; services provided by associations, entities, groups (including "economic interest groupings) and other legal persons to their members when they are exclusively integrated by taxable persons carrying out economic activities exempted or not subject to VAT; certain social assistance services provided by public bodies or not-for-profit organisations.	Cultural and sporting services provided for taxable persons different from public bodies and non-profit making organisations; letting of commercial buildings; building land; supply of new buildings.
Sweden	Common exemptions[2]; public television and radio; public cemetery services; social services; creative artists.	Most cultural services; letting of commercial buildings in certain cases (optional).
Switzerland	Common exemptions[2]; cultural services and the supply of cultural works by their creators, such as authors, composers, film makers, painters, sculptors and services supplied by publishers and collecting societies in order to circulate these works; the supply of used movable goods, which were used exclusively for the provision of supplies exempt from the tax without credit; the sale of agricultural, forestry and market garden products cultivated in their own business by farmers, foresters or gardeners, the sale of cattle by cattle dealers, and the sale of milk by milk collection points to milk processing plants; publicity services, which charitable organisations provide for the benefit of third parties or third parties for the benefit of charitable organisations; the exercise of arbitration functions.	The dispensing of artificial limbs and orthopaedic equipment; renting of exhibition stands and individual rooms in exhibition and congress buildings.
Turkey	Importation of goods for cultural and educational purposes or for social purposes; restoration project related to cultural object; delivery of goods and provision of services to military factories, shipyards and factory plants; exempted taxpayers according to Income Tax Law; mergers and transfer according to Corporate Tax Law; transactions on leasing of real properties not included in economic enterprises; banking and insurance transaction; transactions of the Mint House and the Stamp Printing House; supply of precious mine and waste; supply of water used in agriculture; services supplied in free trade area; transportation of foreign oil and gas by pipelines; supply of land and workplace for organised industrial zone; supply of goods within the scope of financial restructuring; the transactions of Savings Deposit Insurance Fund; news service provided to General Directorate of Press and Information; renting work place in customs area; delivery and leasing of immovable property by the Treasury; transfers and deliveries resulting from the sales of shares and real properties that have been included for at least two years in the assets of institutions; transfer of movable and immovable assets and intangible assets to the asset leasing company and the leasing of assets by asset leasing company; services provided by "Insurance Arbitration Commission" about settling disputes.	Private education; private cultural services and sporting services; private hospital and medical care and dental care; human blood; transport of sick/injured persons(lower rate); postal services; sale of commercial buildings; letting; radio and television broadcasting; betting, lotteries and gambling; financial services that made by financial corporation; supply of land and buildings included in economic enterprises (standard rate); public hospital and medical care and dental care; public education; public cultural services and sporting services; tissues and organs; certain charitable work that is made by public organization or certificated institution; insurance and reinsurance; letting of immovable property not included in economic enterprises (exemption); non-commercial activities of non-profit making organisations; certain fund-raising events(non-taxable).
United Kingdom	Common exemptions[2]; burials and cremations; sports competitions; certain luxury hospital care; works of art.	Standard rated: freehold sales of new commercial buildings (standard rated for three years from completion date) and "option to tax" for other ordinarily exempted supplies of commercial buildings; gaming machines and certain gambling in licensed clubs. Zero rated: New housing, including construction of new houses; residential and some charity buildings.

1. **Exemptions:** for the purposes of this table, "exemption" means supplies for which VAT is not levied on the amount charged by the provider while the latter is not allowed to deduct related input tax. In some countries, such supplies are called "input taxed supplies".
2. **Common exemptions:** in this table, "Common exemptions" hereafter refer to exemptions generally applied in most OECD countries: postal services; transport of sick/injured persons; hospital and medical care; human blood, tissues and organs; dental care; charitable work; education; non-commercial activities of non-profit making organisations; sporting services; cultural services (except radio and television broadcasting); insurance and reinsurance; letting of immovable property; financial services; betting, lotteries and gambling; supply of land and buildings; certain fund-raising events
3. **Israel:** the statistical data for Israel are supplied by and under the responsibility of the relevant Israeli authorities. The use of such data by the OECD is without prejudice to the status of the Golan Heights, East Jerusalem and Israeli settlements in the West Bank under the terms of international law.

Source: National delegates; position as at 1 January 2016.

Table 2.A2.5. Restrictions to the right to deduct VAT on specific inputs[1]

Country	Inputs on which the right to deduct VAT is denied or limited
Australia	**Entertainment:** recreational club leisure facility, entertainment, meal entertainment, family maintenance, relative's travel. **Vehicles:** the amount of GST recoverable on the acquisition of a car is limited to that applicable to the car depreciation limit for the income year, currently AUD 57 466. **Others:** penalties, non-compulsory uniforms. GST is not recoverable on the expenses above to the extent they are not eligible for a deduction under the income tax law.
Austria	**Entertainment:** all entertainment expenses. **Vehicles:** vehicles, except used for commercial passenger transport, for leasing purposes or used at least 80% for driving schools.
Belgium	**Entertainment:** full input tax block for restaurant and hotel (with a number of strict exceptions), certain alcoholic beverages (with a number of strict exceptions) and reception and hospitality costs. **Vehicles:** expenses relating to vehicles for transport of persons and/or goods by road. The right to deduct input tax may in principle not exceed 50% (with a number of strict exceptions). **Others:** supplies relating to special VAT scheme (e.g. margin scheme, special VAT scheme for tobacco).
Canada	**Entertainment:** deduction restrictions apply to memberships in dining, recreational or sporting facilities clubs; deduction for food, beverages, and entertainment expenses generally limited to 50% of the GST/HST payable. Food and beverage expenses for long-haul truck drivers are limited to 80%. **Vehicles:** deduction is limited on passenger vehicles acquired as capital property to the GST/HST payable on the capital cost value ($30.000); deduction is limited on passenger vehicles leases to the GST/HST payable on $800 monthly lease payments. **Others:** home office expenses; restriction to the extent that the consumption or use of a property or service of such quality, nature, or cost is unreasonable given the person's commercial activity. **Local limitations:** large businesses (generally those with annual taxable supplies in excess of CAD 10 million) that acquire certain property or services (e.g. energy, telecommunications, road vehicles) for use in the provinces of Ontario and Prince Edward Island are subject to input tax credit restrictions on the provincial portion of the HST. These restrictions are being phased out in Ontario and will be phased out beginning in 2018 in Prince Edward Island.
Chile	**Vehicles:** automobiles, station wagons and similar vehicles as well their lubricants, spare parts, repairs or maintenance unless the regular business activity of the taxpayer is the sale, rental or lease of automobiles or unless the Commissioner of the Internal Revenue Service consider the relevant expenses as deductible for income tax purposes. **Fuels:** products or components that have any form of subsidy for end consumers. **Supermarkets:** expenses made in supermarkets and similar businesses when they exceed 5 Monthly Tax Units (CLP 224 455 – USD 343) and information specified in the law is not given to the tax authority.
Czech Republic	**Entertainment:** representation expenditures as defined in the income tax law for which there is no tax allowance according to the income tax law (except small gifts).
Denmark	**Entertainment:** expenses of entertainment, restaurant and presents. **Vehicles:** supply of vans with a weight of 3000kg or less used for both taxable and non-taxable purpose; cars with room for less than 10 persons; leased cars. **Others:** employee telephones paid by employer; board of employees and owner of the company; other objects in favour of the employees.
Estonia	**Entertainment:** goods or services relating to the reception of guests or the provision of meals or accommodation for employees. This restriction does not apply to accommodation services received during a business trip. **Vehicles:** the right of deduction is limited to 50% on purchase, import, lease or hire of passenger cars not wholly used for business purposes and on the related expenditures, except for cars purchased for resale, hire or lease, for cars used for the transportation of passengers (e.g. taxis) and for cars used for driving lessons.
Finland	**Entertainment:** representation and entertainment expenses. **Vehicles, boats and aircraft:** used for sporting and leisure purposes, cars, motorcycles and caravans. However, any means of transport which are to be resold, rented out or used in professional passenger transport or in driving lessons as well as passenger cars used only for taxable transactions are deductible. **Others:** travelling costs of personnel between home and workplace; goods and services related to dwellings or buildings provided for the recreation of personnel.

Table 2.A2.5. Restrictions to the right to deduct VAT on specific inputs[1] *(cont.)*

Country	Inputs on which the right to deduct VAT is denied or limited
France	**Vehicles:** vehicles or equipment, whatever their nature, designed to carry persons or mixed-use, except those for resale as new; leased, having in addition to the driver's seat more than eight seats used by companies to bring their staff on the workplace, assigned exclusively to the driving instruction, all type of road vehicles exclusively for the operation of ski lifts and ski areas, vehicles acquired by companies of public passenger transport and assigned exclusively to the realisation of such transport. Components, parts and accessories of vehicles and machines previously referred. **Others:** goods and services used by taxable persons for more than 90% for a non-business purpose; gifts above a certain value; goods or services linked to the free supply of housing to officers or employees of a company, except when it's for the security staff on construction sites or in company premises; goods or services used for advertising alcoholic beverages; supply of passenger transport and services ancillary to such transport, except those produced either on behalf of an enterprise of public passenger transport, or under a permanent contract of transport by companies to bring their staff on the workplace; most fuels not subsequently delivered or sold as is or as other petroleum products. **Partial restrictions:** The right to deduction is limited to 50% for gas oil and other hydrocarbons in gaseous state and kerosene used as fuel, when such products are used for vehicles and equipment mentioned above. The right of deduction is limited to 50% for gas oil and other hydrocarbons in gaseous state and kerosene used as fuel, when such products are used for vehicles and equipment mentioned above. The right of deduction is limited to 80% for gas oils and bio ethanol E85 used as fuel for vehicles and equipment mentioned above, except those used for testing for the purposes of making engines of motorised equipment and insofar as they are not subsequently delivered or sold as is or as other petroleum products.
Germany	**Entertainment:** representation expenditures as defined in the income tax law for which there is no tax allowance according to the income tax law (e.g. gifts except small gifts, restaurant, catering, entertainment expenditure except appropriate ones, expenditures on hunting and fishing, sailing yacht or motor yachts and expenditures of similar nature).
Greece	**Entertainment:** receptions, recreation and hospitality in general; accommodation, food, drinks, transport and recreation for the personnel or representatives of the business. **Means of transport:** private motor vehicles of up to 9 seats; motorcycles and mopeds, vessels and aircraftsfor private use intended for recreation or sports, and the related supplies of fuel, repair, maintenance, rental/leasing and circulation in general. The restriction does not apply to the aforementioned means of transport when they are intended for sale, rental/leasing or transport of persons for a fare. **Others:** manufactured tobacco products, spirituous or alcoholic beverages intended to be used in non-taxable activities.
Hungary	**Entertainment:** services of restaurants and other public catering services; entertainment services; food and beverages. **Vehicles:** passenger cars (except hearses), motorcycles above 125 cubic centimetres; yachts and vessels. **Others**: supplies of motor fuels, other fuels, other goods used in connection with the operation or maintenance of passenger cars; residential properties, goods and services used for the construction or remodelling of residential properties; taxi services, parking services, highway toll services; 30% of input tax regarding fixed phone, mobile phone and VOIP service; 50% of input tax regarding the services used for the operation or maintenance of passenger cars.
Iceland	**Entertainment:** all expenses related to catering and food for the taxable person. **Vehicles:** supply, running and rental of passenger cars; delivery trucks, trucks and off-road vehicles whith a weight of 5.000 kg or less, unless used for specially regulated taxable purpose. **Others:** all expenses related to residential property for the owner and the employees of the taxable person. All expenses which come instead of salaries to the owner and the employees of the taxable person. All expenses related to summer houses and similar entertainment for the owner and the employees of the taxable person; presents.
Ireland	**Entertainment:** food, drink, accommodation (except for qualifying conferences), personal services, entertainment. **Vehicles:** purchase or hire of passenger vehicles (20% of the cost is allowed where the car meets certain conditions regarding business use and emission levels). **Others:** petrol
Israel[2]	None
Italy	**Entertainment:** entertainment expenses, food and beverages. **Vehicles:** means of transport and connected services (motor vehicles, aircraft and yachts); passenger transport. **Other:** luxury goods and connected services, buildings.
Japan	None
Korea	**Entertainment:** entertainment expenses and similar expenditures. **Vehicles:** purchase and maintenance of non-business small automobiles
Latvia	**Entertainment:** 60% shall not be deductible from the tax as input tax from the tax amount to be paid into the State budget for the goods acquired and services received for the representation needs. **Vehicles:** 50% shall not be deductible from the tax as input tax from the tax amount to be paid into the State budget for an acquired, leased or imported passenger car the number of seats of which, not including the driver's seat, does not exceed eight seats, as well as the costs related to the maintenance of such car, including expenses for repair of the car and purchase of fuel. Fully non-deductible from the tax amount from the State budget for buying, renting and importing passenger car the number of seats of which, not including the driver's seat, does not exceed eight seats and value higher than EUR 50 000 (exclusive of VAT), as well as the costs related to the maintenance of such car, including expenses for repair of the car and purchase of fuel.
Luxembourg	**Entertainment:** not strictly business expenditures such as luxuries, entertainment or amusements.

Table 2.A2.5. Restrictions to the right to deduct VAT on specific inputs[1] (cont.)

Country	Inputs on which the right to deduct VAT is denied or limited
Mexico	No restrictions list, the law establishes that deductions must come from goods and services "strictly indispensable" for the principal activity. The expenses deductible for VAT purposes must be deductible in terms of the Income Tax Law. The Income Tax Law has list of "Authorized deductions" for each type of regime.
Netherlands	**Entertainment:** restaurant services. Also certain representation and gift expenditures.
New Zealand	**Entertainment:** entertainment expenses are in effect only 50% deductible. Businesses may claim a full deduction when the goods and services are acquired and must annually calculate and repay the deemed 50% private portion.
Norway	**Entertainment:** catering and hiring of locations related to catering; entertainment expenses; the construction, maintenance, renting or operation of real property for accommodation or welfare needs. **Vehicles:** procurement, operation or maintenance of passenger vehicles. **Others:** works of art or antiques; accommodation of- and remuneration in kind to the owner, management, employees or pensioners of an enterprise; business gifts, goods and services for distribution for advertising purposes; cash payments above NOK 10 000 (USD 1040).
Poland	**Entertainment:** restaurant services and accommodation. **Vehicles:** limitation to 50% of the right to deduct VAT on the purchase, intra- Community acquisition, import, hire or lease of motor vehicles as well as VAT charged on expenditure related to those vehicles, where the vehicle is not entirely used for business purposes. **Others:** limitation to 50% of the right to deduct VAT on the purchase of motor fuels, fuel oil &and natural gas used by aforementioned vehicles.
Portugal	**Entertainment:** transport, accommodation or meals (except connected with conferences, seminars, fairs or exhibitions, which, under certain conditions, are deductible in 25% or 50%). Luxury and entertainment expenses **Vehicles:** acquisition or hiring of light vehicles deemed to be used for non-business purposes, as well as pleasure boats, helicopters, aircrafts and motorcycles (except if intended for sale or constitute the core of the business activity). **Others:** fuel used in motor vehicles (other than gas oil, liquefied petroleum gas, natural gas and bio fuels, which are deductible at 50%; or fully deductible if used in certain heavy vehicles or tractors).
Slovak Republic	**Entertainment:** goods and services for the purposes of treat and entertainment **Others:** suspense items (Suspense items means expenses paid on behalf and for the account of the purchaser or the customer, which the supplier charges to the purchaser or the customer.
Slovenia	**Entertainment:** entertainment expenses (where entertainment expenses shall include only the costs of entertainment and amusement during business or social contacts); meals (including drinks) and accommodation expenses, except expenses incurred by taxable person in connection with these supplies in the ordinary course of his business. **Vehicles:** yachts and boats intended for sport and recreation; aircrafts other than those used for transport of passengers and goods, leasing, renting and resale. Passenger cars and motorcycles other than: vehicles used for transport of passengers and goods, leasing, renting and resale, vehicles used in driving schools for the provision of the driver's training program in accordance with the regulations in force and combined vehicles for carrying out an activity of a public line and special line transport, and special vehicles adapted exclusively for the transport of deceased people. **Others:** fuels, lubricants, spare parts and services which are closely linked to vehicles above.
Spain	**Entertainment:** access to shows and services of a recreational character; travel, accommodation and catering services, unless they are deductible as a cost in income taxes. **Others:** jewellery, gold and platinum objects, pearls, precious stones; food, drinks and tobacco; goods or services used as gifts to clients, employees or third parties;
Sweden	None
Switzerland	None
Turkey	**Cars**: purchases of cars except when used by car renting companies **Others**: Missing and stolen stocks (excluding those lost due to fire in places of compelling reason declared by Ministry of Finance).
United Kingdom	**Entertainment:** business entertainment; in general terms the free provision of any hospitality to business contacts is not recoverable. The exception is where the entertainment is provided to non UK customers. However it is likely that if recovery is granted it would be off-set by a private use charge that would effectively cancel out any credit obtained. **Vehicles:** motor cars in general, except motor cars that are stock in trade (car dealers etc.); tools of the trade (driving schools etc.) or exclusively used for business purposes with no availability for private use (leasing companies etc.); lease of a motor car (right to deduction is limited to 50%).

1. **Restrictions to the right to deduct VAT on specific inputs:** the table includes limitations of the right to deduct input VAT on specific goods, services and intangibles ***because of their nature,*** generally with a view to ensure (input) taxation of their ***deemed*** final consumption. The table does **not** include input tax blockings related to the exemption of outputs (e.g. limited right of deduction for inputs used to provide financial and insurance services, medical care, education, etc listed in Table 3.11 on VAT exemptions) or to inputs not connected with the taxable activity of the business.
2. **Israel:** the statistical data for Israel are supplied by and under the responsibility of the relevant Israeli authorities. The use of such data by the OECD is without prejudice to the status of the Golan Heights, East Jerusalem and Israeli settlements in the West Bank under the terms of international law.

Source: National delegates; position as at 1 January 2016.

Table 2.A2.6. **Usage of margin schemes**

	Usage of margin schemes[1]
Australia	Margin scheme can be used on certain sales of new residential or commercial property. It is generally based on the difference between the tax inclusive sale price and the original purchase price. Special rules apply in certain cases, such as sales between associates or members of the same GST group. Gambling: GST applies to the gambling margin calculated based on the total amount wagered less total monetary prizes awarded. Second hand goods when second-hand dealers adopt a special "global" accounting method. It applies when (1) second-hand goods are acquired from an unregistered supplier and are divided up for re-supply and (2) the dealer exercises the option to apply the global method over a specified category of second-hand good.
Austria	Travel agencies; second-hand goods, works of art, collector's items and antiques (EU Directive)
Belgium	Travel agencies; second-hand goods, works of art, collector's items and antiques (EU Directive)
Canada	-
Chile	-
Czech Republic	Travel agencies; second- hand goods; works of art; collector's items and antiques (EU Directive)
Denmark	Travel agencies; second-hand goods, works of art, collector's items and antiques (EU Directive)
Estonia	Travel agencies; second-hand goods, works of art, collector's items and antiques (EU Directive)
Finland	Travel agencies; second-hand goods, works of art, collector's items and antiques (EU Directive)
France	Travel agencies; second-hand goods, works of art, collector's items and antiques (EU Directive); real estate agents.
Germany	Travel agencies; second-hand goods, works of art, collector's items and antiques (EU Directive)
Greece	Travel agencies; second-hand goods, works of art, collector's items and antiques (EU Directive); sales by public auction
Hungary	Travel agencies; second-hand goods; works of art, antiques, collectors' items (EU Directive).
Iceland	-
Ireland	Optional margin scheme for antiques, works of art and second hand goods (EU Directive). Mandatory margin scheme for auctioneers and travel agents.
Israel[2]	Sale of used furniture by a dealer whose business is the sale of such furniture. Sale of used vehicle, motorcycle or cross-country vehicle by a dealer whose business is a purchase and sale of used vehicles. Sale of dwellings by a real estate dealer who acquired it from a person who is not a non-profit organisation, a financial institution or a dealer. Sale of coins and medals, which the seller has purchased such coins and medals from a non-licensed dealer (i.e. not VAT registered business). Sale of postage stamps and revenue stamps by a person whose business is the sale of such stamps (deemed to be a service). Sale of foreign currency, securities or other negotiable instruments, including the acquisition of aforesaid securities and instruments in order to collect their redemption or retirement price, by a dealer whose business is the sale of such assets or the sale of foreign currency, shall be deemed to be a brokerage service rendered by the dealer, between the dealer's supplier and the dealer's customer.
Italy	Travel agencies; second-hand goods, works of art, collector's items and antiques (EU Directive)
Japan	-
Korea	-
Latvia	Travel agencies; second-hand goods, works of art, collector's items and antiques (EU Directive)
Luxembourg	Travel agencies; second-hand goods, works of art, collector's items and antiques (EU Directive)
Mexico	Sale of used cars, previously acquired previously acquired by a company from an individual
Netherlands	Travel agencies; second-hand goods, works of art, collector's items and antiques (EU Directive)
New Zealand	-
Norway	Voluntary margin scheme for second hand goods, works of art, collectors' items and antiques.
Poland	Travel agencies; second-hand goods; works of art; collector's items and antiques (EU Directive).
Portugal	Travel agencies; second-hand goods, works of art, collector's items and antiques (EU Directive) and fuel retailers..
Slovak Republic	Travel agencies; second-hand goods, works of art, collector's items and antiques (EU Directive)
Slovenia	Travel agencies; second-hand goods, works of art, collector's items and antiques (EU Directive)
Spain	Travel agencies; second-hand goods, works of art, collector's items and antiques (EU Directive)
Sweden	Travel agencies; second-hand goods, works of art, collector's items and antiques (EU Directive)
Switzerland	None, but deemed input tax deduction for used, individual, movable goods for supplies within the jurisdiction.
Turkey	Travel agencies (commission taken from tour sold abroad is exempt; commission taken from tour sold in Turkey is subject to tax.)
United Kingdom	Travel agencies; second-hand goods, works of art, collector's items and antiques (EU Directive)

1. **Margin scheme:** In this context, a margin scheme means a scheme where the tax base is calculated on the difference between the price paid by the taxpayer for an item and the price of resale rather than on the full selling price. The reseller is not allowed to deduct the input VAT embedded in the buying price of the items resold under the margin scheme.
2. **Israel:** The statistical data for Israel are supplied by and under the responsibility of the relevant Israeli authorities. The use of such data by the OECD is without prejudice to the status of the Golan Heights, East Jerusalem and Israeli settlements in the West Bank under the terms of international law.

Source: National delegations; position as at 1 January 2016.

Chapter 3

Measuring performance of VAT

This chapter describes how the VAT Revenue Ratio (VRR) provides an indicator of the effect of exemptions, reduced rates and non-compliance on government revenues. It presents the updated VRR estimates for OECD countries and explains how the VRR is calculated and how it should be interpreted. It is complemented with technical notes on the measurement of final consumption expenditure, on the VAT treatment of public sector activities and on the VAT exemption for financial services.

The statistical data for Israel are supplied by and under the responsibility of the relevant Israeli authorities. The use of such data by the OECD is without prejudice to the status of the Golan Heights, East Jerusalem and Israeli settlements in the West Bank under the terms of international law.

3.1. Introduction

The measurement of VAT performance is challenging. It has traditionally been measured by the "efficiency ratio", defined as the ratio of VAT revenues to GDP divided by the standard rate (expressed as a percentage). Although the efficiency ratio is widely used as a diagnostic tool in evaluating VATs, its limitations are significant. In particular, the measure suffers from a fundamental weakness: a "perfect" efficiency ratio of 100% could be achieved by a product-type VAT levied at a uniform rate. However, this is misleading since the norm is a consumption-type VAT. This difficulty is addressed by taking final consumption as a reference for the potential tax base rather than production (Ebrill et al., 2001). If measured by the ratio of revenue from the tax to the product of the standard VAT rate and aggregate consumption, a benchmark VAT levied at a uniform rate on all consumption would have "C-Efficiency" of 100% provided that all the tax due is collected by the tax administration.

Building on the concept for measuring the "C-efficiency ratio" of VAT regimes as used by the International Monetary Fund (IMF), this chapter presents the estimates for OECD countries of the VAT Revenue Ratio (VRR). It provides an indicator that combines the effect of loss of revenues as a consequence of exemptions and reduced rates, fraud, evasion and tax planning. Although the VRR has to be interpreted with care and erosion of the tax base may be caused by a variety of factors, it may support policymakers in assessing the revenue raising performance of their VAT system and in identifying opportunities to raise additional revenues by improving the performance of VAT systems.

This chapter first explains what the VRR is intended to measure and how it is calculated (Section 3.2). It then presents the estimates for OECD countries of the VRR in 2014 and a high-level analysis of these estimates (Section 3.3). This is followed by some guidance for the interpretation of the VRR and explains that the use of this measure is subject to a range of caveats (Section 3.4). This is complemented by three technical notes that provide further detailed insight into two specific aspects of VAT policy design that may often have a significant impact on a country's VRR and that may therefore assist readers in interpreting the VRR estimates (Section 3.5). The first technical note deals with the differences between the measurement of final consumption expenditure that is used to calculate the VRR and the potential tax base of a "pure" VAT regime; the second technical note discusses the VAT exemption for financial services and the third note looks at the VAT treatment of public bodies.

3.2. What does the VRR measure and how is it calculated?

What does the VRR measure?

The aim of the VRR is to provide a comparative measure of a country's ability to secure effectively the potential tax base for VAT. The VRR measures the difference between the VAT revenue actually collected and what would theoretically be raised if VAT was applied at the standard rate to the entire potential tax base in a "pure" VAT regime and all revenue was collected:

$$VRR = \frac{VR}{B \,.\, r}$$

Where: VR = actual VAT revenues; B = potential tax base and r = standard VAT rate

The "standard" rate refers to the default rate applicable to the tax base, unless otherwise advised by legislation. Legislation can (and many countries do) provide that lower (or higher) rates are applicable to a defined list of products. Reduced VAT rates are still widely used in OECD countries, mainly for equity or social objectives (basic essentials, health, education, etc.). No OECD countries apply higher VAT rates (see Chapter 2).

Assessing the tax base

The main methodological difficulty in the calculation of the VRR lies in the assessment of the potential tax base, since no standard assessment of the potential VAT base for all OECD countries is available. The potential VAT base includes all supplies of goods, services and intangibles made for consideration (or deemed to be made for consideration) by businesses or any other entity acting as a business (e.g. individuals, government entities providing supplies for direct consideration, etc.) to final consumers. In principle, the tax base ultimately corresponds to the expenditure made by final consumers to obtain goods, services and intangibles. In practice, however, many VAT systems impose VAT burden not only on final household consumption, but also on various entities that are involved in non-business activities or in VAT exempt activities (see Chapter 1 and 2). In such situations, VAT can be viewed alternatively as treating such entities as if they were end consumers, or as "input taxing" the supplies made by such entities on the presumption that the burden of the VAT imposed will be passed on in the prices of the outputs of those non-business activities. The tax ultimately collected by the government in these situations is the tax on these inputs.

In the absence of a standard assessment of the potential VAT base for all OECD countries, the closest statistic for that base is final consumption expenditure as measured in the national accounts, since VAT is, ultimately, a tax on final consumption. Final consumption expenditure is calculated according to a standard international norm, the System of National Accounts (SNA 2008) under Item P3 (except for Turkey, Chile and Japan that still use SNA 1993).

The final consumption expenditure (domestic demand) consists of the following components:

- P31-S14: Private final consumption expenditure of households.
- P31-S15: Final consumption expenditure of non-profit organisations serving households (NPSH).
- P3-S13: Final consumption expenditure of general government, including:
  - P31-S13: Individual consumption expenditure of general government.
  - P32-S13: Collective consumption expenditure of general government.

The differences between the final consumption expenditure as measured in the national accounts and the potential VAT base for OECD countries, and how these differences may influence the VRR estimate for a given country, are discussed in more detail in Section 3.5. This explanation may be helpful in interpreting the VRR estimates and in acquiring a deeper understanding of the various factors that may influence the result for a given country.

The formula used to estimate the VRR of OECD countries

In the VRR calculation formula as presented above, the potential tax base (B) is measured by the final consumption expenditure under Item P3 in the national accounts. However, since the SNA measures consumption expenditures at market prices, i.e. including VAT, revenues from VAT should be deducted from the amount under P3. Indeed, the theoretical basis for taxation should not include the tax itself.

As a result, the VRR estimates presented in Table 3.A3.1 have been calculated as follows:

$$VRR = \frac{VR}{(FCE - VR).r}$$

Where: VR = actual VAT revenues; FCE = Final Consumption Expenditure (Item P3 in National Accounts); and r = standard VAT rate.

3.3. The VRR estimates for OECD countries

Across the OECD, the unweighted average VRR has remained relatively stable at 0.56, compared to 0.55 in 2012, meaning that 44% of the potential VAT revenue is not collected. Behind this average, Table 3.A3.1 shows the considerable variation in the VRR estimates across OECD countries.* In 2014 the estimates varied from 0.32 (Mexico) to 1.23 (Luxembourg). Two countries have a VRR far above the others: Luxembourg (1.23) and New Zealand (0.97) while two countries have a VRR estimate considerably below the OECD average, Mexico (0.31) and Greece (0.37). The majority of countries (28 of 34) have a VRR below 0.65 and almost half (16 of 34) have a ratio below 0.50. This suggests that a considerable part of the potential VAT revenue remains uncollected in many OECD countries.

This VRR notably reflects the fact that preferential treatments, such as reduced rates and exemptions, are still widely used in OECD countries (see Tables 2.A2.2 and 2.A2.4). This is confirmed by available data on tax expenditures, reflecting the cost of tax concessions (OECD 2010).

It appears that there is no direct correlation between the level of the standard VAT rate and the VRR. Countries with very different VAT rates may have comparable VRRs. Australia and Ireland, for example, both have a VRR of 0.49 while their standard VAT rates are respectively 10% and 23%. Although about two thirds of countries (21 of 34) have a VRR between 0.45 and 0.65, they have standard VAT rates which vary widely, from 5% (Canada) to 25% (Denmark, Norway, Sweden). Denmark, Norway and Sweden combine a high standard VAT rate (25%) with a VRR above the OECD average (respectively 0.59, 0.56 and 0.56) while Mexico and Turkey combine lower standard VAT rates (respectively 16% and 18%) with a VRR estimate considerably below the OECD average (respectively 0.32 and 0.42). Japan combines a low VAT rate (5%) and absence of a domestic zero rate with a high VRR (0.70).

* For a number of countries, VRR figures presented in this edition may be slightly different from those presented in previous editions (including for figures before 2009) due to the update of the SNA methodology (*www.oecd.org/std/na/sna-2008-main-changes.htm*).

Figure 3.1. **VAT Revenue Ratio in OECD countries 2014**

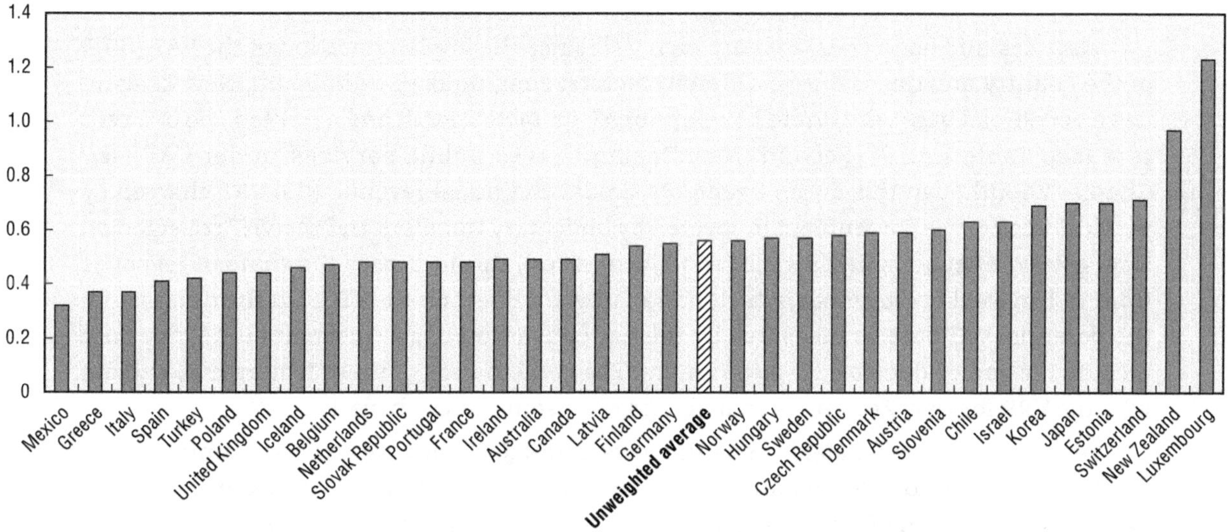

Source: Author's own calculations based on Revenue Statistics 2016 and National Accounts. The VAT revenue ratio (VRR) is defined as the ratio between the actual value-added tax (VAT) revenue collected and the revenue that would theoretically be raised if VAT was applied at the standard rate to all final consumption (see Table 3.A3.1).

StatLink http://dx.doi.org/10.1787/888933419971

The respective weight of the different factors that affect the VRR may vary widely across countries depending on the circumstances. The two countries with the highest VRR, Luxembourg and New Zealand, are both far above the OECD average (with respectively 1.23 and 0.97 compared to an average of 0.56) and even significantly above the country that follows immediately (Switzerland with a VRR of 0.71). However, the reasons behind such high ratios are very different.

The VRR for Luxembourg has constantly increased since the late 1990s, from 0.56 in 1996 to 1.23 in 2014. This increase is correlated with deep changes in the EU marketplace, in particular the liberalisation of financial services and the boom of e-commerce. It is reasonable to assume that these market factors and their specific VAT treatment have had a strong upward effect on Luxembourg's VRR. It may be assumed that Luxembourg's position as an international financial centre has resulted in additional VAT revenue for the country. According to EU VAT rules, the supply of financial services is generally exempt from VAT in Luxembourg without right to deduct the input tax, including when supplied to customers in other EU Member States. This means that the VAT incurred by the providers of the financial service providers in Luxembourg increase Luxembourg's VAT revenues while a large share of the corresponding final consumption occurs in other EU Member States as a result of the increasing cross-border trade in financial services. Luxembourg has over time also become an international centre for e-commerce, notably as a consequence of the VAT treatment of this activity under EU VAT legislation. According to this legislation, e-commerce supplies to final consumers in other EU Member States were taxed (until the 1 January 2015) in the Member State where the supplier is established. The low standard VAT rate in Luxembourg, the lowest of the EU (15% in 2014), has acted as an incentive to e-suppliers to establish in Luxembourg. This has generated additional revenue for the country, which has continued to increase over time as a result of the strong growth of the internet economy. The change in the place of taxation rule on 1 January 2015, where suppliers have now to charge VAT to EU consumers on the basis of the rate applicable in their Member State of residence, is likely to trigger a decline in the VRR for Luxembourg from 2015 onwards.

New Zealand has a constant very high VRR since the implementation of the VAT (GST) in the country and this is due to different factors. First, unlike Luxembourg, New Zealand has a very broad base with limited exemptions (see Table 2.A2.4) and a limited use of a zero rate (see Table 2.A2.2). Second, New Zealand taxes public services under VAT (see Chapter 2). Although this doesn't generate actual additional revenue (the VAT charged by public bodies to the government is covered by budgetary transfers and the VAT collected on local government activities is included in local taxes), this increases the share of revenues from VAT in total tax revenues, which has an upward effect on the VRR. On the other hand, the potential VAT base as measured by the national accounts (see section above) does not include the value added by the government. The combination of these factors may explain why the VRR for New Zealand is so high and even sometimes above 1.

At the opposite end, Mexico has the lowest VRR (0.32) amongst OECD countries. This is likely to be due to a combination of factors such as the scope of VAT exemptions, the extensive application of a domestic zero rate and a low compliance rate (Mexico's VAT gap for 2010 has been estimated at 21.7%; see CIAT, 2012). A VAT reform was implemented in 2014 to eliminate the reduced VAT rate of 11% in border areas so that the standard VAT rate of 16% now applies throughout the country. The reform also removed the zero rate on hotel and related services to foreigners, now taxed at the standard rate, and adjusted the regime of inward processing arrangements (*maquiladores*) to reduce the risk of fraud. The VRR for Mexico increased from 0.31 in 2012 and 0.28 in 2013 to 0.32 in 2014.

Although the unweighted average of the VRR has remained relatively stable over time, the impact of the economic crises is visible in a many countries, particularly among those that have been hardest hit by the impact of the global financial and economic crisis. Between 2007 and 2012, the VRR decreased in 28 OECD countries and increased in only 7 countries. The fell was particularly strong (more than 0.1) in 4 countries (Estonia, Greece, Iceland, Ireland, Latvia, Poland, Slovak Republic, Slovenia and Spain). The reductions in VRR may be explained by a combination of factors including non-compliance and changes in consumption patterns resulting from the economic crisis. Indeed, if the share of total households' expenditure for basic items (subject to reduced rates or exemptions – food, health, housing, etc.) increases compared to the share of expenditure for other items (new houses, cars, leisure), the VRR decreases.

3.4. How to interpret the VRR estimates?

Factors that may influence the VRR

In theory, the closer the VAT system of a country is to a "pure" VAT regime, the closer its VRR is to 1. A lower value reflects such factors as the effects of reduced rates, exemptions or a failure to collect all tax due. A VRR above 1 is possible in theory where almost all the tax base is covered by the standard rate and a number of exemptions without right to deduction apply so that the cascading effect of the exemption provides additional revenue for the government that exceeds the cost of the exemption. A VRR close to 1 is taken as an indicator of a VAT bearing uniformly on a broad base with effective tax collection. In practice, the VRR rarely equals 1 and a number of complex factors, alone or in combination, may influence the results positively or negatively. These include:

- The application of lower VAT rates to a number of goods and services and the level of such lower rates that reduce the tax revenue and have a negative impact on the VRR.
- The level of the registration and/or collection threshold under which small businesses do not account for VAT. These thresholds reduce the amount of VAT collected, although it could be argued that the adverse revenue consequences of such thresholds are likely to be limited since the businesses under the thresholds will generally not be able to deduct any input VAT and their value added can be expected to be modest.
- The scope of the exemptions. Exemptions may reduce the tax revenue (when exemption applies to goods and services directly supplied to final consumer e.g. healthcare) or may increase that revenue when exemption occurs early in the supply chain (e.g. financial services made to businesses) and the revenue arising from the cascading effect exceeds the potential tax arising from taxation at standard rates with deduction of input tax. Depending on the features of the exemptions and market structures, exemptions may influence the VRR upwards or downwards. The application of a VAT exemption for financial services may often have a considerable impact on the VRR, given the importance of the financial services output in many countries (for more detail, see the technical note on financial services in Section 3.5).
- The VAT treatment of public sector activities. Final consumption by government is the second largest final use in national accounts after household consumption. From a VAT perspective, governments' activities are exempt or outside the scope of VAT in most countries, New Zealand being the notable exception treating all governments activities as taxable. As a consequence, public bodies cannot deduct the input VAT paid on their taxable expenditure, again with the exception of New Zealand that provides a full right to deduct input tax for government activities. A number of countries have created mechanisms for balancing the adverse effects of the exemption, such as targeted VAT refunds, full or partial right to deduct input VAT, budgetary compensations or extended taxation of government activities. The different options chosen by governments may have varied impacts on the VRR. Compensations outside of the VAT system (e.g. a simple budgetary compensation) have no direct effect on the VRR since the government activities are still fully input taxed, generating the corresponding VAT revenue. On the other hand, extended right to deduction may reduce the VAT collection by the government and hence influence the VRR downwards. From the opposite perspective, extended taxation of government activities like is the case in New Zealand will increase the amount of VAT collected since its outputs will be taxed rather than its inputs (for more detail, see the technical note on public sector in Section 3.5).
- Place of taxation rules for international trade may diverge from the destination principle and may not always allow the full taxation of the potential tax base in the destination country (e.g. services taxed in the country where the supplier is established while customers are located abroad). Depending on the position of the country –net exporter or net importer- the VRR can be influenced upwards or downwards. Inconsistent place of taxation rules may also lead to double taxation of cross-border trade.
- The capacity of the tax administration to manage the VAT system efficiently and the degree of compliance by taxpayers influences the VRR as low compliance has a negative

impact on actual VAT revenue. Taxpayers' insolvencies and bankruptcies can also influence the VRR downwards.

- The failure of the tax administration to pay VAT refunds to businesses when they are in a tax credit situation (e.g. exporters can claim a tax credit on their inputs while exports are made tax-free), which is contrary to the fundamental principle of VAT-neutrality, may influence the VRR upwards.
- The evolution of the consumption patterns may also affect the tax revenue. The VRR can for instance be reduced, all other things equal, when the share of consumption of necessities that are taxed at the lower rate increases, e.g. as a result of an economic crisis.
- Finally, also the possible impact of the differences between the measurement of final consumption expenditure in the national accounts and countries' potential VAT base should be taken into account when interpreting the VRR (see Section 3.5).

Assessing the relative impact of the various factors that may impact the VRR

The level of the VRR rarely depends on one factor in isolation but rather on the interaction between them. For example, a high standard rate may create an incentive for evasion while multiple lower rates may lead to revenue loss due to misclassifications. Exemption of certain sectors of activity may create distortions and incentives for avoidance, which require additional administrative capacities that cannot be used for the efficient collection of VAT. Inefficient tax administration, burdensome administrative requirements and complex VAT mechanisms may reduce the degree of compliance of taxpayers.

These potentially influencing factors can be divided in two main categories:

- those resulting from policy decisions, mainly affecting the tax base or the coverage of the standard rate (i.e. reduced VAT rates and exemptions), and
- those related to the efficiency of the tax collection and compliance levels.

Measuring only the impact of policy decisions on a country's VAT revenue, sometimes called the "Policy Efficiency Ratio", can be achieved by comparing the theoretical VAT revenue under the actual tax base and rates (assuming perfect compliance) with that under a uniform tax on all consumption:

Policy Efficiency Ratio = (VAT theoretical revenue from actual tax law)/(final consumption x Standard VAT rate).

On the other hand, a measure of compliance, sometimes called the "Compliance Efficiency Ratio" or the "VAT Gap" in the EU would compare actual revenue with the theoretical VAT revenue under the legislated tax base and rates:

Compliance Efficiency Ratio = (VAT revenue)/(theoretical VAT revenue from actual tax law)

The VRR is a combination of the "Policy Efficiency Ratio" and the "Compliance Efficiency Ratio". Methods may be developed to produce breakdowns of the composition of the VRR. One method may consist in using the tax expenditure (i.e. the revenue cost of departure from the application of the standard rate to the "entire" tax base) for calculating the policy efficiency ratio. The remaining difference between 1 and the actual VRR would provide the compliance efficiency ratio by deduction. However, given the number of other factors that may influence the VRR the figures should be used with caution.

Another method would be to calculate the "tax gap" i.e. the difference between tax collected and the tax that should be collected if all consumers and businesses fully complied with the law. This method is employed for the VAT in the EU (CASE 2016), where the VAT Gap is defined as the difference between the amount of VAT actually collected and the theoretical tax liability according to tax law (VAT Total Tax Liability VTTL). The VAT Gap is estimated using a "top-down" approach that applies respective VAT rates to the relevant components of consumption (including final consumption of households; final consumption of government and non-profit institutions, intermediate consumption for partially exempt businesses; expenditure on housing, country-specific, adjustments, etc.). Australia uses a similar method (ATO, 2015). The EU survey (CASE, 2016) also provides an estimate of the policy gap and its decomposition in "rate gap" and "exemption gap" where it appears that if many Member States have some scope for broadening the VAT base at standard rate, better enforcement remains a key component of any strategy to improve the VAT system.

3.5. Technical notes

Differences between final consumption expenditure and the VAT base that may influence the VRR

The main measure of consumption in national accounts is final consumption expenditure. This includes the consumption by households, non-profit organisations and general government. It includes a number of items that are not considered part of the tax base in any OECD country, such as the imputed rents on owner-occupied housing (part of consumption of households) and the services provided free of charge by the public administration (part of government consumption). On the other hand, it does not include items that are subject to VAT in some OECD countries, most notably housing construction.

Given the differences between final consumption expenditure and the VAT base, one can take the view that VAT is a general tax on consumption and that this implies that its revenues should be compared with those that would be raised if it were applied to the national accounts definition of consumption – its natural base. Alternatively, an adjustment of the national accounts measure of consumption to bring it closer to a typical VAT base would allow for a better interpretation of a country's VRR as it would better reflect the revenue impact of deviations from a generally accepted VAT base.

Whichever approach is taken, a number of more detailed issues will need to be addressed. This is most obvious for the second approach, where detailed decisions would have to be made as to what constitutes a "standard VAT base". This problem is similar to the problem of defining a benchmark tax system against which tax expenditures are judged, and it might well be as difficult to solve. The sections below look at the main differences between final consumption expenditure in national accounts and the typical VAT base and some additional factors that may influence the VRR.

Private final consumption expenditure of households

Households' final consumption expenditure includes purchases of the goods and services used by households to meet their everyday needs (clothing, household durables, rent, transport, personal services and so on), which represent by far the largest part of their consumption expenditure. The way final consumption expenditure is accounted for in SNA matches the potential VAT base. Also, by convention, all goods and services are considered to have been entirely consumed once they have been acquired by household and are therefore regarded as "final consumption", which is consistent with the way VAT works (see Chapter 1).

The treatment of private dwellings is the main area where final consumption expenditure in SNA deviates from the potential VAT base. Indeed, purchases of dwellings are not recorded as final consumption expenditure under item P3, but rather in gross fixed capital formation (under item P5). This doesn't exactly match the potential VAT base as it should normally include the sale of new dwellings by businesses to final consumers. National accountants also regard the owners of dwellings as producing housing services either for themselves or for tenants. The purchase of repair materials or services of plumbers and electricians needed to keep the dwelling in good condition are not considered as final consumption but as intermediate consumption. From a VAT perspective, when dwellings are made available for rent by their owners, rentals should be recorded as final consumption expenditure by tenants since they normally belong to the potential VAT base. On the other hand, final consumption in the national accounts includes the imputed value of the housing services for owner-occupiers (imputed rents) but, since they don't result from any transaction, they can't be subject to VAT and do not belong to the potential tax base.

Adjusting the denominator of the VRR for taking these differences into account may be challenging for a number of reasons: the value of imputed rents is not available in national accounts of a number of member countries. Second, adjustments may be complex. For example, expenditures incurred by the owner for maintenance and repair of its own occupied dwelling should be considered to be final consumption while the same expenditures aimed at maintaining rented dwellings should not; sale of private dwellings should be included, but only the sale of dwellings by businesses (e.g. builders) and not the ownership transfer between households. In addition, if expenditures on fixed assets in the form of dwellings were completely included in the potential tax base, there would be some double counting in respect of rentals of dwellings. As a result, in respect of private dwellings, no adjustment is made of the potential VAT base as measured by final consumption expenditure.

Final consumption expenditure by the non-profit organisations servicing households (NPSH)

NPSH are units formed by groups of households in order to supply services to themselves or to other households on a non-commercial basis. NPSH include political parties, trade unions, religious organisations, sports clubs, cultural associations, charities and associations with philanthropic aims (Red Cross, etc.) and certain charitable foundations. In some countries, a number of universities are also classified in this sector. On the other hand, non-profit institutions which are not directly financed by households but, for example, by enterprises (Chambers of Commerce, professional associations, etc.) are classified in the enterprise sector. Those controlled or financed by general government are classified in the general government sector. NPSH constitute only a small sector in the national accounts.

Like general government, the NPSH provide "non-market" services. For this reason, their treatment in the national accounts is similar to that of general government (see below). The output of services by NPSHs is valued at cost, and by convention the NPSH "consume" the services they produce. Final consumption expenditure of the NPSH is therefore equal to their operating costs. There is no need to divide between individual expenditure and collective expenditure here since these organisations are at the service of households and all their expenditure is therefore considered as individual. Such treatment under SNA corresponds to the VAT treatment, where in most countries NPSH are VAT exempt without the right to deduction of input tax and VAT is ultimately collected on their inputs.

Final consumption expenditure of general government

Final consumption by government is the second largest final use in national accounts after household consumption. Expenditures by general government are considered by convention as forming part of final consumption by government itself. For example, current expenditure on police and education is regarded as consumption by general government. This convention reflects the fact that, although these expenditures benefit households and enterprises, it is not possible to attribute them precisely to the beneficiaries, since they do not buy them, even though they pay the taxes that finance them. It has therefore been convention not to attempt to allocate these expenditures to their beneficiaries but to attribute all these expenditures to general government itself. Among other advantages, this makes it possible to remain closer to the actual monetary flows.

General government consumption expenditure includes collective consumption expenditure (expenditure related to the activities of general government that are not attributable uniquely to households but that also benefit enterprises such as National Assemblies, Parliaments, ministries of foreign affairs, safety and order, defence, home affairs, economic affairs, etc.) and individual consumption expenditure where individual beneficiaries could in principle be identified (expenditure that is clearly carried out for the benefit of households such as public education and public healthcare; spending on aid for social housing; operating expenses of museums and other government services to households). In accounting terms, final consumption expenditure by government is equal to its cost, defined by the following sum: compensation of employees of the government; *plus* purchases by government of materials and other intermediate consumption items; *plus* consumption of government fixed capital; *plus* the purchases of goods and services by the government for the benefit of households (for example, reimbursement of healthcare services, housing allowances, etc.); *minus* partial payments by households or firms for services provided by government (entry to museums, purchases of government publications, etc.).

From a VAT perspective, governments' activities are exempt or outside the scope of VAT in most countries, New Zealand being the notable exception treating all governments activities as taxable. As a consequence, public bodies cannot deduct the input VAT paid on their taxable expenditure and this non-deductible VAT is therefore part of the cost of government consumption, again with the exception of New Zealand that provides a full right to deduct input tax for government activities. Final consumption expenditures by NPSH and general government is regarded as final consumption for VAT purposes since these organisations are at the last step in the VAT supply chain. They pay VAT on their inputs but cannot, in principle, deduct this input VAT since their output is generally exempt or outside the scope of VAT. This approach broadly fits with the definition of the tax base provided above, which covers expenditure to attain consumption (rather than actual consumption itself). The cost (or size) of the government may have an impact on the VRR. For example, if the salary cost of producing the same service to the population (e.g. justice) is 100 units in Country A and 120 units in Country B, the potential VAT base as measured by Item P3 (P32-S13) will be higher in Country B, which will mathematically show a lower VRR than Country A, all other things equal.

A number of countries have created mechanisms for balancing the adverse effects of exemption, such as targeted VAT refunds, full or partial right to deduct input VAT, budgetary compensations or extended taxation of government activities. As indicted above, New Zealand, treats all government activities as taxable and provides for the corresponding full right to deduct input tax. The different options chosen by governments may have varied impacts on the VRR. Compensations outside of the VAT system (e.g. a simple budgetary compensation) have no direct effect on the VRR since the government activities are still fully input taxed, generating the corresponding VAT revenue. On the other hand, extended right to deduction may reduce the VAT collection by the government and hence influence the VRR downwards. From the opposite perspective, extended taxation of government activities will increase the amount of VAT collected since its outputs will be taxed rather than its inputs. The extreme example is the New-Zealand system, which generates significant additional VAT revenue due to the full taxation of government outputs, even though it ultimately does not generate actual revenue since the VAT is paid by the government itself (central government) or is included in other taxes (i.e. in local government taxes). In the latter case, the VRR is clearly influenced upwards.

Other differences that may influence the VRR

Other elements may potentially influence the VRR. These include the distortion that may arise from the inclusion in the calculation of the potential VAT base of imputed transactions (other than imputed rents) that are considered as part of final consumption expenditure by national accounts. Some of those transactions (e.g. goods that households produce for themselves such as agricultural products and do-it-yourself services) are not part of the potential tax base while others (e.g. exchange of goods and services undeclared to the authorities) could arguably be considered within the scope of VAT. However, the global impact on the potential tax base is very difficult to measure from the national accounts. Another element is the inclusion of business-to-consumer supplies of second-hand goods, such as motor vehicles, in final consumption expenditure. The consumption figures of households include the full price paid by the household for the good. Since VAT applies only to the margin of the reseller in most cases, this may distort. Finally, cross-border shopping may also marginally influence the VRR since final consumption expenditure arises in one country while the tax accrues to another.

The VAT treatment of public sector activities

In most countries, government entities and public sector bodies are VAT-exempt, i.e. they don't account for VAT on their outputs and cannot deduct the input tax. This means that, from a tax revenue perspective, they are treated as final consumers and VAT collected on their taxable purchases only (i.e. the supplies provided to them by taxable persons) and the value-added by the public sector itself is not taxed.

The reasons for such an exclusion from the VAT are both substantial and practical. Indeed, in most modern VAT systems, the intended tax base is final private consumption expenditure, which excludes collective consumption expenditure (i.e. services that are provided simultaneously to all citizens and that are automatically consumed without any specific action of their part). Collective consumption expenditure notably includes security (police, army); collective health (prevention policies); education and culture (state's schools, free libraries and monuments); and town planning (maintenance and development of public space). From a legal point of view, most VAT systems provide that supplies are only taxable where there is a direct connection between an identifiable supply and a specific consideration, which is generally not the case for collective consumption items. Finally public entities, when acting as such, are not engaged in an economic activity and therefore do not qualify as taxpayers.

On the other hand, public sector activities are generally taxable in situations where the exemption would create substantial distortions of competition with the taxable private sector providing similar services or when public entities are engaged in a commercial activity. Services provided by public entities against a specific fee considered as a consideration directly connected with the service can also be treated as taxable supplies. In those cases, public entities are considered to be taxable persons as a result of this activity, whatever their legal status.

Despite the conceptual and practical rationale for exemptions of public sector activities, difficulties may arise in situations where it is not easy to draw the line between taxable and exempt activities as exemptions are determined by a combination of elements such as the nature of the activity, the legal status of the supplier or the market circumstances. The exemption can also create distortions with the private sector, prevent the emergence of competitive businesses and create a bias against outsourcing of support or back-office functions. Indeed, since they are tax exempt i.e. "input taxed", public entities will bear the burden of the VAT on supplies of outsourced functions by taxable businesses while this will not be the case for internally produced services. Exemption can also create tax cascading effects and distortions in the cross-border trade in services and intangibles, as exemptions in the financial sector do (see section above).

There are two main options for addressing the adverse effects of the exemption: refunding (part of) the input tax incurred by public bodies and extending the concept of taxable activity to public services. A refund system would allow bodies who perform exempt activities to reduce or eliminate the VAT burden on their inputs to minimise the bias towards self-supply. Within the EU, eight Member States (Austria, Denmark, Finland, France, Netherlands, Portugal, Sweden and the United Kingdom) have introduced systems designed to compensate public bodies for the inability to deduct input VAT. These compensation systems appear in different forms, for the most part being outside the national VAT regime (for detailed description see Copenhagen Economics 2013). Depending on the countries, the input VAT refund may be allocated to public bodies, irrespective of their activities (e.g. Denmark, Finland) or to a wider span of bodies, but covering certain sectors only such as health and social security (Austria) or army, political parties, churches, social solidarity bodies and fire departments (Portugal). The allocation of refunds can also be limited to municipalities, provincial authorities and regional governments (Netherlands). In addition to refunds for input VAT, the system can also compensate public bodies for the VAT embedded in the price of services provided to them by private exempt suppliers e.g. in the health area (Finland, Sweden). The refund can also take the form of a fixed percentage of expenses (e.g. in France where legal entities governed by public authorities receive such compensation for the VAT that they pay on their investment expenses). Some countries also place a *de minimis* limit where certain bodies can be refunded input VAT if the proportion of this input VAT incurred is insignificant in relation to input VAT attributable to taxable non-exempt transactions (United Kingdom). In Canada, public service bodies such as non-profit organisations, municipal authorities, public education bodies or hospital authorities may be eligible to claim a full or partial GST/HST rebate for the tax paid on their inputs (Gendron, 2013). In addition, systems can be put in place to address specificities of the federal VAT system. In Canada for instance the Constitution prevents federal and provincial governments from taxing each other, so sales from taxable businesses to Provinces are zero-rated (for provinces that do not participate to the Harmonised Sales Tax – HST) while the governments of the five participating HST provinces have agreed to pay the GST/HST on their taxable inputs.

However, while partially remedying the bias against outsourcing, the VAT refunds to public bodies may increase the distortion of competition with the private sector by adding a compensation for non-deductible input VAT to an exemption of the output. It also adds a compliance burden on public bodies in order to track the amount of non-deductible input VAT for compensation purposes.

As an alternative to a rebate system, New Zealand applies a "full taxation system" where all supplies by public bodies are considered taxable with deduction of input tax (that system is described in detail in Millar, 2013). Under that approach, many (but not all) flows of government money are treated as consideration for taxable supplies. In that system, the concepts of "taxable person", "supply" and "taxable activity" are adjusted to include the central government; local authorities and the grants and subsidies they provide. In that system, the public authorities of the central government are considered taxable persons carrying out taxable activities. Public bodies are deemed to be supplying taxable services (security, justice, education, health, etc…) to the government, which gives them a budget (considered as a consideration for VAT purposes) for delivering such services. As a concrete example, a public body receives a budget of NZD 1 million for reforming the government procurement performance. The public body in charge of the reform will invoice NZD 1 million plus NZD 150 000 GST. If the body in charge of the project needs inputs from other public bodies or from private businesses to deliver the supply, the GST charged on those inputs will give rise to an input tax credit claimed by the public body. The central government outputs for collective or individual consumption by citizens are not invoiced to them directly (there is no GST on income taxes) but to the government, unless the public body charges a specific fee to individual citizens as consideration for a specific individual supply. As a result of this system, supplies between public authorities are taxable but are ultimately paid from the government's budget itself and no net revenue is generated.

The full taxation system applied to local government works more like regular businesses. Local governments charge local taxes (essentially a property tax) to owners of land to fund both collective and individual consumption. Those property owners may be resident/non-resident, GST registered businesses, unregistered businesses and end consumers. The amount of tax charged to a particular taxpayer may not reflect the value of his individual consumption of local government services. According to the GST law, these local taxes are treated as consideration for taxable supply of services to owners of land. Unlike for central government bodies, the GST is charged directly to those owners, who pay GST on the local tax. GST registered businesses are entitled to an input credit for the GST on those taxes (unless they are input taxed) while end consumers are not and the system generates, in this instance, net revenue for the government. Most other supplies made by the local government (e.g. fees and charges for the supplies of permits and licences, specific grants and subsidies, etc.) to individual consumers are also taxable. Of course the local government is entitled to a full input tax credit for the GST incurred on its inputs.

The VAT exemption of financial services

Financial (banking and insurance) services are generally exempt from VAT mainly because of the difficulty to assess the tax base on a transaction-by-transaction basis for the complex intermediation services that constitute the bulk of financial activity. Ideally, the VAT would be levied only on the intermediation charge, which reflects the actual value added by the financial institution and not on the interest rate, premium or return that has to be paid by the financial institution's customers. However, in practice, this distinction is not easily made. Although taxing financial services under VAT would improve the efficiency of the system, it is often argued that, in the absence of a simple and robust approach to assessing the tax base, such taxation might lead to high tax compliance, administration and enforcement costs.

The exemption of financial services from VAT creates a number of distortions with respect to both consumer and business decisions. Exemptions cause a break in the VAT chain, meaning that financial institutions incur significant amounts of irrecoverable VAT paid on their inputs as they cannot charge VAT on their onward supplies. This creates cascading tax effects since the irrecoverable VAT embedded in the charges that banks make to their business customers cannot be recovered and will be carried through to final prices for domestic consumption. The incidence of the non-recoverable VAT can also affect profits in the financial sector and/or lead to higher prices for consumers depending on the degree of competition in the market. The exemption also provides financial institutions with a tax-induced incentive to self-supply to avoid incurring irrecoverable VAT, which would be the case if they obtained these supplies from other businesses. Thus, the tax system provides an incentive for vertical integration.

This break in the VAT chain also creates distortions of competition between domestic services (exempt with no right of deduction/input taxed) and services imported from a VAT country (where export of such services are free of VAT) or from a non-VAT country (e.g. USA). Exemption also creates incentives for "channelling" some supplies through foreign jurisdictions or for artificially changing the nature of a supply with a view to increasing the deductible proportion. Such difficulties are reinforced by the absence of coherence for the VAT treatment of financial services between countries e.g. on their definition, the scope of the exemption, the calculation of deductible proportion, etc.

Since financial institutions provide many kinds of services, some being taxed while others are exempted without right of deduction, they need to assess which of their inputs (or which share of certain inputs) are used for providing onwards taxable supplies and thus give right to deduction and which do not. In a highly complex environment, such allocation of inputs to taxable outputs or the computation of a deductible proportion involve high administrative and compliance costs as well as uncertainty for businesses and tax administrations. In addition, it is increasingly difficult to draw a bright line between taxable and exempt services as new products and services emerge.

One way of correcting the cascading effect of the exemption would be to apply a zero rate to B2B financial transactions either directly as in New Zealand or indirectly as in Australia and Singapore. On the other hand, taxing all explicit fees to final consumers would allow for taxation of at least part of the final consumption of financial services. However, such a solution would still involve an under-taxation of non-fee based B2C financial services and would harm the self-policing feature of VAT.

Although it appears that the best technical solution would be to fully tax financial services under VAT with full deduction of input tax the fundamental question remains designing a practical mechanism for effecting such an outcome. Actually, the main difficulty for achieving a proper taxation of financial services under VAT does not lie in the VAT per se but in the application of the invoice-credit system to services priced on the basis of margin spreads rather than explicit fees (Zee, 2013). This difficulty, combined with political and historical factors has led most countries to exempt such services from the VAT.

Considerable work has been done over the years on the development of an appropriate method, mainly the subtraction method; the truncated cash flow method (TCA); and the modified reverse charge mechanism (MRC). However, none has found universal favour. The case for the actual feasibility of the reform has still not been fully made i.e. in terms of administrative burdens or compliance. In addition, comprehensive evaluation of the merits of the reform i.e. the removal of the distortions and its potential costs, in particular in terms of revenue for governments seems still missing. Further, political sensitivities around taxation of banks also need to be considered. However, given new technologies and accounting standards it should be possible to devise a methodology which taxes margin-based financial services in a fair, reliable and cost effective manner. This could be done in a manner which strikes a balance between simplicity and excessive attention to detail (Kerrigan, 2010).

References

ATO (2015), *Measuring tax gaps in Australia 2014-15*, Australian Taxation Office, November 2015, *www.ato.gov.au/About-ATO/Research-and-statistics/In-detail/Tax-gap/Measuring-tax-gaps-in-Australia,-2014-15*.

Ebrill, L. et al. (2001), *The Modern VAT*, International Monetary Fund, Washington DC.

CASE (2016), *Study and Reports on the VAT Gap in the EU 28 Member States: 2016 Final Report*, Institute for Advances Studies, Warsaw, August 2016.

CIAT (2012), *Estimating non-compliance in Latin America 2000-10*, Working Paper No. 3/2012.

Copenhagen Economics (2013) *VAT in the Public Sector and Exemptions in the Public interest*, Report for the European Commission, Copenhagen January 2013.

HMRC (2013), *Measuring Tax Gaps 2013*, HM Revenue and Customs, London.

Keen, M (2013), *The anatomy of the VAT*, IMF Working Paper WP/13/111, May 2013, Washington.

Kerrigan, A (2010), *The elusiveness of neutrality – why is it so difficult to apply VAT to financial services?* International VAT Monitor, Vol. 21, No. 2 (18. March 2010).

Millar, R. (2013), Smoke and Mirrors: Applying the Full Taxation Model to Government under the Australian and New Zealand GST Laws, *VAT exemptions, consequences and design alternatives*, Rita de la Feria, Wolters Kluwer 2013, New York.

OECD (2010), *Choosing a Broad Base – Low Rate Approach to Taxation*, OECD Tax Policy Studies, No. 19, OECD Publishing, Paris, *http://dx.doi.org/10.1787/9789264091320-en*.

OECD (2006), *Understanding National Accounts*, OECD Publishing, Paris, *http://dx.doi.org/10.1787/9789264027657-en*.

Reckon (2009), *Study to quantify and analyse the VAT gap in the EU-25 Member States*, London.

United Nations (2009), *System of National Accounts*, New York.

Warren, N (2008), *A Review of Studies on the Distributional Impact of Consumption Taxes in OECD Countries*, OECD Social, Employment and Migration Working Papers n°64, June 2008, OECD, Paris.

Zee, H. (2013), Further thoughts on reforming the VAT: treatment of financial intermediation services, *VAT exemptions, consequences and design alternatives*, Rita de la Feria, Wolters Kluwer 2013, New York.

ANNEX 3.A3

VAT Revenue Ratio

Table 3.A3.1. VAT Revenue Ratio (VRR)

	Standard VAT rate 2014	1976	1980	1984	1988	1992	1996	2000	2005	2006	2007	2008	2009	2010	2011	2012	2013	2014	Difference 2007-12	Difference 2012-14
Australia	10.0								0.56	0.54	0.54	0.49	0.51	0.50	0.48	0.47	0.50	0.49	-0.07	0.02
Austria	20.0	0.66	0.65	0.64	0.62	0.61	0.60	0.61	0.59	0.57	0.58	0.59	0.58	0.58	0.58	0.59	0.59	0.59	0.01	0.00
Belgium	21.0	0.56	0.60	0.49	0.5	0.49	0.46	0.50	0.50	0.50	0.51	0.48	0.46	0.48	0.48	0.48	0.47	0.47	-0.03	0.00
Canada	5.0					0.43	0.47	0.49	0.49	0.46	0.50	0.49	0.49	0.50	0.47	0.47	0.48	0.49	-0.03	0.02
Chile	19.0					0.63	0.68	0.64	0.67	0.64	0.67	0.70	0.59	0.62	0.63	0.64	0.63	0.63	-0.03	-0.01
Czech Republic	21.0						0.43	0.42	0.56	0.53	0.54	0.57	0.55	0.53	0.55	0.57	0.57	0.58	0.03	0.02
Denmark	25.0	0.63	0.60	0.60	0.60	0.56	0.57	0.59	0.62	0.64	0.65	0.61	0.58	0.58	0.59	0.59	0.58	0.59	-0.06	0.00
Estonia	20.0						0.73	0.72	0.70	0.81	0.80	0.67	0.73	0.67	0.67	0.69	0.66	0.70	-0.11	0.01
Finland	24.0						0.54	0.61	0.60	0.61	0.60	0.58	0.56	0.55	0.56	0.56	0.55	0.54	-0.04	-0.02
France	20.0	0.65	0.69	0.62	0.62	0.53	0.52	0.50	0.52	0.51	0.51	0.50	0.47	0.47	0.48	0.48	0.48	0.48	-0.03	0.00
Germany	19.0	0.55	0.56	0.51	0.49	0.61	0.60	0.60	0.54	0.56	0.54	0.55	0.55	0.54	0.55	0.55	0.54	0.55	0.01	0.00
Greece	23.0				0.46	0.47	0.43	0.49	0.47	0.46	0.48	0.46	0.39	0.44	0.37	0.37	0.36	0.37	-0.11	0.00
Hungary	27.0					0.30	0.43	0.52	0.48	0.55	0.59	0.57	0.62	0.53	0.52	0.53	0.53	0.57	-0.06	0.04
Iceland	25.5					0.56	0.54	0.59	0.61	0.64	0.59	0.53	0.45	0.43	0.44	0.45	0.45	0.46	-0.14	0.01
Ireland	23.0	0.30	0.21	0.44	0.42	0.45	0.52	0.61	0.66	0.67	0.63	0.55	0.46	0.48	0.46	0.44	0.45	0.49	-0.18	0.04
Israel	18.0						0.66	0.62	0.61	0.62	0.65	0.64	0.65	0.65	0.65	0.64	0.65	0.63	-0.01	-0.01
Italy	22.0	0.44	0.4	0.38	0.4	0.37	0.39	0.43	0.39	0.41	0.41	0.39	0.36	0.40	0.40	0.38	0.37	0.37	-0.03	-0.01
Japan	5.0					0.68	0.70	0.68	0.71	0.70	0.68	0.68	0.67	0.69	0.69	0.69	0.71	0.70	0.01	0.01
Korea	10.0					0.64	0.58	0.59	0.64	0.63	0.63	0.63	0.65	0.67	0.67	0.69	0.67	0.69	0.06	0.00
Latvia	21.0							0.51	0.57	0.60	0.61	0.49	0.38	0.42	0.42	0.46	0.49	0.51	-0.15	0.05
Luxembourg	15.0	0.59	0.61	0.64	0.66	0.46	0.56	0.70	0.87	0.84	0.96	0.97	0.97	1.00	1.07	1.12	1.18	1.23	0.16	0.11
Mexico	16.0		0.33	0.27	0.25	0.31	0.24	0.28	0.30	0.33	0.33	0.34	0.30	0.32	0.31	0.31	0.28	0.32	-0.02	0.01
Netherlands	21.0	0.47	0.51	0.49	0.54	0.57	0.55	0.57	0.56	0.58	0.59	0.57	0.52	0.55	0.53	0.53	0.48	0.48	-0.07	-0.05
New Zealand	15.0				0.89	0.96	0.99	0.99	1.03	1.03	0.96	0.96	0.97	1.10	0.93	0.94	0.95	0.97	-0.02	0.04
Norway	25.0	0.66	0.66	0.63	0.69	0.58	0.60	0.67	0.57	0.61	0.63	0.57	0.54	0.56	0.56	0.57	0.57	0.56	-0.06	0.00
Poland	23.0						0.42	0.42	0.48	0.51	0.53	0.50	0.45	0.47	0.47	0.43	0.42	0.44	-0.10	0.01
Portugal	23.0				0.45	0.49	0.55	0.60	0.56	0.51	0.51	0.49	0.43	0.48	0.45	0.47	0.46	0.48	-0.04	0.01
Slovak Republic	20.0						0.48	0.44	0.61	0.57	0.53	0.53	0.47	0.46	0.48	0.43	0.46	0.48	-0.10	0.05
Slovenia	22.0							0.67	0.66	0.68	0.69	0.68	0.59	0.59	0.59	0.58	0.64	0.60	-0.11	0.02
Spain	21.0				0.6	0.60	0.43	0.52	0.57	0.57	0.53	0.43	0.32	0.45	0.39	0.41	0.39	0.41	-0.12	0.00
Sweden	25.0	0.44	0.36	0.38	0.42	0.41	0.50	0.53	0.55	0.56	0.57	0.58	0.57	0.59	0.58	0.56	0.56	0.57	-0.01	0.01
Switzerland	8.0						0.68	0.74	0.72	0.74	0.73	0.74	0.70	0.72	0.71	0.71	0.71	0.71	-0.02	0.00
Turkey	18.0				0.45	0.44	0.43	0.45	0.38	0.39	0.36	0.35	0.34	0.39	0.43	0.40	0.45	0.42	0.04	0.01
United Kingdom	20.0	0.42	0.41	0.44	0.48	0.43	0.44	0.44	0.44	0.44	0.44	0.42	0.43	0.43	0.43	0.43	0.43	0.44	-0.01	0.01
Unweighted average	19.1	0.53	0.51	0.50	0.53	0.52	0.55	0.57	0.58	0.59	0.59	0.57	0.54	0.55	0.55	0.55	0.55	0.56	-0.04	0.01

Calculation formula: VRR = VAT Revenue/[(Consumption – VAT revenue) x standard VAT rate]. Consumption = Final Consumption Expenditure (Heading P3) in national accounts. VAT rates used are standard rates applicable as at 1 January of each year.

Time series: Since data beyond 2014 is not available for all countries at the time of publication, VRR is not calculated after this date.

Canada: VRR Calculation includes federal VAT only..

Canada and Japan: Annual final consumption expenditure in national accounts was adjusted to ensure matching between the fiscal year (Q2 Y to Q1 Y+1) for the tax revenue and the civil year for final consumption figures.

Israel: The statistical data for Israel are supplied by and under the responsibility of the relevant Israeli authorities. The use of such data by the OECD is without prejudice to the status of the Golan Heights, East Jerusalem and Israeli settlements in the West Bank under the terms of international law. Although VAT was implemented in Israel in 1976, the VRR is only calculated from 1996 onwards since tax revenue figures are not available before that year.

Japan: given the substantial VAT rate hike on 1 April 2014, an average VAT rate was used to calculate the VRR for 2014 i.e. (5X3+8X9)/12=7.25%.

New Zealand had a high VRR of 1.10 in 2010 because of the increase in GST rate from 12.5% to 15% in October 2010.

Source: OECD.

StatLink http://dx.doi.org/10.1787/888933420100

Chapter 4

Selected excise duties in OECD countries

This chapter describes the main features of selected excise duties and their impact on revenue, customer behaviour and markets. It explains the respective impact of ad quantum and ad valorem taxes and how they interact. It shows the detailed excise tax rates on beer, wine, alcoholic beverages, tobacco, and mineral oil products in OECD countries.

The statistical data for Israel are supplied by and under the responsibility of the relevant Israeli authorities. The use of such data by the OECD is without prejudice to the status of the Golan Heights, East Jerusalem and Israeli settlements.

4.1. Introduction

Although excise taxes may cover a very wide range of products, excise taxes on alcohol, tobacco and hydrocarbon oils are common to all OECD countries and raise significant revenues for governments. In recent decades, governments have increasingly used these taxes to influence customer behaviour where consumption of certain products are considered harmful to health or to the environment.

This chapter presents an overview of the key characteristics of excise duties and the evolution in their use by governments in some areas (Section 4.2). It then looks in some detail at the excise rates structure for four main categories of products: alcoholic beverages (Section 4.3), tobacco products (Section 4.4) and mineral oil products (Section 4.5). This is followed by a brief description of the impact of differences in excise rates between countries on cross-border trade (Section 4.6) and on their distributional effects (Section 4.7).

4.2. Key characteristics and revenue trends

Excise, unlike value added taxes (VAT)[1] and other general consumption taxes, is levied only on specific goods. Although many products can be subject to excise, such as chocolate, coffee and orange juice, only a few are considered in this chapter, since they are taxed in all OECD countries. The three principal product groups that are liable to excise in all OECD countries are alcoholic beverages, mineral oils and tobacco products.

Before looking at these three groups in terms of their characteristics and their comparative treatment by different countries, a number of general characteristics on excise may be noted:

- Excise duty is generally calculated by reference to the weight, volume, strength, or quantity of the product, combined in some cases with the value, but sometimes on a value basis only.
- Excise duty does not normally become payable until the goods enter free circulation. Transfers of ownership can take place while goods remain in a controlled warehousing environment or between registered operators without creating an excise charge.
- The excise system is characterised by a small number of taxpayers, who are active in the manufacturing, wholesale stage or importation of the three main product groups.

Unlike VAT, which is collected through a staged collection process by all the stakeholders in the value chain until the final consumer (see Chapter 1), excise duties are normally collected only once from one registered operator at the time the goods are released for consumption. In the European Union, the movement of excisable products between Member States is made under a duty-suspension arrangement until the moment they are released for free circulation. In the United States, where both federal and local excise exist, they are levied by the federal government and by many states and local governments. Federal excise taxes are collected by the Internal Revenue Service while states may impose the tax according to their own rules and rates.

Excise is normally part of the VAT tax base, meaning that VAT is usually levied on the duty-paid value of the excise products. Therefore, an increase of excise duty rates implies an increase of both excise and VAT burden.

The share of excise duties in total tax revenue has been subject to a long decline since 1965, when they accounted for 14.2% on average to 7.6% in 2014 (see Table 4.A4.9). Behind the OECD average there are large differences between countries, with excise accounting for 2.6% of total tax revenue in New Zealand and 18.1% in Turkey. In two thirds of the OECD countries (24 out of 35), the weight of excise duties is between 5% and 10% of total tax revenue while it accounts for less than 5% in 5 countries (Belgium, Canada, New Zealand, Switzerland and the United States) and for more than 10% in 6 countries (Estonia, Greece, Latvia, Poland, Slovenia and Turkey).

Ad valorem vs. ad quantum excises

In addition to the rates and tax bases, the weight and impact of excise are substantially affected by its structure. There are two main ways in which excisable products can be taxed: *ad valorem* and *ad quantum*. Under an *ad quantum* excise, a fixed amount of tax is levied per unit of the product (e.g. USD 1 per litre), which means that this is a tax on the volume of sales. Under *ad valorem* excise, the tax is levied as a proportion of the product price (e.g. 20% of the selling price) and this is a tax on the value of sales. In a number of instances (e.g. tobacco taxes as presented in Table 4.A4.4) the total excise tax results from a mix of ad valorem and specific taxes. The *ad quantum* tax requires a precise definition of the nature and characteristics of the tax base (e.g. a litre of unleaded gasoline with 94 RON) while the *ad valorem* tax is simply based on the price.

Most products naturally present a bundle of different characteristics (volume, weight, strength, octane, alcoholic or carbon content, etc.). *Ad quantum* taxes remain unaffected by changes in the product characteristics that have not been defined as being relevant for the tax base, whereas *ad valorem* taxes bear on all the characteristics of the product that are reflected in the price. Depending on the type of tax, the impact on production and consumption is different. For example, a specific tax on beer (per % absolute alcohol in volume) may encourage brewers to develop varieties of beer, including more luxurious products that could be offered at higher prices while remaining subject to the same level of excise as the cheaper product. On the other hand, *ad valorem* taxes may discourage costly improvements in product quality or encourage consumers to switch to low-cost products. *Ad quantum* taxes may be easier to administer, because it is necessary only to determine the physical quantity of the product taxed. They also produce a more predictable revenue stream than *ad valorem* taxes, as revenue does not vary with the price of the product (WHO 2015). On the other hand, *ad valorem* taxes may keep pace with inflation better than *ad quantum* taxes, though it also possible to index *ad quantum* taxes for inflation. Being subject to price variations, *ad valorem* taxes are possibly more volatile than *ad quantum* taxes. In addition, empirical evidence has found that *ad quantum* taxes tend to be more than fully passed through to the consumer (prices rise by more than the tax increase), whereas *ad valorem* taxes tend to be less than fully passed through (Sassi, et al., 2013).

If distributional goals are taken into account in the design of a specific tax, there may be a case for *ad valorem* rather than *ad quantum* taxation as such a policy option can be expected to increase the tax burden on high-income taxpayers relative to low-income taxpayers, assuming that high-income taxpayers purchase more expensive products. But this is not entirely straightforward: the exact distributional impact will depend on consumption patterns, and even with an *ad valorem* tax, high-income taxpayers may still end up paying less tax relative to their income than poor households. Addressing redistributive goals is likely to be better achieved through the progressive personal income tax which directly links taxes paid to income (Thomas, A. and Brys, B. 2016) (see also Section 4.6 below).

There may be a case for a combination of *ad quantum* and *ad valorem* taxes if a goal of the tax is to discourage consumption of, or maximise revenue from, both high and low value products. Where there are large differences in prices of a product, an *ad quantum* tax will be less likely to reduce demand for the high value product, and will raise less revenue from it than an *ad valorem* tax. Additionally, higher income consumers who are more likely to consume high value products may be less responsive than low-income groups to the imposition of a given tax (although *ad quantum* taxes may reduce the price differentials). Imposing a higher aggregate tax on these expensive products will therefore be necessary to affect behaviour. To achieve this, an *ad valorem* tax can be combined with an *ad quantum* tax, which is common with tobacco taxation (see Section 4.3 below).

Setting the "optimal" balance between *ad quantum* and *ad valorem* components of excise will depend of the products concerned, the market structure and the government's objective, hence there is no optimal balance between the two taxes in absolute (Keen, 1998). The aim can be the maximisation of tax revenue; to ensure the predictability and stability of the revenue; and/or to influence consumer behaviour.

Excises as instruments to influence behaviour

While the original reason for introducing excise duties was to raise revenue, they are now increasingly used to discourage consumption of certain products that are considered harmful to health or the environment. Regardless of the reason for which they are implemented, excise taxes affect consumer behaviour. The case put forward in relation to alcoholic beverages and tobacco products is that drinking and smoking are health hazards and increased excise duties help to reduce consumption. For mineral oils, reasons for levying excise taxes relate to energy security concerns and social externalities from energy use, particularly environmental costs. Over the last decade, environmental concerns have played an increasing role in determining the nature and application of taxes e.g. to road fuel, motor vehicles (see Chapter 5) and CO_2 emissions. OECD analysis (OECD, 2010) confirms the advantages of environmental taxes over many other environmental policy instruments in terms of environmental effectiveness, economic efficiency, the ability to raise public revenue, and transparency. Also, environmental taxes have been successfully used to address a wide range of issues including waste disposal, water pollution and air emissions. It also shows how the way they are designed and implemented is crucial to their success (OECD, 2011).

A related rationale for applying excise duties on energy is their (cost-) effectiveness in mitigating global warming. At the United Nations Climate Change Conference in Paris (COP21) 195 countries agreed to decarbonise the global economy by the second half of this century (UN, 2015). While energy use accounted for 69% of total greenhouse gas emissions in 2010 (IEA, 2014), excise duties on fossil fuel based energy increase its price, so reducing demand for it. In addition, if excise duties are levied proportionally on the carbon content of fuels, they encourage substitution towards less carbon-intensive forms of energy. Taking electricity as an example, producers can switch from coal to less carbon-intensive natural gas, or carbon-free solar and wind power. Besides specific excise duties on energy, carbon taxes (often also levied as excise duties) and tradable emission permits put a price on the carbon content of energy. The principal appeal of using prices to abate carbon emissions is that this encourages abatement where it is cheapest.

Effective Carbon Rates (OECD, 2016), presents the first full analysis of the use of carbon prices in 41 OECD and G20 economies, covering 80% of global energy use and of CO_2 emissions. Only 10% of emissions are priced above EUR 30 per tonne, a conservative minimum of the climate cost of carbon. Specific excise duties on energy contribute most to average effective carbon rates, clearly dominating carbon taxes and tradable emission permits.

While the main characteristics and objectives ascribed to excise duties are approximately the same across OECD countries, their implementation, especially in respect to tax rates and structure, gives rise to significant differences between countries.

Giving an order of magnitude of the tax burden differences between countries is not straightforward. Although taxes (other than VAT) on alcoholic beverages and tobacco consist almost exclusively of excise duties (*ad quantum* or *ad valorem*), their structure may vary widely across countries. For example, standard excise rates on beer may be tempered by the application of reduced rates on small breweries. Different duty rates applicable to substitutes (cigarettes and rolling tobacco) may also blur the picture. If the objective is to measure total burdens on automotive transport services, cross-country comparisons of road fuels show only a part of automotive taxation policy that also includes road tolls, taxes on registration and use of vehicles, taxes on insurance, etc.

4.3. Alcoholic beverages

A wide variety of alcoholic beverages exist across the world that can be produced from a range of different ingredients (grapes, apples, malt, rice, etc.) that are fermented or distilled. The Customs Combined Nomenclature Code (CN) provides a classification of alcoholic beverages with which excise categories are intrinsically linked. The CN includes six main categories of alcoholic beverages: beer made from malt (code 22.03); wine of fresh grapes, including fortified wines (code 22.04); vermouth and other wine of fresh grapes flavoured with plants or aromatic substances (code 22.05); other fermented beverages (for example, cider, perry, mead), mixtures of fermented beverages and mixtures of fermented beverages and non-alcoholic beverages (code 22.06); undenatured ethyl alcohol of an alcoholic strength of 80% pure alcohol by volume (abv) or higher (code 22.07) and undenatured ethyl alcohol of an alcoholic strength of less than 80% abv (code 22.08). There are inevitably sub-divisions within each of these broad categories but the use of the internationally accepted nomenclature provides for consistency and helps to avoid contradictory definitions in applying rates. Member States of the European Union also apply a harmonised structure for excise duties on alcohol and alcoholic beverages (Council Directive 92/83/EEC). Except otherwise mentioned in country notes, Tables 4.A4.1 and 4.A4.2 cover products under CN codes 22.03 and 22.04. Table 4.A4.3 covers products not included in Tables 4.A4.1 and 4.A4.2.

Given the long history of alcohol taxation, several methods and measures were developed over time for assessing the alcoholic content of a product. Nowadays, the alcohol by volume (abv) is a standard measure of how much alcohol (ethanol) is contained in an alcoholic beverage. It is defined as the number of litres of pure ethanol present in 100 litres of solution at 20 °C, expressed as a percentage of total volume. As a result, the alcoholic content in Tables 4.A4.1 and 4.A4.2 is expressed in % abv. In some countries, the alcoholic content of beer is still calculated in degree Plato (measuring the density of beer wort in terms of percentage of extract by weight). In order to provide comparable excise data, the amounts of tax per degree Plato were converted amount per % abv. There is no precise conversion between degrees Plato and degrees of absolute alcohol but for tax purposes it is assumed that 1% abv is equivalent to 2.5 degrees Plato. As a result, tax rates expressed in degree Plato have been multiplied by 2.5 to obtain the rates in degree abv.

Excise is applied to alcoholic beverages in two main ways. The duty can be either *ad quantum* in relation to the alcoholic content of the product or *ad valorem* calculated according to the value of the product. The two methods are combined to include both the volume (based on alcohol content) and value. One exception is Mexico where the rate of tax is calculated exclusively on the value of the product for alcoholic beverages, with a graduated rate for beer based on the alcoholic content of the product. The high inflation rate in Mexico may have played a role in this decision. Besides countries in the EU levy a circulation tax per hectolitre on alcoholic beverages with the exception of beers and spirits on which the ad quantum method is also applied.

Tables 4.A4.1, 4.A4.2 and 4.A4.3 in respect of excise duties on beer, wine and other alcoholic beverages show the complicated computations for excise duties in many instances. Due to the existence of differing sub-categories and specific rates (e.g. for low-alcohol products and for small breweries) and calculations according to both the value and the nature of the product, it is difficult to be precise about the price differentials from a consumer point of view. However, Tables 4.A4.1, 4.A4.2 and 4.A4.3 show the large differences that exist between countries: excise on wine (Table 4.A4.2) may vary from zero (Austria, Czech Republic, Germany, Hungary, Israel, Italy, Luxemburg, Portugal, Slovak Republic, Slovenia, Spain and Switzerland) up to more than USD 7 a litre of still wine (Norway) and more than USD 13 a litre of sparkling wine (Turkey). Excise on beer (Table 4.A4.1) also varies from about USD 2 per hectolitre per % abv (Germany and Luxembourg) up to USD 35 (Finland) and even USD 59 (Israel).

4.4. Tobacco products

Historically, as for alcohol taxation, the primary motivation for tobacco taxation was the efficient generation of government revenue, with nearly all countries having taxed tobacco products for many decades or, in some cases, centuries. The relatively low elasticity of demand for tobacco products (i.e. the less than proportionate response of tobacco product consumption to moderate increase in prices), the small number of producers and significant consumption had made tobacco products particularly attractive targets for excise and other taxation. In recent decades, as evidence on the health consequences of tobacco has accumulated, the use of tobacco taxation as a tool for improving public health has gained prominence, as economic evidence showed the effectiveness of increased tobacco product taxes and prices in reducing tobacco use (WHO, 2016).

As with alcohol and mineral oils, there is a sub-division of tobacco products into a number of categories – cigarettes, cigars, cigarette rolling tobacco and pipe tobacco.

Unlike for excises on alcoholic beverages and mineral oils, which are almost exclusively *ad quantum*, the majority of countries use a combination of specific and *ad valorem* elements to calculate excise on tobacco products.

Table 4.A4.4 shows large differences between countries. Differences may also exist within a federal structure such as the USA where e.g. local excise rates on cigarettes (on the top of the federal tax) range from USD 0.17 in Missouri to USD 4.35 in New York per pack of 20 cigarettes (FTA, 2016). However, the individual rates or amounts of each tax (*ad valorem/ ad quantum* excise, VAT, duties, etc.) on tobacco products shown separately (provided in Table 4.A4.4) do not provide sufficient information to assess the overall tax burden on those products. Indeed, a high *ad valorem* tax can be balanced with a low *ad quantum* excise (or vice versa) when a mixed excise tax structure applies (i.e. made of both an *ad quantum* and an *ad valorem* excise). *Ad valorem* excise can be assessed on different bases (producer price, import price, retail price) and the combined effect of the VAT rate with excise duties will not be reflected.

A better understanding of the relative taxation levels may be gained by calculating the total tax burden (TTB) as a share of the total retail selling price (RSP) to the final consumer. Table 4.A4.5 shows the total tax burden (*ad quantum* excise + *ad valorem* excise + VAT) for cigarettes as a share of the retail selling price of a pack of 20 cigarettes in OECD countries (for the calculation methodology, see note to Table 4.A4.5). This table shows that the total tax burden for a pack of 20 cigarettes varies widely between countries, from 42.54% of the RSP in the United States (national average estimate of federal and local taxes) and 56.76% in Australia to 84.10% in the United Kingdom and 86.51% in Ireland. However, in all the OECD countries (except the US), the tax burden is above 50% of the RSP and above 80% for 10 countries (Chile, Estonia, Finland, France, Greece, Ireland, Latvia, Poland, Turkey and the United Kingdom). Table 4.A4.5. also shows that there are substantial differences in the pre-tax prices, depending on the structure of the market, the geographic location (in particular with respect to cross-border shopping) and the structure of taxes. For example, pre-tax prices tend to be higher in countries where there are no or low *ad valorem* taxes.

The level of the rate plays a crucial role in achieving the objectives of the tax. If the tax is primarily intended to raise revenue then the tax rate would vary depending on the level of revenue required and the elasticity of the demand for the taxed products. A moderate rate may be sufficient to generate stable revenue without creating significant political economy difficulties. If the tax is intended to have a significant impact on customer behaviour then a higher tax rate may be required to achieve the desired health outcomes. In the specific case of tobacco, research has shown that higher taxes and prices on tobacco reduce both prevalence (i.e. from users quitting) and intensity of use (i.e. users consuming less), in particular on vulnerable populations (young people and low income households). In addition, the monetary burden of higher tobacco taxes appears to fall more heavily on the wealthiest users, whose tobacco use declines less, while most of the health and economic benefits from reductions in tobacco use accrue to the most disadvantaged populations, whose tobacco use declines more when taxes increase (WHO 2015). Political economy factors (e.g. industry lobbying, public opposition) may make imposing a high rate difficult to achieve. Earmarking (part of) the revenue from the taxes for specific health related purposes such as funding health programmes and/or tobacco control activities may increase public support, although it reduces the flexibility in government budgeting (OECD, 2016a). Concerns about cross-border trade and bootlegging between countries with high price differentials may also make it difficult to impose a high tax rate in some countries unless regional co-operation is implemented.

4.5. Mineral oil products

Mineral oils are usually sub-divided into product categories in relation to technical specifications such as unleaded gasoline, diesel oil, and heavy fuel oil. Some OECD countries also tax other energy products under an excise tax regime (or under specific taxes on energy products, for example carbon taxes) such as natural gas, electricity and coal. The European Union (EU) Energy Tax Directive (2003/96/EC) sets the EU framework for the taxation of energy products and electricity. The Directive sets minimum tax rates for energy products for all energy products including coal, natural gas and electricity. *Taxing Energy Use* (OECD, 2015 and 2013) provides a comprehensive overview of specific taxes on energy for 41 OECD and G20 countries and *Effective Carbon Rates* (OECD, 2016b) elaborates on the role that specific taxes on energy, carbon taxes and tradable emission permits play in mitigating climate change.

A significant feature of excise on mineral oils is the fact that duty rates have been used to influence consumer behaviour to a greater degree than in many other areas. Excise on transport fuels has been around for many years although it was originally motivated by non-environmental needs (such as general revenue generation or sometimes earmarked for infrastructure spending). When the more environmentally-friendly unleaded gasoline appeared on the market it was more expensive to produce and as a consequence not commercially competitive with leaded gasoline as a retail product. This handicap was soon overcome through tax differentials making unleaded gasoline cheaper at the pump. Today, leaded gasoline has disappeared and is even not allowed any more on the market. On the other hand, lower taxes on Liquefied Petroleum Gas (LPG) used as propellant had a much less significant effect on consumer choices since the characteristics of this fuel (not liquid at standard temperature and atmospheric pressure, more difficult to stock, need for specifically equipped stations) have hindered its development. The use of LPG is globally very low compared to diesel and gasoline.

Excise taxes on transport fuels usually are much higher than on mineral oils and, more generally, fossil fuels used in other sectors (OECD, 2013). This can be for various reasons, including a lower elasticity of the tax base in transport, the use of excises to cover (more or less directly) some external costs that are relevant only in transport (most notably congestion), and equity concerns that may lead to lower tax rates on diesel used for household heating (see Table 4.A4.8). Indeed, the vast majority of OECD countries (except the Czech Republic, Hungary, Israel and the Netherlands) tax heating oil for households at a lower rate than diesel for transport use even though these two products are more or less identical.

EU member states have implemented the Energy Taxation Directive (2003/96/EC), which sets out common rules for the taxation of energy products. The Directive is intended to reduce distortions of competition, both between member states as a result from divergent rates of tax on energy products, and between mineral oils and the other energy products. It is also intended to increase incentives to use energy more efficiently. The Directive sets common taxation rules for a range of fuels, including many oil products, coal and natural gas, and for electricity consumption. For each, it sets a minimum level of tax expressed in terms of the volume, weight, or energy content of the fuel. For example minimum rates on road fuels are as follows: EUR 0.359/l for unleaded gasoline; EUR 0.330/l for gas oil and EUR 0.125/kg for LPG. On the other hand, the Directive does not specify which taxes should be employed to attain the minimum level and they may include a diversity of specific taxes such as excise, carbon tax, energy tax, etc.

The revenues raised from these taxes are significant, as a result of the considerable level of consumption in the OECD countries and high tax rates in many of them. Although there are large differences between countries, the level of taxation for fuel relative to the base is very high compared to other taxes within the overall economy. For premium unleaded gasoline (Table 4.A4.6), the total tax burden (mainly excise plus VAT) exceeds 100% of pre-tax prices in all the OECD countries, except Australia, Canada, Mexico, New Zealand and the United States.

Excise levels for diesel fuel are lower than those for gasoline in most countries. Only two countries – Chile and Switzerland – levy a higher excise duty on diesel than on gasoline and only two countries apply the same excise rate to both fuels (Australia and United Kingdom). From an environmental point of view, this is peculiar, as diesel consumption in vehicles has a much greater environmental impact than unleaded gasoline, largely due to the significant differences in NO_x[2] and particulate emissions. With more stringent motor vehicle regulations, the difference is becoming less pronounced for new vehicles, although there are concerns about differences between test cycle and on-road performance and the stock of vehicles is still weighted toward older, more polluting diesel vehicles (OECD, 2010; Harding, 2014a).

Excise rates on automotive fuels should not be considered in isolation in assessing the overall tax burden on automotive transport. Vehicles are also subject to registration taxes and recurrent circulation taxes and many countries differentiate those taxes according to the type of fuel used or according to CO_2 emissions per unit distance (see Chapter 5). Furthermore, the tax treatment of company car use is often more favourable – sometimes considerably so – than that of other car use (Harding, 2014b).

The rates shown in Tables 4.A4.6 to 4.A4.8 are taken from the International Energy Agency and do not reflect excise duties exclusively but also include in some countries a number of taxes such as contributions to emergency stock funds.

4.6. Impact on cross-border trade

Differences in excise rates between countries often result from national traditions, social and health policy, local production and government's financing needs. Such differences are not without impact on the cross-border movement of goods. The development of integrated markets (e.g. the European Union) and elimination of border controls at frontiers have shed light on the disparate excise rates between neighbouring countries to the extent that market forces are affected. In such circumstances the effects of cross-border shopping can have a significant economic impact on businesses and put pressure on the relevant tax authorities to seek closer approximation of excise duty rates with their neighbours. Differences between certain neighbouring countries may also encourage cross-border "bootlegging" activities (McKee et al., 2004). Although some would argue that market forces should encourage moves towards convergence of rates, this is contradictory with other policy factors when issues such as health are taken into account in setting the rates.

4.7. Distributional impact of excise

The distributional impact of excise taxes is a concern to many policy makers. Knowing the distributional effects of excise duties allows for better fine-tuning of the distributional impacts of the overall system. The distributional impact of excise taxes varies across the goods on which they are imposed. A recent study for 20 mainly European OECD countries showed that the combined impact of excise taxes on alcohol, tobacco and transport fuels tends to be regressive whether measured as a percentage of income or expenditure (OECD, 2014). On the other hand, research on the distributional impact of excise taxes on transport fuels has shown that these taxes are not regressive (Flues and Thomas, 2015). These results imply that as households earn more they spend a smaller proportion of their income and total expenditure on excise taxes on alcohol and tobacco. Exact burdens can vary depending on tax design. For example, if richer households consume more expensive alcohol and tobacco than poorer households, richer households will face relatively higher tax burdens with an *ad-valorem* tax that taxes the value of the product compared to an *ad quantum* tax that taxes the quantity consumed. The non-regressive nature of taxes on transport fuels can be explained both by a smaller likelihood of lower income households owning a car and by driving less if they own a car.

Notes

1. VAT may also be referred to as Goods and Services Tax (GST). For ease of reading, all value added taxes will be referred to as VAT in this chapter.
2. NO_x is a generic term for the various nitrogen oxides produced during combustion. These are considered to be important air pollutants.

References

Flues, F. and A. Thomas (2015), "The distributional effects of energy taxes", *OECD Taxation Working Papers*, No. 23, OECD Publishing, Paris, *http://dx.doi.org/10.1787/5js1qwkqqrbv-en*.

FTA (2014), Federation of Tax Administrators, *State Excise Taxes*, Washington 2016 *www.taxadmin.org*.

Harding, M. (2014a), "The Diesel Differential – Differences in the tax treatment of gasoline and diesel for road use", *Tax Policy Working Papers*, No. 21, OECD Publishing, Paris, *http://dx.doi.org/10.1787/5jz14cd7hk6b-en*.

Harding, M. (2014b), "Personal Tax Treatment of Company Cars and Commuting Expenses: Estimating the Fiscal and Environmental Costs", *Tax Policy Working Papers*, No. 20, OECD Publishing, Paris, *http://dx.doi.org/10.1787/5jz14cg1s7vl-en*.

IEA (2014), *CO_2 emissions from fuel combustion – Highlights – 2014 Edition*, OECD/IEA, Paris.

IEA (2010), *Energy prices and taxes, 2010*, International Energy Agency, Paris.

Keen (1998), *The Balance Between Specific and Ad Valorem Taxation*, Fiscal Studies Vol. 19, No. 1 pp. 1-37, London.

McKee, M.; Mac Lehose, L.; Nolte, E. (2004), *Health policy and EU enlargement*, European Observatory on Health Systems and Policy Series, Open University Press, Buckingham.

Thomas, A. and Brys, B. (2016), *Health-related taxes on food and non-alcoholic beverages in OECD countries: key design issues, OECD Taxation Working Paper*, forthcoming.

OECD (2016), *Effective Carbon Rates: Pricing CO_2 through Taxes and Emissions Trading Systems*, OECD Publishing, Paris, *http://dx.doi.org/10.1787/9789264260115-en*.

OECD (2015), *Taxing Energy Use 2015: OECD and Selected Partner Economies*, OECD Publishing, Paris, *http://dx.doi.org/10.1787/9789264232334-en*.

OECD/KIPF (2014), The Distributional Effects of Consumption Taxes in OECD Countries, OECD Publishing, Paris. *http://dx.doi.org/10.1787/9789264224520-en.*

OECD (2013), *Taxing Energy Use: A Graphical Analysis*, OECD Publishing, Paris, *http://dx.doi.org/10.1787/9789264183933-en.*

OECD (2011), *Environmental Taxation, a Guide for Policy Makers*, OECD, Paris, *www.oecd.org/env/tools-evaluation/48164926.pdf.*

OECD (2010), *Taxation, Innovation and the Environment*, OECD Publishing, Paris, *http://dx.doi.org/10.1787/9789264087637-en.*

Sassi, F., A. Belloni and C. Capobianco (2013), *The Role of Fiscal Policies in Health Promotion*, *OECD Health Working Papers*, No. 66.

UN (2015), *Adoption of the Paris Agreement*, United Nations, *https://unfccc.int/resource/docs/2015/cop21/eng/l09r01.pdf.*

WHO (2008), *Methods for evaluating tobacco control policies*, International Agency for Research on Cancer, Geneva.

WHO (2015), *Using price policies to promote healthier diet*, World Health Organisation, Geneva.

WHO (2016), *Report on the Global tobacco Epidemic, Raising Taxes on Tobacco*, World Health Organisation, Geneva.

ANNEX 4.A4

Data on excise rates

Table 4.A4.1. **Taxation of beer**

Country	Currency	Specific excise per hectolitre per % abv[1]		Lower excise for small independent breweries			Excise duty on low alcohol beer (not exceeding 2.8% abv) Excise per hectolitre of product		VAT rate	Excise rates which are progressive by strength
		National currency	USD	Annual production (hl)	National currency	USD	National currency	USD	%	
Australia*	AUD	Country note		Country note			Country note		10.0	Yes
Austria	EUR	5.00	5.55	< 12 500	3	3.33	–	–	20.0	No
				< 25 000	3.5	3.88			20.0	
				< 37 500	4	4.44			20.0	
				≤ 50 000	4.5	4.99			20.0	
Belgium	EUR	5.01	5.56	≤ 12 500	4.36	4.84	–	–	21.0	No
				≤ 25 000	4.50	4.99			21.0	
				≤ 50 000	4.65	5.16			21.0	
				≤ 75 000	4.79	5.32			21.0	
				≤ 200 000	4.94	5.48			21.0	
Canada*	CAD	Country note		Country note			Country note		5.0/13.0/14.0/15.0	Yes
Chile*	CLP	Country note		Country note			Country note		19.0	No
Czech Republic	CZK	80.00	3.25	≤ 10 000	40.00	1.63	–	–	21.0	No
				≤ 50 000	48.00	1.95			21.0	
				≤ 100 000	56.00	2.28			21.0	
				≤ 150 000	64.00	2.60			21.0	
				≤ 200 000	72.00	2.93			21.0	
Denmark*	DKK	56.02	8.33	≤ 3 700	Country note		0.00	0.00	25.0	No
				≤ 20 000	Country note				25.0	
				< 200 000	Country note				25.0	
Estonia	EUR	8.30	9.21	≤ 3 000	4.15	4.61	–	–	20.0	No
Finland*	EUR	32.05	35.57	≤ 5 000	16.03	17.79	8.00	8.88	24.0	No
				≤ 30 000	22.44	24.90			24.0	
				≤ 55 000	25.64	28.46			24.0	
				≤ 100 000	28.85	32.01			24.0	
France*	EUR	7.41	8.22	≤ 200 000	7.41	8.22	3.70	4.11	20.0	No
Germany	EUR	1.97	2.19	≤ 5 000	1.10	1.22	–	–	19.0	No
				≤ 10 000	1.32	1.47			19.0	
				≤ 20 000	1.54	1.71			19.0	
				≤ 40 000	1.65	1.83			19.0	
Greece	EUR	6.50	7.21	≤ 200 000	3.25	3.61	–	–	23.0	No
Hungary	HUF	1 620.00	5.80	< 8 000	810.00	2.90			27.0	No
Iceland*	ISK	Country note		–	–	–	Country note	–	11.0	Yes
Ireland*	EUR	22.55	25.03		Country note		Country note		23.0	No
Israel*	ILS	231.00	59.43	–	–	–	Country note		17.0	No
Italy*	EUR	7.60	8.44	–	–	–	Country note	–	22.0	No
Japan*	JPY	Country note					–	–	8.0	No
Korea*	KRW	Country note					Country note		10.0	No
Latvia*	EUR	3.80	4.22	≤ 10 000	1.90	2.11			21.0	No
Luxembourg*	EUR	1.98	2.20	≤ 50 000	0.98	1.09	–	–	17.0	No
				≤ 200 000	1.12	1.24	–	–	17.0	
Mexico*	MXN	26.50%					–	–	16.0	Yes
Netherlands*	EUR	Country note		–	–	–	–	–	21.0	Yes
New Zealand*	NZD	27.20	18.97				Country note		15.0	No
Norway*	NOK	See note					Country note		25.0	Yes

Table 4.A4.1. **Taxation of beer** *(cont.)*

Country	Currency	Specific excise per hectolitre per % abv[1]		Lower excise for small independent breweries			Excise duty on low alcohol beer (not exceeding 2.8% abv) Excise per hectolitre of product		VAT rate	Excise rates which are progressive by strength
		National currency	USD	Annual production (hl)	National currency	USD	National currency	USD	%	
Poland*	PLN	19.48	5.17	Country note			–	–	23.0	No
Portugal*	EUR	See note		Country note			Country note		23.0	Yes
Slovak Republic	EUR	3.59	3.98	≤ 200 000	2.65	2.94	–	–	20.0	No
Slovenia*	EUR	12.10	13.43				–	–	22.0	No
Spain*	EUR	Country note		–	–	–	Country note		21.0	Yes
Sweden	SEK	194.00	23.02	–	–	–	–	–	25.0	No
Switzerland*	CHF	Country note					Country note		8.0	Yes
Turkey*	TRY	0.63	–	–	–	–	–	–	18.0	No
United Kingdom*	GBP	18.37	28.09	Country note			8.10	12.39	20.0	No
United States*	USD	Country note					–	–		No

* See country notes in Box 4.A4.1.

Note: Conversion of national currency in USD: conversion rates are average market rates (2015) published in OECD Monthly Monetary Statistics (stats.oecd.org).

1. % abv = percentage of pure alcohol by volume at 20°C. In some countries the excise rate on beer is calculated per hectolitre per degree Plato. For ease of reading, all amounts have been converted in % abv. There is no precise conversion between degrees Plato and % abv but for tax purposes it is often assumed that 1% abv is equivalent to 2.5 degrees Plato. As a result, tax rates expressed in degree Plato have been multiplied by 2.5 to obtain the % abv.

Source: National Delegates; position as at 1 January 2016.

StatLink http://dx.doi.org/10.1787/888933420114

Box 4.A4.1. **Country notes**

Australia: The excise rates for beer in individual containers not exceeding 48 litres are: AUD 41.08 per litre of alcohol where volume of alcohol does not exceed 3%, AUD 47.85 where volume of alcohol exceeds 3% but does not exceed 3.5% and AUD 47.85 where volume exceeds 3.5%. The rates for beer in individual containers exceeding 48 litres are: AUD 8.21 per litre of alcohol where volume of alcohol does not exceed 3%, AUD 25.73 where volume of alcohol exceeds 3% by volume of alcohol but not more than 3.5%, and AUD 33.70 where volume exceeds 3.5%. These rates apply as of 1 February 2016. Each rate is calculated on the amount by which the alcohol content exceeds 1.15% by volume of alcohol. Beer that does not contain more than 1.15% cent by volume of alcohol is free of excise. These rates are indexed to inflation in February and August each year. Independent brewers receive an excise refund of 60% of the excise paid up to a maximum of AUD 30 000 per financial year for beer sold directly from the brewery.

Canada: Excise duty rates for beer are imposed per hectolitre of product (*not* per hectolitre per degree alcohol). Provincial and territorial governments also charge various mark-ups and levies on beer, generally at rates that exceed the federal level. Federal excise duty rates: (1) On all beer or malt liquor containing more than 2.5% absolute ethyl alcohol by volume, CAD 31.22 per hectolitre. (2) On all beer or malt liquor containing more than 1.2% absolute ethyl alcohol by volume but not more than 2.5% absolute ethyl alcohol by volume, CAD 15.61 per hectolitre. (3) On all beer or malt liquor containing not more than 1.2% absolute ethyl alcohol by volume, CAD 2.591 per hectolitre. Reduced rates of excise duty apply on the first 75 000 hectolitres of beer produced per year by Canadian brewers at the following rates: (1) On the first 2 000 hectolitres of beer and malt liquor brewed in Canada: (a) if it contains more than 2.5% absolute ethyl alcohol by volume, CAD 3.122 per hectolitre; (b) if it contains more than 1.2% absolute ethyl alcohol by volume but not more than 2.5% absolute ethyl alcohol by volume, CAD 1.561 per hectolitre; and (c) if it contains not more than 1.2% absolute ethyl alcohol by volume, CAD 0.2591 per hectolitre. (2) On the next 3 000 hectolitres of beer and malt liquor brewed in Canada: (a) if it contains more than 2.5% absolute ethyl alcohol by volume, CAD 6.244 per hectolitre; (b) if it contains more than 1.2% absolute ethyl alcohol by volume but not more than 2.5% absolute ethyl alcohol by volume, CAD 3.122 per hectolitre; and (c) if it contains not more than 1.2% absolute ethyl alcohol by volume, CAD 0.5182 per hectolitre. (3) On the next 10 000 hectolitres of beer and malt liquor brewed in Canada:(a) if it contains more than 2.5% absolute ethyl alcohol by volume, CAD 12.488 per hectolitre; (b) if it contains more than 1.2% absolute ethyl alcohol by volume but not more than 2.5% absolute ethyl alcohol by volume, CAD 6.244 per hectolitre; and (c) if it contains not more than 1.2% absolute ethyl alcohol by volume, CAD 1.0364 per hectolitre. (4) On the next 35 000 hectolitres of beer and malt liquor brewed in Canada: (a) if it contains more than 2.5% absolute ethyl alcohol by volume, CAD 21.854 per hectolitre; (b) if it contains more than 1.2% absolute ethyl alcohol by volume but not more than 2.5% absolute ethyl alcohol by volume, CAD 10.927 per hectolitre; and (c) if it contains not more than 1.2% absolute ethyl alcohol by volume, CAD 1.8137 per hectolitre. (5) On the next 25 000 hectolitres of beer and malt liquor brewed in Canada: (a) if it contains more than 2.5% absolute ethyl alcohol by volume, CAD 26.537 per hectolitre; (b) if it contains more than 1.2% absolute ethyl alcohol by volume but not more than 2.5% absolute ethyl alcohol by volume, CAD 13.269 per hectolitre; and (c) if it contains not more than 1.2% absolute ethyl alcohol by volume, CAD 2.2024 per hectolitre.

Chile: The sale of alcoholic beverages (including wine, beer, distilled alcoholic beverages and other alcoholic beverages) is subject to 19% VAT and also to a surtax on the sale or import of alcoholic beverages. The rate applied to beer is of 20.5% and does not depend upon the degree of alcohol that the beer contains. The tax is applied to the VAT base, that is the sale`s price (excluding VAT itself) and levies sales made between wholesale dealers. For sales between wholesalers, the tax paid to the vendor is creditable against the tax applied on sales at each stage of the value chain (including imports) until the last sale to the final retailer. The sale from the retailer to the final consumer is not subject to the surtax and the retailer cannot deduct the input tax.

Box 4.A4.1. **Country notes** *(cont.)*

Denmark: Lower rates on small independent breweries: production ≤ 3 700 hl receives a tax reduction of DKK 77.08 per hl; production > 3 700 hl but ≤ 20 000 hl (X) receives a tax reduction of DKK 259.939/(X + 6.83) per hl; production > 20 000 hl receives a tax reduction of DKK 22.02 – (X/9083) per hl. An additional duty is placed on products which contain a mixture of beer and non-alcoholic drinks. Rates: DKK 9.38/l. of mixture with alcohol content ≤ 10% vol. in the final product and DKK 16.39/l. of mixture with alcohol content > 10% vol. in the final product. Beer with alcohol content less than 2.8% vol. is free of excise tax.

Finland: Beer with an alcoholic content less than 0.5% vol. is free of excise.

France: Beer with alcoholic content above 18% support an additional taxation for social budget: EUR 2.96/ degree of alcohol/hectolitre

Iceland: The duty in Iceland is ISK 112 per centilitre of alcohol per litre minus 2.25 centilitres. For example, one litre of beer that has 6% abv has 6 centilitres alcohol per litre. So the duty for one litre of beer that contains 6% abv would be as follows: (6-2.25) * 112 = ISK 420 per litre. As a result of this formula, beer with less than 2.25% abv is not taxed.

Ireland: There is remission or repayment of 50% alcohol products tax (excise duty) on beer brewed in independent small breweries producing up to 30 000 hl a year. For low alcohol beer, the rate is 0.00 (beer ≤ 1.2% abv) and EUR 11.27 (beer > 1.2% abv up to 2.8% abv).

Israel: The duty was set as ILS 231 on 1 January 2016. The amount is updated each year according to the change in the Consumer Price Index (CPI). There is no duty on beer under 2% alcohol (or under 3.8% alcohol if marketed in reusable bottles). The statistical data for Israel are supplied by and under the responsibility of the relevant Israeli authorities. The use of such data by the OECD is without prejudice to the status of the Golan Heights, East Jerusalem and Israeli settlements in the West Bank under the terms of international law.

Italy: Beer with volume of alcohol does not exceed 0.5 percent is not taxed.

Japan: Excise rates are JPY 22 000 per hectolitre of product. Small brewers who produce no more than 13 000 hectolitre of beer per year pay JPY 18 700 per hectolitre on the first 2000 hectolitres for the first five years of the license (temporary measure).

Korea: The rate of Liquor Tax on beer is 72% of the manufacturer's price. In addition, Education Tax (30% on the amount of Liquor Tax levied) is also levied.

Latvia: Starting from 1 March 2016 the excise per hectolitre per % abv is EUR 4.2; excise per hectolitre per % abv for small independent breweries is EUR 2.1 (not less than EUR 7.8 per hectolitre of beer). The reduced rate for small independent breweries (annual production up to 50 000 hl) is applied for the first produced 10 000 hl of beer.

Luxembourg: Rates for small breweries (annual production up to 200 000 hl) range from EUR 0.40 to EUR 0.45. Additional rate for alcopops: EUR 600 per hectolitre.

Mexico: The rates apply to the value of the goods as follows: 26.5% for beer and other alcoholic beverages up to 14° Gay-Lussac (GL); 30% for beverages above 14° G.L. and up to 20° G.L.; 53% for beverages above 20° G.L. As a mechanism to discourage the use of disposable containers, taxpayers should pay the greater amount between the result of applying the corresponding rate to the value or a MXN 3 per litre fee (taxpayers that use re-usable containers can reduce an amount of MXN 1.26 per litre).

Netherlands: Most beers in the Netherlands are in the range 11°-15° Plato, usually 12° Plato, with an excise duty of EUR 37.96:12 = EUR 3.16 per degree Plato. Excise duty rates are as follows per hectolitre of product: a) Up to 7° Plato EUR 8.83; b) 7°-11° Plato EUR 28.49; c) 11°-15° Plato EUR 37.96; d) 15 or more degrees Plato EUR 47.48. Rates for small breweries (annual production up to 200 000 hl) are as follows: a) up to 7° Plato the above mentioned rate; b) 7°-11° Plato EUR 26.35; c) 11-15 degrees Plato EUR 35.11; d) 15 or more degrees Plato EUR 43.92. For beer with a maximum alcohol content of 0.5% a consumer tax of EUR 8.83 per hectolitre is applicable and a VAT rate of 6%.

Box 4.A4.1. **Country notes** *(cont.)*

New Zealand: The excise rate for beer containing more than 2.5% abv is NZD 27.870 per litre of alcohol in finished product. The rate for beer containing more than 1.15% abv but not more than 2.5% abv is NZD 41.797 per litre of product. There is no excise duty on beer containing less than 1.15% abv.

Norway: Excise rates are as follows per hectolitre of product: a) 0.0-0.7% abv: NOK 0; b) 0.7-2.7% abv: NOK 327; c) 2.7-3.7% abv: NOK 1 229; d) 3.7-4.7% abv: NOK 2 129. The excise rate for beer with an alcoholic content of more than 4.7% abv is NOK 476 per degree of alcohol and hectolitre.

Poland: Allowances for small breweries: sale ≤ 20 000 hl a year tax is reduced by PLN 30 /hl; sale ≤ 70 000 hl a year tax is reduced by PLN 15/hl; sale ≤ 150 000 hl a year tax is reduced by PLN 12.00/hl and by PLN 9.00/hl if the producer sells no more than 200 000 hl a year. However, the amount of exemption cannot exceed 50% of the amount of excise duty calculated with the standard rate of excise duty on beer.

Portugal: Excise rates for beer are as follows per hectolitre of product: (a) > 0.5.% ≤ 1.2% abv EUR 7.98; (b) > 1.2 ≤ 2.8% abv EUR 10.0; (c) > 2.8° ≤ 4.4% abv EUR 15.98; (d) > 4.4° ≤ 5.2% abv EUR 20.0; (e) > 5.2° ≤ 6% abv EUR 23.99; (f) > 6% abv EUR 28.06 (rates as at 31 March 2016). Rates for small breweries (annual production up to 200 000 hl) are 50% of the normal rates.

Slovenia: Specific excise per hectolitre per degree abv: EUR 12.10.

Spain: Excise rate according to strength is: beer < 1.2% abv is free of excise; beer between 1.2% and 2.8% abv is EUR 2.75/hl; beer between 2.8% abv and 11° Plato is EUR 7.48/hl; beer with a degree Plato > 11 and not > 15 = EUR 9.96/hl; beer with a degree Plato > 15 and not > 19 = EUR 13.56/hl; beer with a degree Plato > 19 = EUR 0.91/hl and per degree Plato. There is no tax on Beer in Ceuta and Melilla (Spanish cities situated in the North of Africa).

Switzerland: Rates per hectolitre: light beer (up to 10.0° Plato): CHF 16.88, regular and special beer (10.1 to 14.0° Plato): CHF 25.32, strong beer (from 14.1° Plato): CHF 33.76. Reductions for small breweries from 40% (annual production max. 15 000 hl) to 0% (annual production min. 55 000 hl). Beer with more than 15% vol. is taxed as an alcoholic beverage (CHF 2900 per hectolitre of absolute alcohol).

Turkey: The minimum tax amount is TL 103 per hectolitre/degree. If the amount computed according to the tax rate (63%) is lower than the minimum tax amount, the minimum tax amount is paid.

United Kingdom: Beer with an alcoholic content not exceeding 1.2% abv is free of excise. Lower strength beer duty applies to beer 1.3 to 2.8% abv. High strength beer duty was introduced from 1 October 2011 and is a duty applied to all beer exceeding 7.5% abv in addition to general beer duty. Reduced duty rates apply for independent breweries producing: less than 5 000 hectolitres, 50% of the standard rate of duty; between 5 000 hectolitres and and 30 000 hectolitres = annual production -2500 /annual production X standard rate of duty; between 30 000 hectolitres and 60 000 hectolitres = annual production (2500-8.33% of annual production in excess of 30 000) /annual production X standard rate of duty. No further reduction of the Lower Strength Beer Duty rate can be claimed by a small brewer.

United States: The weighted average Federal and State excise tax rate is USD 22 per hectolitre of product. The Federal tax is USD 18.00 per barrel (31 gallons). 1 barrel = 1.1735 hectolitres. Small domestic brewers who produce less than 2 million barrels of beer per calendar year pay USD 7.00 in federal tax per barrel on the first 60 000 barrels. There is no progressive rate structure based on alcohol content and no Federal VAT.

Table 4.A4.2. **Taxation of wine**

		Still wine			Sparkling wine			Low-alcohol (still) wine (< 8.5% abv)		
	Currency	Excise per hectolitre of product		VAT	Excise per hectolitre of product		VAT	Excise per hectolitre of product		VAT
		National currency	USD	%	National currency	USD	%	National currency	USD	%
Australia*	AUD	Country note	-	10.00	Country note	-	10.00	Country note	-	10.00
Austria	EUR	0.00	0.00	20.00	100.00	110.99	20.00	0.00	0.00	20.00
Belgium	EUR	74.91	83.14	21.00	256.32	284.48	21.00	23.91	26.54	21.00
Canada*	CAD	62.00	48.51	5.0/13.0/14.0/15.0	62.00	48.51	5.0/13.0/14.0/15.0	Country note	-	5.0/13.0/14.0/15.0
Chile*	CLP	Country note	-	19.00	Country note	-	19.00	Country note	-	19.00
Czech Republic	CZK	0.00	0.00	21.00	2 340.00	95.15	21.00	0.00	0.00	21.00
Denmark*	DKK	1 161.00	172.64	25.00	1 496.00	222.45	25.00	534.00	79.41	25.00
Estonia*	EUR	111.98	124.28	20.00	84.67	93.97	20.00	48.55	53.88	20.00
Finland*	EUR	339.00	376.25	24.00	339.00	376.25	24.00	Country note	-	24.00
France*	EUR	3.77	4.18	20.00	9.33	10.36	20.00	3.77	4.18	20.00
Germany*	EUR	0.00	0.00	19.00	136.00	150.94	19.00	0.00	0.00	19.00
Greece	EUR	20.00	22.20	23.00	20.00	22.20	23.00	20.00	22.20	23.00
Hungary	HUF	0.00	0.00	27.00	16 460.00	58.96	27.00	0.00	0.00	27.00
Iceland*	ISK	Country note	-	11.00	Country note	-	11.00	Country note	-	11.00
Ireland*	EUR	424.84	471.52	23.00	849.68	943.04	23.00	141.57	157.13	23.00
Israel*	ILS	0.00	0.00	17.00	See note	-	17.00	0.00	0.00	17.00
Italy	EUR	0.00	0.00	22.00	0.00	0.00	22.00	0.00	0.00	22.00
Japan	JPY	8 000.00	66.11	8.00	8 000.00	66.11	8.00	8 000.00	66.11	8.00
Korea*	KRW	See note	-	10.00	Country note	-	10.00	Country note	-	10.00
Latvia*	EUR	70.00	77.69	21.00	70.00	77.69	21.00	Country note		21.00
Luxembourg*	EUR	0.00	0.00	14 or 17	0.00	0.00	17.00	0.00	0.00	14.00
Mexico*	MXN	26.5%/30%	-	16.00	26.5%/30%	-	16.00	26.5%	-	16.00
Netherlands*	EUR	88.36	98.07	21.00	254.41	282.36	21.00	44.18	49.03	21.00
New Zealand*	NZD	Country note	-	15.00	Country note	-	15.00	Country note	-	15.00
Norway*	NOK	5 712.00	708.33	25.00	5 712.00	708.33	25.00	Country note	-	25.00
Poland	PLN	158.00	41.91	23.00	158.00	41.91	23.00	158.00	41.91	23.00
Portugal	EUR	0.00	0.00	13.00	0.00	0.00	23.00	0.00	0.00	23.00
Slovak Republic*	EUR	0.00	0.00	20.00	79.65	88.40	20.00	0.00	0.00	20.00
Slovenia	EUR	0.00	0.00	22.00	0.00	0.00	22.00	0.00	0.00	22.00
Spain*	EUR	0.00	0.00	21.00	0.00	0.00	21.00	0.00	0.00	21.00
Sweden*	SEK	2 517.00	298.61	25.00	2 517.00	298.61	25.00	Country note	0.00	25.00
Switzerland*	CHF	0.00	0.00	8.00	0.00	0.00	8.00	0.00	0.00	8.00
Turkey*	TRY	557.00	204.55	18.00	3 763.00	1 381.93	18.00	557.00	204.55	18.00
United Kingdom*	GBP	273.31	417.91	20.00	350.07	535.28	20.00	84.21	128.76	20.00
United States*	USD	47.00	47.00	-	116.00	116.00	-	Country note	-	-

* Country notes: see Box 4.A4.2.

Note: Conversion of national currency in USD: conversion rates are average market rates (2015) published in OECD Monthly Monetary Statistics (stats.oecd.org).

Source: National delegates; position as at 1 January 2016.

StatLink http://dx.doi.org/10.1787/888933420124

Box 4.A4.2. Country notes

Australia: All wine (including still, sparkling and low alcohol wine) is liable for the wine equalisation tax (WET). WET applies at 29% of the value of the wine at the last wholesale sale (before adding GST). A rebate of WET paid, or the amount of WET that would have been paid had the buyer not quoted, applies to eligible producers, up to a maximum of AUD 500 000 each financial year. The Australian Government announced in the 2016-17 Budget that the maximum rebate amount will be reduced to AUD 350 000 from 1 July 2017 and to AUD 290 000 from 1 July 2018 and eligibility will be narrowed from 1 July 2019.

Canada: (1) A rate of CAD 0.62 per litre applies to wine with more than 7% abv. The rate is CAD 0.295 per litre on wine of more than 1.2% abv, but not more than 7% abv; and for all wine with 1.2% abv or less the rate is CAD 0.0205 per litre. (2) Fortified wine in excess of 22.9% abv would not be included in the definition of "wine" (and, therefore, fall within the definition of "spirits"). Provincial and territorial governments also charge various mark-ups and levies on wine, generally at rates that exceed the federal level.

Chile: The sale of alcoholic beverages is subject to a surtax of 20.5% on the sale or import of wine, sparkling wine, champagne, cider and other alcoholic beverages (among others). The tax is applied to the VAT base, that is the sale`s price (excluding VAT itself), and levies sales made between wholesale dealers. For sales between wholesalers, the tax paid to the vendor is creditable against the tax applied on sales at each stage of the value chain (including imports) until the last sale to the final retailer. The sale from the retailer to the final consumer is not subject to this surtax and the retailer cannot deduct the input tax nor is levied with this tax the sale of wine in bulk made by producers to a taxpayer seller subject to this surtax.

Denmark: The rate for high-alcohol wine > 15% abv – maximum 22% abv is DKK 1 555 per hectolitre. Medium-alcohol wine < 6% abv – maximum 15% abv is DKK 1 161 per hectolitre. Low-alcohol wine < 1.2% abv – maximum 6% abv is DKK 534 per hectolitre. The rates for sparkling wine correspond to the rates for still wine plus DKK 335 per hectolitre. An additional duty is placed on products which contain a mixture of wine and non-alcoholic drinks. Rates: DKK 7.13 per litre of mixture with alcohol content ≤ 10% abv in the final product and DKK 11.50 per litre of mixture with alcohol content > 10% abv in the final product.

Estonia: Excise rate for low alcohol up to 6% vol. still and sparkling wine is EUR 48.55 (rates as at 1 February 2016).

Finland: Excise rates for low alcohol wine are as follows: a) over 1.2% abv and up to 2.8% abv EUR 22.00; b) over 2.8% abv and up to 5.5% abv EUR 169.00; c) over 5.5% abv and up to 8.0% abv EUR 241.00.

France: A reduced rate applies to the following categories of low-alcohol wine: cider, perry, mead, grapes juice lightly sparking.

Germany. Excise rate for low alcohol sparkling wine < 6% abv is EUR 51.00. Intermediate products with a volume of alcoholic degree between 1.2% and 22% abv are taxed according to the following rates: > 15% abv – 22% abv = EUR 153/hl; <= 15% abv = EUR 102/hl; <= 15% abv and sparkling = EUR 136/hl.

Iceland: The duty rate is ISK 102 per centilitre of alcohol per litre minus 2.25 centilitres for wine up to 15% abv. For example, one litre of wine that has 15% abv has 15 centilitres alcohol per litre. So the duty for one litre of wine that contains 6% abv would be as follows: (15-2.25) * 102 = ISK 1 300.50 per litre.

Ireland: The rate for low alcohol wine applies to wine with an alcoholic content of less than 5.5% abv. The rate for still wine with alcoholic content > 15% abv is EUR 616.45.

Israel: The statistical data for Israel are supplied by and under the responsibility of the relevant Israeli authorities. The use of such data by the OECD is without prejudice to the status of the Golan Heights, East Jerusalem and Israeli settlements in the West Bank under the terms of international law.

Korea: The rate of liquor tax on wine is 30% on the manufacturer's price (or imported price). In addition, Education Tax (10% of the amount of Liquor tax levied) is also levied. These rates are applicable to both still and sparkling wine regardless of alcohol content.

Box 4.A4.2. **Country notes** *(cont.)*

Latvia. Starting from 1 March 2016 the excise for wine (still and sparkling) is EUR 74 per hectolitre. There is no specific rate for low-alcohol (still) wine (< 8.5% abv).

Luxembourg: The reduced VAT rate (12%) applies to still wine with alcoholic content ≤ 13% abv. Additional rate for alcopops: EUR 600 per hectolitre.

Mexico: All rates apply to the value of the goods, and not per hectolitre of product, as follows: 26.5% for beer and other alcoholic beverages up to 14° Gay-Lussac (GL); 30% for beverages above 14° G.L. and up to 20° G.L.; 53% for beverages above 20° G.L.

Netherlands: Excise duty rate for still wine > 15% abv is EUR 129.81/hl. Excise duty rate for low alcohol (max 8.5% abv) sparkling wine is EUR 48.25/hl. For low alcohol wine < 1.2% abv the VAT rate is 6%.

New Zealand: The excise rate for unfortified wine is NZD 2.7870 per litre of product.

Norway: The rate shown in Table 4.2 is the rate for wine with an alcoholic content of 12% abv. Excise rates for wine with an alcoholic content of 4.7%-22% abv = NOK 476 per vol. pct. alcohol and per hectolitre.

Slovak Republic: The rate of EUR 54.16/hl applies to sparkling fermented beverages with an alcoholic strength by volume not exceeding 8.5% abv. The rate for intermediate products is EUR 84.24/hl.

Spain: Intermediate products - products to which distilled alcohol has been added – and with a volume of alcoholic degree between 1.2% abv and less than 22% abv are taxed according to the following rates: alcoholic degree > 1.2% abv and less than 15% abv = EUR 36.65/hl. Others = EUR 61.08/hl.

Sweden: Excise rates for low alcohol wine are as follows: a) < 2.25% abv: SEK 0; b) 7%-8.5% abv: SEK 1797; c) 4.5%-7% abv SEK 1306; d) 2.25%-4.5% abv SEK 884. No special rates for sparkling wine.

Switzerland: In general wine with more than 15% abv is taxed as an alcoholic beverage (CHF 2 900 per hectolitre of absolute alcohol). Natural wines made from fresh grapes with more than 18% abv are taxed as an alcoholic beverage (CHF 1 450 per hectolitre of absolute alcohol up to 22% abv then CHF 2 900 per hectolitre of absolute alcohol).

Turkey: The excise rate is 0%.

United Kingdom: Reduced rates for lower strength drinks (wine categories) are as follows: a) exceeding 1.2% – not exceeding 4% abv = GBP 84.21; b) exceeding 4% – not exceeding 5.5% abv = GBP 115.80; and c) low strength sparkling wine exceeding 5.5% – less than 8.5% abv = GBP 264.61. d) sparkling wine and made wine at least 8.5% abv but not exceeding 15% abv = GBP 350.07. Rate in the band exceeding 15% abv but not exceeding 22% abv = GBP 364.37 (wine and made wine). The duty rates on wine changed on 21 March 2016 to: Excise duty rate on still wine 277.84, reduced rate for lower strength drinks (wine categories) a) exceeding 1.2% – not exceeding 4% abv = GBP 85.60; b) exceeding 4% – not exceeding 5.5% abv = GBP 117.72; and c) low strength sparkling wine exceeding 5.5% – less than 8.5% abv = GBP 268.99 d) sparkling wine and made wine at least 8.5% abv but not exceeding 15% abv = GBP 355.87. Rate in the band exceeding 15% abv but not exceeding 22% abv = GBP 370.41 (wine and made wine).

United States: The weighted average Federal and State excise tax rate is USD 47 per hectolitre of product for still wine up to 14% abv and USD 116 for sparkling wine. The Federal excise rates are as follows: a) up to 14% abv: USD 1.07 per gallon; b) 14%-21% abv: USD 1.57 per gallon; c) 21%-24% abv: USD 3.15 per gallon; d) artificially carbonated wine USD 3.30 per gallon; and e) sparkling wine USD 3.40 per gallon. 26.42 US gallons = 1 hectolitre. There is no Federal VAT.

Table 4.A4.3. **Taxation of alcoholic beverages**[1]

	Currency	Tax per hectolitre of absolute alcohol			
		Excise		VAT rate %	Small distillery rate
		National currency	USD		
Australia*	AUD	8 105.00	6 089.41	10.00	No
Austria*	EUR	1 200.00	1 331.85	20.00	Yes
Belgium	EUR	2 992.79	3 321.63	21.00	No
Canada*	CAD	1 169.60	915.18	5.0, 13.0, 14.0 or 15.0	No
Chile*	CLP	See note	-	19.00	No
Czech Republic	CZK	28 500.00	1 158.87	21.00	No
Denmark*	DKK	15 000.00	2 230.48	25.00	No
Estonia	EUR	2 172.00	2 410.65	20.00	No
Finland*	EUR	4 555.00	5 055.49	24.00	No
France*	EUR	1 737.56	1 928.48	20.00	No
Germany*	EUR	1 303.00	1 446.17	19.00	Yes
Greece*	EUR	2 450.00	2 719.20	23.00	No
Hungary*	HUF	333 385.00	1 194.10	27.00	Yes
Iceland*	ISK	1 380 000.00	10 462.79	11.00	No
Ireland	EUR	4 257.00	4 724.75	23.00	No
Israel*	ILS	See note	-	17.00	No
Italy*	EUR	1 035.52	1 149.30	22.00	No
Japan*	JPY	See note	-	8.00	No
Korea*	KRW	See note	-	10.00	No
Latvia*	EUR	1 360.00	1 509.43	21.00	No
Luxembourg	EUR	1 041.15	1 155.55	17.00	No
Mexico*	MXN	53%	-	16.00	No
Netherlands*	EUR	1 686.00	1 871.25	6.0 or 21.0	No
New Zealand*	NZD	See note	-	15.00	No
Norway	NOK	73 100.00	9 064.98	25.00	No
Poland	PLN	5 704.00	1 513.00	23.00	No
Portugal*	EUR	1 327.94	1 473.85	23.00	Yes
Slovak Republic*	EUR	1 080.00	1 198.67	20.00	No
Slovenia*	EUR	1 320.00	1 465.04	22.00	No
Spain*	EUR	913.28	1 013.63	21.00	Yes
Sweden	SEK	51 148.00	6 068.10	25.00	No
Switzerland*	CHF	2 900.00	3 014.55	8.00	Yes
Turkey*	TRY	15 071.00	5 534.70	18.00	No
United Kingdom*	GBP	2 766.00	4 229.36	20.00	No
United States*	USD	995.00	995.00	-	No

* Country notes: see Box 4.A4.3.

Note: Conversion of national currency in USD: conversion rates are average market rates (2015) published in OECD Monthly Monetary Statistics (stats.oecd.org).

1. Alcoholic beverages other than those included in Tables 4.1 and 4.2.

Source: National delegates; position as at 1 January 2016.

StatLink http://dx.doi.org/10.1787/888933420138

Box 4.A4.3. **Country notes**

Australia: The excise duty of AUD 81.05 per litre of alcohol applies to spirits and other excisable beverages (except beer). A lower rate of AUD 75.70 per litre of alcohol applies to brandy (distilled from grape wine). These rates apply as of 1 February 2016 and are indexed to inflation in February and August of each year. The Australian Government announced in the 2016-17 Budget that it would provide a refund of 60 per cent of excise paid up to AUD 30 000 per financial year to domestic distilleries and producers of low strength alcoholic beverages from 1 July 2017.

Austria: For small distilleries producing not more than 4 hl pure alcohol per year the rate is EUR 648.(54% of the standard rate).

Canada: (1) Spirits are subject to excise duty at the rate of CAD 11.696 per litre abv. Spirits containing not more than 7% abv are subject to excise duty at the rate of CAD 0.295 per litre. (2) Beer with an alcoholic strength in excess of 11.9% abv is deemed to be Spirits. Provincial and territorial governments also charge various mark-ups and levies on spirits, generally at rates that exceed the federal level.

Chile: Alcoholic beverages are subject to a surtax on the sale or import. The rates applied are the following: 31.5% on liquors, brandy, vermouth, pisco, whiskey and other distilled alcoholic beverages; 20.5% on beer, wine, sparkling wine, champagne, cider and other alcoholic beverages. The tax is applied to the VAT base, that is the sale`s price (excluding VAT itself) and levies sales made between wholesale dealers. For sales between wholesalers, the tax paid to the vendor is creditable against the tax applied on sales at each stage of the value chain (including imports) until the last sale to the final retailer. The sale from this retailer to the final consumer is not subject to the surtax and the retailer cannot deduct the input tax nor is levied with this tax the sale of wine in bulk made by producers to a taxpayer seller subject to this surtax.

Czech Republic: The reduced rate of CZK 14 300 per hectolitre of pure alcohol applies for small fruit grower's distilleries producing no more than 30 litres of fruit spirit per year per household. The excise duty of CZK 2 340 per hectolitre of product is applicable for intermediate products.

Denmark: An additional duty is placed on products which contain a mixture of spirits and non-alcoholic drinks, Rates: DKK 4.21 per litre of mixture.

Finland: Excise rates are as follows: (a) CN – code 2208. alcoholic content between 1.2% abv and 2.8% abv. EUR 800; (b) Other products EUR 4 555.

France: Additional taxation for social budget: EUR 557.90/hectolitre of pure alcohol.

Germany: The rates for small distilleries are EUR 730 or EUR 1 022. Additional rate for alcopops: EUR 5 550 per hectolitre of absolute alcohol.

Greece: The rate for ouzo and ethyl alcohol (derogation possible for several regions but only applied in the department of Dodecanese) is EUR 1225 per hectolitre of pure alcohol.

Hungary: A reduced rate of 50% applies to ethyl-alcohol produced by fruit growers' distilleries from fruit supplied to them by private fruit growers. The application of reduced rate is limited to 43 litres of pure alcohol for private consumption per fruit grower household per year.

Iceland: Excise rate shown in the table is the rate for other alcohol than beer or wine up to 15% abv. The rate is ISK 138 per each centilitre of alcohol by volume exceeding 2.25% abv.

Israel: The excise rates for all kinds of alcoholic beverages is ILS 84.24 per litre of absolute alcohol. The statistical data for Israel are supplied by and under the responsibility of the relevant Israeli authorities. The use of such data by the OECD is without prejudice to the status of the Golan Heights, East Jerusalem and Israeli settlements in the West Bank under the terms of international law.

Italy: Taxation applies for beverages of alcoholic strength exceeding 1.2% abv. The rate of EUR 88.67 applies to intermediate products.

Box 4.A4.3. **Country notes** *(cont.)*

Japan: Excise rates are as follows: a) Whiskey and brandy (40% abv) JPY 40 000; b) Spirits (37% abv) JPY 37 000; c) Shochu Group A and B (25% abv) JPY 25 000.

Korea: As Excise Tax for liquor is based on the value of the product, the rate does not vary with alcohol content. For whiskey, brandy, general distilled spirits, liquor, diluted soju and distilled soju, the Liquor tax is 72% and the Education tax is 30%.

Latvia: Starting from 1 March 2016 the excise rate is EUR 1400 per hectolitre of absolute alcohol.

Luxembourg: Additional rate for alcopops: EUR 600 per hectolitre.

Mexico: The excise tax is set at an ad valorem rate and not per hectolitre of product. The rates for alcoholic beverages apply to the value of the goods as follows: 26.5% up to 14° Gay-Lussac (G.L.); 30% above 14° G.L. and up to 20° G.L.; 53% above 20° G.L.

Netherlands: For low alcohol spirits with an alcoholic content < 1.2% the VAT rate is 6%.

New Zealand: For alcoholic beverages with 9-14% abv, the excise rate is NZD 2.7870 per litre. For alcoholic beverages above 14% abv, the excise rate is NZD 50.759 per litre of absolute alcohol (with the exception of unfortified wine and vermouth which has the rate of NZD 2.7870 per litre of product).

Portugal: Intermediate products are taxed at EUR 72.86/hl; Ethyl alcohol/spirits: EUR 1 327.94/hl (rates applicable as at 31 March 2016). A reduced rate of 50% for small distilleries applies.

Slovak Republic: A reduced rate of 50% of the national rate of excise duty on ethyl alcohol, applies to ethyl alcohol produced by fruit growers' distilleries. The application of the reduced rate is limited to 43 litres of ethyl alcohol for personal consumption of the fruit growers' household per year.

Slovenia: Tax per hectolitre of absolute alcohol is EUR 1 320.

Spain: The excise rate in the Canary Islands is EUR 714.63 per Hl of pure alcohol. There is a special regime for small distilleries for which the rate is EUR 799.19 per hl (or EUR 622.23 in the Canary Islands).

Switzerland: Under certain conditions farmers do not pay tax on the first 5 litres of pure alcohol produced per year for their personal consumption. A reduced rate of 30% is applied to the first 30 litres of pure alcohol produced per year by small producers. Normal rate: CHF 2900 per hectolitre. Special rate for certain types of wines: CHF 1450 per hectolitre. Special rate for alcopops: CHF 11 600 per hectolitre (Alcopop -also called ready to drink (RTD) or designer drink) is a mix of alcohol and soda.

Turkey: The excise rate is 0%. If the tax amount computed according to the tax rate is lower than the minimum tax amount specified in the table, then the minimum tax amount is paid.

United Kingdom: All drinks over 22% abv are taxed as spirits. Most other mixtures of spirits with other types of alcohol are also taxed as spirits. Still cider and perry exceeding 1.2% – not exceeding 7.5% abv = GBP 38.87, still cider and perry exceeding 7.5% – less than 8.5% abv = GBP 58.75, sparkling cider and perry exceeding 1.2% – not exceeding – 5.5% abv = GBP 264.61, sparkling cider and perry exceeding 5.5% – less than 8.5% abv = GBP 264.61. The duty rates on sparkling cider and perry exceeding 5.5% – less than 8.5% abv changed on 21 March 2016 to GBP 268.99.

United States: The weighted average Federal and State excise tax rate is USD 995 per hectolitre. The Federal excise rate is USD 13.50 per proof gallon. A proof gallon is a US gallon (3.785 litres) containing 50% alcohol. There is no Federal VAT.

Table 4.A4.4. **Taxation of tobacco**

	Currency	Cigarettes			Cigars[2]			Rolling tobacco for cigarettes			VAT
		Specific excise per 1 000		Excise on value	Specific excise per 1 000		Excise on value	Specific excise per 1 000 grams		Excise on value	
		National currency	USD	% of RSP[1]	National currency	USD	% of RSP[1]	National currency	USD	% of RSP	%
Australia*	AUD	530.96	398.92	0.00	Country note	-	0.00	663.72	498.66	0.00	10.00
Austria*	EUR	45.00	49.94	40.00	0.00	0.00	13.00	0.00	0.00	56.00	20.00
Belgium	EUR	39.52	43.86	45.84	0.00	0.00	10.00	23.70	26.30	31.50	21.00
Canada*	CAD	105.15	82.28	Country note	22.89	17.91	Country note	131.44	102.85	Country note	5.0/13.0/14.0/15.0
Chile*	CLP	46 323.00	70.80	30.00	0.00	-	52.60	0.00	-	59.70	19.00
Czech Republic	CZK	1 290.00	52.45	27.00	1 420.00	57.74	-	1 896.00	77.10	-	21.00
Denmark*	DKK	1 182.50	175.84	1.00	500.00	74.35	10.00	788.50	117.25	0.00	25.00
Estonia*	EUR	46.50	51.61	34.00	211.00	234.18	0.00	61.00	67.70	0.00	20.00
Finland*	EUR	37.50	41.62	52.00	0.00	0.00	31.00	26.00	28.86	52.00	24.00
France	EUR	48.75	54.11	49.70	19.00	21.09	23.00	67.50	74.92	32.00	20.00
Germany	EUR	98.20	108.99	21.69	14.00	15.54	1.47	48.49	53.82	14.76	19.00
Greece	EUR	82.50	91.56	20.00	0.00	0.00	35.00	156.70	173.92	0.00	23.00
Hungary*	HUF	15 700.00	56.23	25.00	0.00	0.00	14.00	14 000.00	50.14	0.00	27.00
Iceland*	ISK	22 990.00	174.30	0.00	Country note	-	0.00	16 450.00	124.72	0.00	24.00
Ireland*	EUR	271.96	301.84	9.20	Country note	-	0.00	291.68	323.73	0.00	23.00
Israel*	ILS	395.00	101.62	Country note	0.00	0.00	Country note	454.03	116.81	0.00	17.00
Italy	EUR	17.34	19.25	58.70	0.00	0.00	23.00	0.00	0.00	58.50	22.00
Japan*	JPY	12 244.00	101.19	0.00	12 244.00	101.19	0.00	12 244.00	101.19	0.00	8.00
Korea*	KRW	145 450.00	109.25	64.64	Country note	-	0.00	103 200.00	77.52	0.00	10.00
Latvia*	EUR	54.20	60.16	25.00	42.69	47.38	-	58.00	64.37	-	21.00
Luxembourg	EUR	18.39	20.41	46.65	0.00	0.00	10.00	10.00	11.10	34.30	17.00
Mexico*	MXN	350.00	22.05	38.77	Country note	-	Country note	Country note	-	Country note	16.00
Netherlands	EUR	178.28	197.87	1.09	0.00	0.00	5.00	78.68	87.33	4.60	21.00
New Zealand*	NZD	Country note	-	0.00	Country note	-	0.00	386.14	269.27	0.00	15.00
Norway	NOK	2 500.00	310.02	0.00	2 500.00	310.02	0.00	2 500.00	310.02	0.00	25.00
Poland*	PLN	206.76	54.84	31.41	393.00	104.24	-	141.29	37.48	31.41	23.00
Portugal*	EUR	90.85	100.83	17.00	0.00	0.00	25.00	78.00	86.57	20.00	23.00
Slovak Republic*	EUR	59.50	66.04	23.00	71.11	78.92	-	71.11	78.92	0.00	20.00
Slovenia*	EUR	68.82	76.38	21.18	0.00	0.00	6.00	40.00	44.40	35.00	22.00
Spain	EUR	24.10	26.75	51.00	0.00	0.00	15.80	22.00	24.42	41.50	21.00
Sweden	SEK	1 500.00	177.96	1.00	1 320.00	156.60	0.00	1 833.00	217.46	0.00	25.00
Switzerland*	CHF	118.32	122.99	25.00	5.60	5.82	1.00	38.00	39.50	25.00	8.00
Turkey*	TRY	221.00	81.16	65.25	221.00	81.16	40.00	221.00	81.16	65.25	18.00
United Kingdom*	GBP	189.49	289.74	16.50	236.37	361.42	0.00	185.74	284.01	0.00	20.00
United States*	USD	135.00	135.00	Country note	Country note	-	-	Country note	-	-	-

* Country notes: see Box 4.A4.4.

Note: Conversion of national currency in USD: conversion rates are average market rates (2015) published in OECD Monthly Monetary Statistics (stats.oecd.org).

1. RSP. Retail selling price.
2. Cigars. Denmark and Japan tax cigars at a rate per 1 000 pieces and not according to weight. In Denmark it is assumed that a cigar weighs 3 grams and in Japan 1 gram.

Source: National delegates and European Commission; position as at 1 January 2016.

StatLink http://dx.doi.org/10.1787/888933420145

Box 4.A4.4. **Country notes**

Australia: The excise rate of AUD 0.53096 per stick applies to cigarettes or cigars (in stick form) not exceeding in weight 0.8 grams per stick actual tobacco content. Other tobacco products are subject to an excise rate of AUD 663.72 per kilogram of tobacco content.

Austria: The excise duty on cigars is 13% of RSP, at least EUR 100 for 1 000 pieces. Minimum excise duty on rolling tobacco for cigarettes is EUR 80 per kg. The minimum excise duty on cigarettes is 98% of the total excise duty burden on cigarettes falling under the WAP.

Canada: The excise duty on cigars is CAD 22.88559 per 1 000 cigars plus an additional excise duty based on the greater of CAN 0.08226 per cigar and 82% of the sale price. Each Province and Territory also levies a tobacco tax at varying rates on all tobacco products. Retail sales prices are then subject to GST/HST and, in some cases, when the HST is not applicable, to a provincial sales tax.

Chile: The sale of tobacco products is subject to 19% VAT and to a tax on the sale or import of processed tobacco, cigarettes and cigars. The tax applied to processed tobacco is of 59.7% on the sales' price. Cigarettes are taxed at a rate of 30% over the pack` sales price and with an additional rate of 0.0010304240 of a Monthly Tax Unit per cigarette contained in the pack (a Monthly Tax Unit equals approximately CLP 44 955 or USD 68.71). Cigars are taxed at a rate of 52.6%. The tax base of the excise tax is the sale' price to the final consumer, including VAT and the tax levied on tobacco, cigarettes and cigars.

Denmark: The excise tax for other smoking tobaccos is DKK 738.5/1 000 g. for coarse-cut tobacco

Estonia: For cigarettes, the minimal excise amount to be paid is EUR 90 per 1 000 items (cigarettes)

Finland: Cigarette paper: excise 60% of RSP. Other smoking tobacco: EUR 28.75/kg and 48% of RSP. Minimum excise tax is 188.50 per 1000 pieces for cigarettes and EUR 114.50/kg for fine cut rolling tobacco for cigarettes. As of 1 July 2016, the excise tax on cigarettes is EUR 41.50 per 1000 cigarettes and 52% of RSP. Minimum excise tax is EUR 200 per 1000 cigarettes. For cigars excise tax is 32% of RSP. For fine cut rolling tobacco for cigarettes EUR 28.50/kg and 52% of RSP. Minimum excise tax for fine cut rolling tobacco is EUR 121.50/kg. Other smoking tobacco: EUR 33.00/kg and 48% of RSP.

Hungary: Minimum excise tax is HUF 28 000 per 1000 pieces for cigarettes, HUF 4 000 per 1000 pieces for cigar and cigarillo. VAT as % of tax included retail selling price is 21.26%.

Iceland: There is no specific excise rate for a piece of cigar. The rate is ISK 16 450 per 1 000 grams of cigars (i.e. the same rate as for rolling tobacco).

Ireland: The rate of excise duty on cigarettes in Ireland is EUR 271.96 per 1000 cigarettes together with an amount equal to 9.20% of the price at which the cigarettes are sold by retail or EUR 307.61 per 1000 cigarettes, whichever is the greater. The rate of excise duty on cigars is EUR 315.359 per kilogram. The rate of excise duty on fine-cut tobacco for the rolling of cigarettes is EUR 291.683 per kilogram. Other smoking tobacco is subject to excise duty at a rate of EUR 218.783 per kilogram.

Israel: Excises on value for cigarettes and for cigars are 270% and 90% of the wholesale price, respectively. The statistical data for Israel are supplied by and under the responsibility of the relevant Israeli authorities. The use of such data by the OECD is without prejudice to the status of the Golan Heights, East Jerusalem and Israeli settlements in the West Bank under the terms of international law.

Japan: The tax consists of a national element, a prefectural element and a municipal element.

Korea: The excise tax on cigars is KRW 294800/1000g. National tax (Individual Consumption Tax) levies on tobacco since 2015.

Latvia: Starting from 1 July 2016 the specific excise is EUR 56.20 per 1000 cigarettes and 25% of RSP. Minimum excise EUR 93.70 per 1000 cigarettes.

Box 4.A4.4. **Country notes** *(cont.)*

Mexico: An ad-valorem rate of 160% on the producer or importer price applies for all categories. A reduced rate of 30.4% applies for cigars or rolling tobacco as long as these products are fully handmade. The ad-valorem tax applies at the stage of the producer or importer but on the retail price. In addition a charge of MXN 0.35 should be paid for each sold or imported cigarette. This charge also applies for cigars and other tobacco (MXN 0.35 per each 0.75 grams), with the exemption of those that are fully handmade.

New Zealand: The excise rate for 1 000 cigarettes with actual tobacco content not exceeding in weight of 0.8 kg is NZD 545.39. The excise rate for Cigarettes exceeding 0.8 kg in actual tobacco content per 1 000 cigarettes is NZD 777.18 The excise rate per kilo of tobacco content for other tobacco products, such as snuff, cigars, cheroots and cigarillos is NZD 681.72.

Poland: Since 1 January 2015 the excise duty rate for cigars is calculated on per kilogramme basis.

Portugal: Rates applicable since 31 March 2016. Excise tax on cigarettes is reduced to (1) EUR 18.50 and 41% for cigarettes sold in Azores Islands and made by small producers from the Azores and Madeira Islands; (2) 78.37 and 20% for cigarettes sold in Madeira Island and made by small producers from the Azores and Madeira Islands.

Slovak Republic: Tax on rolling tobacco for cigarettes includes other smoking tobacco. The excise for cigars is EUR 71.11/kg.

Slovenia: Minimum excise duty is EUR 106 per 1 000 cigarettes. Minimum excise duty is EUR 88 per kilo of rolling tobacco for cigarettes. Minimum excise duty for cigars is EUR 40 per kilo.

Switzerland: If the Retail Selling Price for 1 000 cigarettes is CHF 375.00 or less, minimum excise duty (specific + on value) yields CHF 212.10 for 1 000 pieces. Specific excise per 1 000 grams of rolling tobacco for cigarettes: the minimum excise duty (specific + on value) yields CHF 80.00 per 1 000 grams.

Turkey: Minimum tax amount per 1000 cigarettes is TL 221.00. Specific tax amount is 0.2468 for 1 pack of cigarettes. Tax on cigarettes and other tobacco products computed according to the tax rate cannot be less than the minimum tax amount. After calculating the tax according to minimum tax amount system, specific tax amount is added to the tax for 1 pack of cigarettes.

United Kingdom: Specific excise rate for cigars is given per kilogramme and not for 1 000 units. Specific rates exist for "other smoking tobacco" and "other chewing tobacco" which are currently both set at GBP 84.98 per kilo.

United States: State taxes vary widely. The weighted average of Federal and State taxes per thousand cigarettes is USD 135.00. Federal specific excise tax rates on tobacco are: USD 50.33 per thousand for small cigarettes (no more than 3 pounds per thousand); USD 105.69 per thousand for large cigarettes; USD 50.33 per thousand for small cigars weighing no more than 3 pounds per thousand; 52.75% of the manufacturers price but not more than USD 402.60 per thousand for large cigars; and USD 24.78 per pound (54.63 per kg) for roll-your-own tobacco. Some states also tax on an ad valorem basis.

Table 4.A4.5. **Tax burden as a share of total price for cigarettes**[1]

	Ex-tax price (USD)[2]	Specific excise % RSP[3]	Excise on value % RSP[4]	VAT/GST/RST % RSP[5]	Total tax share % RSP	Price of a 20 cigarettes pack[6]		
						Currency	Price (RSP in local currency)	Price (RSP in USD)
Australia	5.54	47.67	0.00	9.09	56.76	AUD	17.05	12.81
Austria	1.08	20.79	40.00	16.67	77.46	EUR	4.33	4.81
Belgium	1.38	13.90	45.84	17.36	77.10	EUR	5.52	6.00
Canada*	2.19	60.93	0.00	9.05	69.80	CAD	9.25	7.24
Chile	0.65	36.76	30.00	15.97	82.73	CLP	2 458.00	3.76
Czech Republic	0.76	32.20	27.00	17.36	76.56	CZK	80.14	3.26
Denmark	1.28	57.89	1.00	20.00	78.89	DKK	40.80	6.07
Estonia	0.65	30.29	34.00	16.67	80.96	EUR	3.07	3.41
Finland	1.06	11.80	52.00	19.35	83.15	EUR	5.68	6.30
France	1.44	14.40	49.70	16.67	80.81	EUR	6.75	7.49
Germany	1.51	36.78	21.69	15.97	74.44	EUR	5.34	5.93
Greece	0.69	44.50	20.00	18.70	83.20	EUR	3.70	4.11
Hungary	0.91	29.67	25.00	21.26	75.93	HUF	1 058.00	3.79
Iceland	3.91	37.54	0.00	19.35	56.89	ISK	1 195.00	9.06
Ireland	1.39	58.61	9.20	18.70	86.51	EUR	9.28	10.30
Israel*	1.71	25.08	39.27	14.53	78.87	ILS	31.50	8.10
Italy	1.17	7.67	51.03	18.03	76.73	EUR	4.52	5.02
Japan	1.27	56.95	0.00	7.41	64.36	JPY	430.00	3.55
Korea	0.89	64.65	0.00	9.09	73.74	KRW	4 500.00	3.38
Latvia	0.61	37.95	25.00	17.36	80.30	EUR	2.79	3.10
Luxembourg	1.84	18.39	46.65	17.00	68.20	EUR	5.20	5.77
Mexico	0.98	14.76	38.77	13.79	67.33	MXN	47.42	2.99
Netherlands	1.42	60.06	1.09	17.36	78.51	EUR	5.94	6.59
New Zealand*	2.69	64.29	0.00	13.04	77.34	NZD	17.00	11.85
Norway	3.90	48.80	0.00	20.40	69.20	NOK	102.00	12.65
Poland	0.66	31.13	31.41	18.70	81.24	PLN	13.30	3.53
Portugal	1.06	42.15	17.00	18.70	77.85	EUR	4.31	4.78
Slovak Republic	0.72	59.50	23.00	16.67	79.30	EUR	3.12	3.46
Slovenia	0.84	39.22	21.18	18.03	78.43	EUR	3.51	3.90
Spain	1.04	10.86	51.00	16.96	78.82	EUR	4.44	4.93
Sweden	1.29	57.38	1.00	20.00	79.31	SEK	52.63	6.24
Switzerland	3.51	27.84	25.00	7.41	60.25	CHF	8.50	8.84
Turkey	0.73	12.34	65.25	15.25	82.62	TRY	11.50	4.22
United Kingdom	1.81	50.94	16.50	16.67	84.10	GBP	7.44	11.38
United States*	3.58	37.38	0.00	5.16	42.54	USD	6.23	6.23

* Canada and the United States, national average estimates calculated for prices and taxes reflect the fact that different rates are applied by state/province over and above the applicable federal tax. For Canada, the weighted rate is as it was on 1 January 2016. The VAT rate will increase in three Canadian provinces during 2016.

* Israel: The statistical data are supplied by and under the responsibility of the relevant Israeli authorities. The use of such data by the OECD is without prejudice to the status of the Golan Heights, East Jerusalem and Israeli settlements in the West Bank under the terms of international law.

* New Zealand: the share of specific excise includes the customs duties of 0.13%.

1. The share of taxes are presented as a % of Retail Selling Price (RSP) for a pack of 20 cigarettes. The RSP is defined as the Weighted Average Price (WAP) i.e. the average consumer price of a tobacco product based on the prices of individual brands and weighted by sales of each brand in the country. Where the WAP is not available, the RSP is defined as the average price of the most sold brand of cigarettes on the market (MSB – see Annex C). This table reflects the situation for the year 2015 since it is based on annual average prices and taxes that are not available for 2016 at the time of this publication.
2. The pre-tax price includes the producer and distributor margins. It is estimated by the deduction of the the total tax share from the RSP.
3. Specific excise: a specific excise tax is a tax on a specific good produced or imported in a country charged as a fixed amout per unit of the product. The amount shown in this table is as a percentage of RSP.
4. Excise on value: an excise on value or ad valorem is a tax on a product produced or imported in a country charged as a percentage of the value of a transaction. Example: 50% of the RSP.
5. VAT/GST: Value added tax or Goods and services tax (see Chapter 1). RST: Retail sales taxes for Canada (in some provinces) and the United States. The amount is shown as a percentage of RSP.
6. Price of a 20 cigarettes pack of cigarettes on the market according to the Weighted Average Price (WAP) method when available and the Most Sold Brand (MSB) method when WAP is not available.

Source: National delegates, European Commission and World Health Organisation; 2015.

StatLink http://dx.doi.org/10.1787/888933420152

Technical note to Table 4.A4.5. Calculation of the total tax burden (TTB)

Total tax burden (TTB) measurement involves the definition of a reference retail price on the market for the product and a methodology to assess the total tax burden in that price. The TTB shown in Table 4.A4.5 is the *weighted average selling price* (WSP), i.e. the average consumer price of a tobacco product based on the prices of individual brands and weighted by sales of each brand in the country. The WAP is considered more appropriate given the dynamics of the market with several popular brands and regular changes in cigarette prices. It also ensures transparency and a level playing field for manufacturers. The WAP has been adopted by the EU as the reference retail price for measuring the tax burden on tobacco products. However, the WAP is not available in all countries. Where the WAP is not available, the RSP is defined as the average price of the most sold brand of cigarettes on the market (see Annex D).

The TTB calculation in Table 4.A4.5 only includes indirect taxes levied on cigarettes (i.e. excise duties or similar taxes, VAT and import duties), which usually have the most significant impact on the price of tobacco products. Certain other taxes, in particular direct taxes such as corporate taxes, can potentially impact tobacco prices to the extent that producers pass them on to final consumers. However, because of the practical difficulty of obtaining information on these taxes and the complexity in estimating their potential impact on price in a consistent manner across countries, they are not considered. The import duty is only used in the calculation of tax shares if the most sold brand of cigarettes was imported into the country.

Table 4.A4.6. **Taxation of premium unleaded (94-96 RON) gasoline (per litre), 2015**[1]

Country	Currency	Ex-tax price[2]	Ex-tax price[2]	Excise[3]		VAT rate[4]	VAT amount	Total tax	Total price	Total tax as % of total price
		National currency	USD	National currency	USD	%	USD	USD	USD	
Australia	AUD	0.851	0.639	0.392	0.295	10.00	0.093	0.388	1.027	37.8
Austria*	EUR	0.450	0.499	0.482	0.535	20.00	0.207	0.742	1.241	59.8
Belgium	EUR	0.603	0.658	0.619	0.687	21.00	0.285	0.972	1.641	59.2
Canada*	CAD	0.755	0.591	0.338	0.264	9.05	0.077	0.342	0.933	36.7
Chile*	CLP	374.30	0.572	317.00	0.484	19.00	0.170	0.654	1.227	53.4
Czech Republic	CZK	11.730	0.477	12.840	0.522	21.00	0.210	0.732	1.209	60.5
Denmark*	DKK	3.852	0.673	4.137	0.615	25.00	0.297	0.912	1.485	61.4
Estonia	EUR	0.448	0.497	0.423	0.469	20.00	0.193	0.663	1.160	57.1
Finland*	EUR	0.451	0.501	0.681	0.756	24.00	0.302	1.057	1.558	67.9
France*	EUR	0.439	0.487	0.624	0.693	20.00	0.236	0.929	1.416	65.6
Germany*	EUR	0.461	0.512	0.655	0.727	19.00	0.235	0.962	1.474	65.3
Greece	EUR	0.463	0.514	0.670	0.744	23.00	0.289	1.033	1.547	66.8
Hungary	HUF	142.580	0.511	120.000	0.430	27.00	0.254	0.684	1.194	57.2
Iceland*	ISK	92.090	0.698	69.860	0.530	24.00	0.295	0.824	1.523	54.1
Ireland	EUR	0.471	0.523	0.588	0.653	23.00	0.270	0.923	1.446	63.8
Israel*	ILS	2.080	0.535	3.056	0.786	17.00	0.224	1.010	1.545	65.4
Italy	EUR	0.469	0.521	0.728	0.808	22.00	0.292	1.100	1.621	67.9
Japan*	JPY	64.800	0.536	56.300	0.465	8.00	0.080	0.545	1.081	50.5
Korea	KRW	881.000	0.779	781.890	0.691	10.00	0.147	0.838	1.617	51.8
Latvia	EUR	0.448	0.498	0.411	0.457	21.00	0.200	0.657	1.155	56.9
Luxembourg*	EUR	0.453	0.503	0.462	0.513	17.00	0.173	0.685	1.188	57.7
Mexico*	MXN	12.158	0.766	0.000	0.000	16.00	0.123	0.123	0.888	13.8
Netherlands	EUR	0.458	0.508	0.744	0.859	21.00	0.287	1.146	1.655	69.3
New Zealand*	NZD	1.054	0.735	0.671	0.468	15.00	0.180	0.648	1.383	46.9
Norway*	NOK	4.940	0.613	5.820	0.722	25.00	0.334	1.055	1.668	63.3
Poland*	PLN	1.883	0.499	1.669	0.443	23.00	0.217	0.659	1.159	56.9
Portugal	EUR	0.491	0.545	0.618	0.686	23.00	0.283	0.969	1.514	64.0
Slovak Republic*	EUR	0.514	0.570	0.515	0.572	20.00	0.228	0.800	1.370	58.4
Slovenia*	EUR	0.432	0.479	0.545	0.605	22.00	0.239	0.843	1.323	63.8
Spain*	EUR	0.496	0.550	0.462	0.513	21.00	0.223	0.736	1.287	57.2
Sweden*	SEK	4.384	0.520	5.575	0.661	25.00	0.295	0.957	1.477	64.8
Switzerland*	CHF	0.596	0.620	0.735	0.764	8.00	0.111	0.875	1.494	58.5
Turkey	TRY	1.510	0.555	2.177	0.799	18.00	0.244	1.043	1.598	65.3
United Kingdom	GBP	0.309	0.472	0.580	0.887	20.00	0.272	1.159	1.631	71.0
United States*	USD	0.492	0.492	0.143	0.143	-	-	0.143	0.635	22.5

* Country notes: see Box 4.A4.6.

Note: Conversion of national currency in USD: conversion rates are average market rates (2015) published in OECD Monthly Monetary Statistics (stats.oecd.org). See also Annex A.

1. Prices and taxes as at 4th Quarter 2015 (1st Quarter 2015 for Iceland).
2. Pre-tax price is the price excluding VAT and excise.
3. Excise taxes are expressed in local currency/USD per litre. They include all non-VAT taxes levied on the product. For the purposes of this table, payments made to specific bodies that use all the amounts collected to accomplish specific missions (e.g. some emergency stock fees) are not considered as "taxes" and are included in the ex-tax price. When different rates apply to the same product depending e.g. on its biofuel or sulphur content, the rate shown is the one applicable to the most commonly used fuel in the country.
4. GST for Australia and New Zealand, sales taxes for the United States and Consumption Tax for Japan. GST/HST and provincial sales taxes for Canada. VAT for all other countries.

Source: International Energy Agency, Energy Prices and Taxes and European Commission Excise Duty Tables Part II.

StatLink http://dx.doi.org/10.1787/888933420162

Box 4.A4.6. Country notes

Austria: the excise amount of EUR 0.482/l applies to unleaded gasoline with minimum 4.6% biofuel content and sulphur content ≤ 10mg/kg. Otherwise the excise duty is EUR 0.515/l.

Canada: excise rates include federal and provincial/urban taxes (the federal rate is CAD 0.1 per litre). The federal GST rate is 5%. The weighted VAT rate including provincial VAT rates was 10.46% on 1 January 2016 and the weighted VAT/sales tax rate was 9.05% The VAT rate will increase in three Canadian provinces during 2016.

Chile: the Fuel Price Stabilisation Mechanism (Mecanismo de Estabilización de Precios de los Combustibles, "MEPCO") introduced in July 2014 is the variable component of the excise, and acts weekly either as a tax or a tax credit to stabilise consumer price compared to international market price variations.

Denmark: the excise amount is for fuel with a minimum amount of 4.8% of biofuels. It includes the Excise Tax, the Environment Tax and the NO_x Tax.

Finland: the excise amount for premium unleaded gasoline includes taxes of energy and CO_2 components and strategic stockpile fee.

France: a rate is determined for each region ranging from EUR 0.6064/l up to EUR 0.6241. An additional tax of max. EUR 0.073/l can be applied by region councils or in Corse to finance sustainable, railway or river navigation substructure.

Germany: the excise amount is for unleaded gasoline with sulphur content ≤ 10mg/kg. Otherwise the excise amount is EUR 0.6698/l.

Iceland: since this country is not member of the IEA or the EU, data is taken from European Automobile Manufacturers Association.

Israel: the statistical data for Israel are supplied by and under the responsibility of the relevant Israeli authorities. The use of such data by the OECD is without prejudice to the status of the Golan Heights, East Jerusalem and Israeli settlements in the West Bank under the terms of international law.

Japan: the excise amount is given for regular unleaded (91RON) instead of premium unleaded. This amount includes the Gasoline Tax and the Road Tax.

Luxembourg: the excise amount is for unleaded gasoline with sulphur content ≤ 10mg/kg. Otherwise the excise amount is EUR 0.464/l.

Mexico: there are no excise duties on volume. A tax (Impuesto Especial de Productos y Servicios) is charged as a percentage of the value of the product at wholesale level. It is included in the ex-tax price.

Netherlands: the amount of EUR 0.774/l excise includes the excise tax of 0.766/l and the stockpiling tax of 0.008/l.

New Zealand: the excise amount includes the National land transport fund tax, the Petroleum engine monitoring levy and the Local authority tax.

Norway: the excise amount includes the Excise tax and the CO_2 tax.

Poland: the excise amount includes the Excise tax and the fuel charge.

Slovak Republic: the excise amount is EUR 0.55052/l for gasoline with biofuel content lower than the minimum.

Slovenia: the excise amount includes the CO_2 tax of EUR 41.47/1000l.

Spain: the excise amount of EUR 0.462/l includes the Excise tax (EUR 0.424/l) and the average Regional authorities tax (EUR 0.038/l).

Sweden: the actual excise amount is EUR 5.850/l (EUR 2.60 Gasoline tax + 3.25 CO_2 tax). However, the amount shown in the table is 95% of this amount to account for the tax-exempt E85 content (5%) of gasoline.

Switzerland: the excise amount includes the Emergency fund tax, the Excise tax and the surcharge for CO_2 emissions.

United States: average federal and state taxes – there is no VAT

European Union: Directive 93/2006/EC sets minimal excise rates for energy products and electricity.

Table 4.A4.7. Taxation of automotive diesel (per litre), 2015[1]

Country	Currency	Ex-tax price[2]	Ex-tax price[2]	Excise[3]		VAT rate[4]	VAT amount	Total tax	Total price	Total tax as % of total price
		National currency	USD	National currency	USD	%	USD	USD	USD	
Australia	AUD	0.749	0.563	0.392	0.295	10.00	0.086	0.380	0.943	40.3
Austria*	EUR	0.476	0.528	0.397	0.441	20.00	0.194	0.634	1.163	54.6
Belgium	EUR	0.516	0.573	0.480	0.533	21.00	0.232	0.765	1.338	57.2
Canada*	CAD	0.724	0.567	0.265	0.207	9.05	0.070	0.277	0.844	32.9
Chile*	CLP	342.500	0.523	802.000	1.226	19.00	0.332	1.558	2.081	74.9
Czech Republic	CZK	13.300	0.541	10.950	0.445	21.00	0.207	0.652	1.193	54.7
Denmark	DKK	3.857	0.574	2.997	0.446	25.00	0.255	0.700	1.274	55.0
Estonia	EUR	0.467	0.518	0.393	0.436	20.00	0.191	0.627	1.145	54.7
Finland*	EUR	0.494	0.548	0.506	0.562	24.00	0.266	0.828	1.376	60.2
France*	EUR	0.420	0.466	0.468	0.519	20.00	0.197	0.717	1.183	60.6
Germany*	EUR	0.547	0.607	0.470	0.522	19.00	0.214	0.736	1.343	54.8
Greece	EUR	0.563	0.625	0.330	0.366	23.00	0.228	0.594	1.219	48.7
Hungary*	HUF	155.070	0.555	110.350	0.395	27.00	0.257	0.652	1.207	54.0
Iceland*	ISK	102.450	0.777	61.840	0.469	24.00	0.299	0.768	1.545	49.7
Ireland	EUR	0.496	0.550	0.479	0.532	23.00	0.249	0.781	1.331	58.6
Israel*	ILS	2.262	0.582	2.928	0.753	17.00	0.227	0.980	1.562	62.7
Italy	EUR	0.475	0.527	0.617	0.685	22.00	0.267	0.951	1.479	64.3
Japan	JPY	70.000	0.579	34.600	0.286	8.00	0.069	0.355	0.934	38.0
Korea	KRW	591.820	0.523	528.750	0.467	10.00	0.099	0.566	1.090	52.0
Latvia	EUR	0.444	0.493	0.333	0.370	21.00	0.181	0.551	1.045	52.8
Luxembourg*	EUR	0.429	0.476	0.335	0.372	17.00	0.144	0.516	0.992	52.0
Mexico*	MXN	10.541	0.664	0.000	0.000	16.00	0.106	0.106	0.770	13.8
Netherlands	EUR	0.476	0.528	0.490	0.544	21.00	0.225	0.769	1.297	59.3
New Zealand	NZD	0.937	0.653	0.004	0.003	15.00	0.098	0.101	0.755	13.4
Norway	NOK	5.090	0.631	4.450	0.552	25.00	0.296	0.848	1.479	57.3
Poland*	PLN	2.002	0.531	1.459	0.387	23.00	0.211	0.598	1.129	53.0
Portugal*	EUR	0.518	0.575	0.402	0.446	23.00	0.235	0.681	1.256	54.2
Slovak Republic*	EUR	0.532	0.590	0.368	0.408	20.00	0.200	0.608	1.199	50.7
Slovenia*	EUR	0.428	0.475	0.462	0.513	22.00	0.217	0.730	1.205	60.6
Spain*	EUR	0.494	0.548	0.368	0.408	21.00	0.201	0.609	1.158	52.6
Sweden*	SEK	5.266	0.625	5.051	0.599	25.00	0.306	0.905	1.530	59.2
Switzerland*	CHF	0.632	0.657	0.763	0.793	8.00	0.116	0.909	1.566	58.1
Turkey	TRY	1.510	0.555	1.595	0.586	18.00	0.205	0.791	1.346	58.8
United Kingdom	GBP	0.333	0.509	0.580	0.887	20.00	0.279	1.166	1.675	69.6
United States*	USD	0.494	0.494	0.150	0.150	-	-	0.150	0.644	23.3

* See country notes in Box 4.A4.7.

Note: Conversion of national currency in USD: conversion rates are average market rates (2015) published in OECD Monthly Monetary Statistics (stats.oecd.org). See Annex A.

1. Prices and taxes as at 4th Quarter 2015.
2. Pre-tax price is the price excluding VAT and excise
3. Excise taxes are expressed in local currency/USD per litre. They include all non-VAT taxes levied on the product. For the purposes of this table, payments made to specific bodies that use all the amounts collected to accomplish specific missions (e.g. some emergency stock fees) are not considered as "taxes" and are included in the ex-tax price. When different rates apply to the same product depending e.g. on its biofuel or sulphur content, the rate shown is the one applicable to the most commonly used fuel in the country.
4. GST for Australia and New Zealand, sales taxes for the United States and Consumption Tax for Japan. GST/HST and provincial sales taxes for Canada. VAT for all other countries.

Source: International Energy Agency, Energy Prices and Taxes and European Commission Excise Duty Tables Part II.

StatLink http://dx.doi.org/10.1787/888933420174

Box 4.A4.7. **Country notes**

Austria: The excise amount of EUR 0.397/l applies to automotive diesel with minimum 6.6% of biofuel and sulphur content ≤ 10mg/kg). Otherwise the excise amount is EUR 0.425/l.

Canada: Excise rates include federal and provincial/urban taxes (the federal rate is CAD 0.04 per litre). The federal GST rate is 5%. The weighted VAT rate including provincial VAT rates was 10.46% on 1 January 2016 and the weighted VAT/sales tax rate was 9.05% The VAT rate will increase in three Canadian provinces during 2016.

Chile: The Fuel Price Stabilisation Mechanism *(Mecanismo de Estabilización de Precios de los Combustibles,* "MEPCO") introduced in July 2014 is the variable component of the excise, and acts weekly either as a tax or a tax credit to stabilise consumer price compared to international market price variations.

Finland: The excise amount of EUR 0.506/l includes the Excise tax for sulphur content (for automotive diesel with low sulphur content < 0.001%), the Energy/CO_2 tax and the Precautionary stock fee.

France: A rate is determined for each region ranging from EUR 0.6064/l up to EUR 0.6241. An additional tax of max. EUR 0.073/l can be applied by region councils or in Corse to finance sustainable, railway or river navigation substructure.

Germany: The excise amount is for diesel with sulphur content ≤ 10mg/kg.

Iceland: Since this country is not member of the IEA or the EU, data is taken from European Automobile Manufacturers Association.

Israel: The statistical data for Israel are supplied by and under the responsibility of the relevant Israeli authorities. The use of such data by the OECD is without prejudice to the status of the Golan Heights, East Jerusalem and Israeli settlements in the West Bank under the terms of international law.

Luxembourg: The excise amount is for diesel with sulphur content ≤ 10mg/kg. Otherwise the excise amount is EUR 0.338/l.

Mexico: Excise taxes on gasoline and diesel in 2015 had three components: (1) the excise-carbon tax, set proportionally to the carbon content of the fuel and implemented through a fixed amount per litre, whose main purpose is to send a carbon price signal to contribute to Climate Change commitments; (2) the excise tax specifically earmarked as transfers to the State's governments, proportional to their consumption, also implemented as a fixed amount per liter; and (3) the main excise tax, which, changed each month in value according to a set of criteria which essentially subtracted from the fuel's controlled price the cost of importing or producing fuel, plus the costs of distribution, logistics, related items, and the retail profit for gas station owners. This general excise tax could even become a negative tax (a subsidy) if domestic prices for fuel were low and international reference prices were high, and this was the case for the first 3 years of the decade. The 2016 excise tax reforms changed completely this latter component. Now, the general excise tax on gasoline and diesel is also a fixed quota tax per liter. During the transition period before full price liberalisation of fuels in 2018, the fixed quota of the excise tax will have a complementary quota component (positive or negative) to ensure that the final fuel prices do not vary outside a price band of +/- 3% of the price they had in 2015. This complementary quota can never become equal in size to the excise tax, so general fossil fuel subsidies would be precluded from happening again.

Netherlands: The amount of EUR 0.490/l excise includes the excise tax of 0.482/l and the stockpiling tax of 0.008/l.

Poland: the excise amount includes the Excise tax and the fuel charge.

Portugal: Automotive diesel used for agriculture is taxed at a lower VAT rate of 13%.

Slovak Republic: The excise amount is EUR 0.386/l for diesel with biofuel content lower than minimum of 6.8%.

Slovenia: The excise amount includes the CO_2 tax of EUR 44.93/1000l.

Box 4.A4.7. **Country notes** *(cont.)*

Spain: The excise amount of EUR 0.368/l includes the Excise tax (EUR 0.331/l) and the average Regional authorities tax (EUR 0.037/l).

Sweden: The tax amount of SEK 5.051/l relates to Class 1 automotive diesel (aromatic content < 5% vol.; max sulphur content of 10 wppm. Higher taxes apply to Class 2 (SEK 5.331/l) and Class 3 (SEK 5.477/l) diesel.

Switzerland: The tax amount of CHF 0.763 includes the Excise tax and the Emergency fund tax.

United States: Average federal and state taxes – there is no VAT.

European Union: Directive 93/2006/EC sets minimal excise rates for energy products and electricity.

Table 4.A4.8. **Taxation of light fuel oil for households (per litre), 2015**[1]

Country	Currency	Ex-tax price[2]	Ex-tax price[2]	Excise[3]		VAT rate[4]	VAT amount	Total tax	Total price	Total tax as % of total price
		National currency	USD	National currency	USD	%	USD	USD	USD	
Australia*	AUD	See note				10.00				
Austria*	EUR	0.438	0.486	0.098	0.109	20.00	0.119	0.228	0.714	31.9
Belgium	EUR	0.389	0.432	0.019	0.021	21.00	0.095	0.116	0.548	21.1
Canada*	CAD	0.892	0.698	0.052	0.041	9.05	0.067	0.108	0.805	13.4
Chile*	CLP	493.030	0.753	0.239	0.000	19.00	0.143	0.144	0.897	16.0
Czech Republic*	CZK	11.762	0.478	10.950	0.445	21.00	0.194	0.639	1.117	57.2
Denmark*	DKK	4.600	0.684	2.667	0.397	25.00	0.270	0.667	1.351	49.4
Estonia	EUR	0.499	0.554	0.111	0.123	20.00	0.135	0.259	0.812	31.8
Finland*	EUR	0.434	0.481	0.187	0.208	24.00	0.165	0.373	0.855	43.7
France	EUR	0.456	0.506	0.076	0.085	20.00	0.118	0.203	0.709	28.6
Germany*	EUR	0.389	0.432	0.061	0.068	19.00	0.095	0.163	0.595	27.4
Greece*	EUR	0.433	0.481	0.230	0.255	23.00	0.169	0.425	0.906	46.9
Hungary*	HUF	103.618	0.371	110.350	0.395	27.00	0.207	0.602	0.973	61.9
Iceland*	ISK	See note				24.00				
Ireland*	EUR	0.427	0.474	0.102	0.114	13.50	0.079	0.193	0.666	28.9
Israel*	ILS	2.107	0.542	2.928	0.753	17.00	0.220	0.973	1.516	64.2
Italy	EUR	0.514	0.570	0.403	0.447	22.00	0.224	0.671	1.242	54.1
Japan*	JPY	67.728	0.560	2.540	0.021	8.00	0.046	0.067	0.627	10.8
Korea*	KRW	729.995	0.645	72.450	0.064	10.00	0.071	0.135	0.780	17.3
Latvia	EUR	0.471	0.523	0.057	0.063	21.00	0.123	0.187	0.710	26.3
Luxembourg*	EUR	0.362	0.402	0.010	0.011	14.00	0.058	0.069	0.471	14.6
Mexico*	MXN	See note								
Netherlands	EUR	0.184	0.204	0.490	0.544	21.00	0.157	0.701	0.905	77.4
New Zealand*	NZD	See note								
Norway	NOK	5.908	0.733	2.490	0.309	25.00	0.260	0.569	1.302	43.7
Poland	PLN	2.017	0.535	0.232	0.062	23.00	0.137	0.199	0.734	27.1
Portugal	EUR	0.463	0.514	0.343	0.380	13.00	0.116	0.497	1.011	49.1
Slovak Republic*	EUR	See note								
Slovenia	EUR	0.392	0.435	0.201	0.223	22.00	0.145	0.368	0.802	45.8
Spain*	EUR	0.316	0.350	0.088	0.097	21.00	0.094	0.191	0.541	35.3
Sweden*	SEK	See note								
Switzerland	CHF	0.498	0.518	0.163	0.170	8.00	0.055	0.225	0.743	30.2
Turkey	TRY	1.240	0.455	0.237	0.087	18.00	0.098	0.185	0.640	28.9
United Kingdom	GBP	0.281	0.430	0.111	0.170	20.00	0.120	0.290	0.720	40.2
United States*	USD	0.986	0.986	0.000	0.000	0.00	0.000	0.000	0.986	0.0

* See country notes in Box 4.A4.8.

Note: Conversion of national currency in USD: conversion rates are average market rates (2015) published in OECD Monthly Monetary Statistics (stats.oecd.org). See also Annex A.

1. Prices and taxes as at 4th quarter 2015.
2. Pre-tax price is the price excluding VAT and excise.
3. Excise taxes are expressed in local currency/USD per litre. They include all non-VAT taxes levied on the product. For the purposes of this table, payments made to specific bodies that use all the amounts collected to accomplish specific missions (e.g. some emergency stock fees) are not considered as "taxes" and are included in the ex-tax price. When different rates apply to the same product depending e.g. on its biofuel or sulphur content, the rate shown is the one applicable to the most commonly used fuel in the country.
4. GST for Australia and New Zealand, sales taxes for the United States and Consumption Tax for Japan. GST/HST and provincial sales taxes for Canada. VAT for all other countries.

Source: International Energy Agency, Energy Prices and Taxes and European Commission Excise Duty Tables Part II.

StatLink http://dx.doi.org/10.1787/888933420185

Box 4.A4.8. **Country notes**

Australia: No data is available.

Austria: Tax amount of EUR 0.098/l applies to light fuel oil with sulphur content ≤ 10mg/kg. Otherwise the excise duty is EUR 0.128/l.

Canada: Excise rates include provincial/urban taxes. There is no federal excise tax on diesel fuel used as heating oil in respect of buildings or for the generation of electricity unless the diesel fuel is used in or by a vehicle of any mode of transportation. The federal GST rate is 5%. The weighted VAT rate including provincial VAT rates was 10.46% on 1 January 2016 and the weighted VAT/sales tax rate was 9.05% The VAT rate will increase in three Canadian provinces during 2016.

Chile: Domestic Kerosene is covered weekly by the Oil Price Stabilisation Fund (Fondo de Estabilización de Precios del Petróleo, "FEPP") which applies a tax or a fiscal credit, measured in USD per m3. The tax is not included in the VAT base at any stage of the import, production, refining, distribution or sale to the consumer, and the fiscal credit is deductible from the taxable base on the first sale or importation.

Czech Republic: Fuel oil marked in accordance with Directive 95/60/EC is subject to reimbursement of an excise duty amount of CZK 10 290/1000l when it has been duly proved that the fuel oil has been used for heating purposes.

Denmark: The amount of DKK 2.667/l includes the Excise tax of DKK 2.215/l; the Environment tax of DKK 0.451/l and the NO_x tax of DKK 0.0009/l.

Finland: The excise amount of EUR 0.1874/l includes the Excise tax Energy/CO_2 tax (EUR 0.1839/l) and the Precautionary stock fee (EUR 0.00353/l).

Germany: The excise amount is for properly marked gas oil with a sulphur content ≤ 50mg/kg.

Greece: The excise of EUR 0.230/l for heating oil for households applies during the winter season (15 October-15 April). Otherwise the excise is 0.330/l.

Hungary: Market prices are not available in IEA/EU Statistics. Price data is extracted from economic information available on *http://countryeconomy.com/energy/prices-gasoline-gas-oil-heating/hungary*.

Iceland: No data is available

Ireland: The rate of 0.102/litre applies to marked gas oil (marked diesel). Marked kerosene is also widely used for heating (including domestic heating) and the rate for that is EUR 0.05073/litre.

Israel: The statistical data for Israel are supplied by and under the responsibility of the relevant Israeli authorities. The use of such data by the OECD is without prejudice to the status of the Golan Heights, East Jerusalem and Israeli settlements in the West Bank under the terms of international law.

Japan: Kerosene for households.

Korea: Kerosene for households

Luxembourg: A reduced VAT rate of 14% applies to heating gas oil.

Mexico: No data is available.

Netherlands: The amount of EUR 0.490/l excise includes the excise tax of 0.482/l and the stockpiling tax of 0.008/l.

New Zealand: No data is provided because the product is not consumed in significant quantities.

Norway: The amount of NOK 2.49/l includes base tax of NOK 1.59/l and CO_2 tax of NOK 0.90/l.

Slovak Republic: No data is provided because the product is not consumed in significant quantities.

Box 4.A4.8. **Country notes** *(cont.)*

Slovenia: The excise amount represents its average value in the 4th Quarter 2015.

Spain: The excise amount of EUR 0.088/l includes the Excise tax (EUR 0.085/l) and the average Regional authorities' tax (EUR 0.003/l).

Sweden: Price data are not available.

United States: Average federal and state taxes – there is no VAT.

European Union: Directive 93/2006/EC sets minimal excise rates for energy products and electricity.

Table 4.A4.9. **Excises (5121) as percentage of total taxation**

	1965	1975	1985	1990	1995	2000	2005	2010	2011	2012	2013	2014
Australia	15.5	11.8	13.9	10.3	9.4	9.2	7.6	7.4	6.7	6.3	6.1	5.5
Austria	9.8	7.9	7.0	6.1	6.1	6.1	6.4	5.8	5.9	5.7	5.5	5.3
Belgium	8.3	6.6	4.7	4.9	5.3	5.1	5.3	5.0	4.8	4.6	4.5	4.6
Canada	9.8	6.3	7.9	5.9	5.6	4.7	4.9	4.5	4.3	4.2	4.1	4.1
Chile				9.3	7.9	10.3	7.8	7.1	6.8	6.8	7.3	7.6
Czech Republic					9.8	9.3	9.8	10.8	11.2	11.1	10.7	8.7
Denmark	26.3	13.8	12.0	10.0	10.7	11.1	10.3	9.1	9.1	9.1	9.1	8.2
Estonia					7.5	9.5	12.2	12.6	13.5	13.9	13.3	13.0
Finland	13.4	11.5	12.0	9.8	9.9	9.0	8.6	8.2	8.8	8.8	8.5	8.3
France	10.8	6.5	6.2	6.2	6.7	6.2	5.7	5.4	5.4	5.3	5.4	5.4
Germany	11.1	8.8	6.8	6.9	7.1	7.5	8.4	7.0	6.9	6.5	6.3	6.1
Greece	17.3	13.6	14.4	12.0	14.4	8.9	8.2	10.0	11.1	10.4	10.6	10.6
Hungary					10.0	10.4	9.7	9.2	9.4	9.3	8.7	8.4
Iceland	1.1	3.0	6.0	2.0	8.9	9.3	9.2	8.6	8.6	8.6	8.2	7.4
Ireland	39.2	26.0	19.0	17.0	15.0	13.2	10.7	10.7	10.4	9.9	9.9	9.3
Israel[1]					3.4	3.5	4.5	5.8	5.5	5.5	5.2	5.0
Italy	14.8	10.2	5.8	7.7	7.9	6.3	5.6	5.4	6.0	6.6	6.5	6.9
Japan	17.2	11.3	10.5	6.6	7.4	7.2	6.9	6.5	6.4	6.2	6.0	5.3
Korea		22.0	13.7	13.2	13.5	13.3	12.0	10.6	7.9	8.3	8.0	7.7
Latvia					6.6	11.6	12.6	12.8	12.4	11.5	11.4	11.2
Luxembourg	9.8	7.3	10.3	9.9	11.9	12.2	11.8	9.3	9.4	9.1	8.4	8.3
Mexico			11.4	9.9	10.9	10.3	4.6	4.6	4.6	4.5	4.4	6.0
Netherlands	8.1	6.3	5.4	5.7	7.7	8.3	8.8	8.1	7.9	7.5	7.3	7.2
New Zealand	12.4	9.4	7.4	7.0	5.8	5.4	3.9	2.9	2.8	2.7	2.5	2.6
Norway	13.9	10.3	14.5	12.4	12.5	8.7	7.4	7.0	6.6	6.3	6.4	6.5
Poland					12.0	11.0	13.0	13.2	12.7	12.4	12.5	12.0
Portugal	15.2	13.0	16.1	13.8	14.7	11.3	11.9	10.4	9.4	8.9	8.1	8.2
Slovak Republic					8.7	9.1	11.5	10.2	9.9	9.6	8.9	8.5
Slovenia					..	8.4	9.0	11.6	11.5	12.3	12.0	11.7
Spain	5.6	2.2	5.4	5.8	7.7	7.5	6.4	6.6	6.4	6.3	6.9	6.8
Sweden	14.9	8.8	9.4	7.3	7.2	6.0	6.1	6.0	5.8	5.7	5.5	5.2
Switzerland	9.0	7.7	6.8	1.8	1.8	5.4	5.1	5.2	4.8	4.9	4.7	4.7
Turkey	23.2	17.6	3.8	0.9	1.0	11.7	21.2	19.9	17.8	18.3	18.6	18.1
United Kingdom	21.8	12.7	11.2	9.7	11.3	10.5	8.8	8.9	8.5	8.5	8.2	8.1
United States	12.7	7.6	6.2	4.2	4.6	3.7	3.9	4.1	4.0	4.0	3.6	3.4
Unweighted average[2]												
OECD-Average	**14.2**	**10.5**	**9.5**	**8.0**	**8.3**	**8.6**	**8.6**	**8.3**	**8.1**	**8.0**	**7.8**	**7.6**

1. **Israel:** The statistical data for Israel are supplied by and under the responsibility of the relevant Israeli authorities. The use of such data by the OECD is without prejudice to the status of the Golan Heights, East Jerusalem and Israeli settlements in the West Bank under the terms of international law.
2. **Unweighted averages:** All member counties are taken into account for the calculation of the unweighted averages, including countries that had not implemented the relevant taxes for the year considered. They are counted with a value of zero in the numerator and 1 in the denominator. However, countries that did not exist at the time considered (Czech and Slovak Republics before 1993; Slovenia before 1991) are not included in the calculation of the averages. Are also excluded from the calculation of the averages the countries for which no data is available for the time considered (Chile before 1990, Estonia, Hungary and Israel before 1995, Korea before 1975; Mexico before 1980; Poland before 1995; and Slovak Republic before 2000).

Source: OECD Revenue Statistics 2016 (1965-2015).

StatLink http://dx.doi.org/10.1787/888933420194

Chapter 5

Taxing vehicles

This chapter describes the main features of vehicle taxes and their use for influencing customer behaviour over the last decades, in particular within the context of environmental policies. It looks in more detail at the taxes on sale and registration of vehicles and recurrent taxes on use of motor vehicles and their components and provides comparative statistics on the level of these taxes.

The statistical data for Israel are supplied by and under the responsibility of the relevant Israeli authorities. The use of such data by the OECD is without prejudice to the status of the Golan Heights, East Jerusalem and Israeli settlements.

5.1. Introduction

Taxes on vehicles were introduced in most OECD countries in the first half of the 20th century and have become an important source of tax revenue for most governments. All member countries rely heavily on a range of tax instruments to ensure significant budgetary receipts from both private and commercial road users. Vehicle taxation in its widest definition represents a prime example of the use of the whole spectrum of consumption taxes including VAT, specific and *ad valorem* taxes. For more than fifteen years, these taxes have been adapted to influence consumer behaviour, mainly to achieve environmental objectives.

Taxes and charges on vehicles include:

- Taxes on the purchase (including VAT and retail sales taxes) and registration of motor vehicles, payable once at the time of acquisition, or first putting into service, of a vehicle (see Table 5.A5.1).
- Periodic taxes payable in connection with the ownership or use of the vehicles (see Table 5.A5.2).
- Taxes on fuels (see Tables 4.A4.6 and 4.A4.7 in Chapter 4).
- Any other taxes and charges that are directly or indirectly connected with the use or ownership of vehicles, such as insurance taxes, road tolls, congestion charges, company car taxation, etc.

The sale and use of motor vehicles generate considerable VAT or sales tax revenues. These taxes are levied on the import and sale of vehicles (in the latter case by application to the full selling price or, for used cars, in respect of the margin between the buying and the selling price). VAT or sales tax will generally also apply to general maintenance and running costs. In addition, they are levied in most cases on the final duty-paid value (e.g. VAT on fuel is levied on the excise-inclusive price See Tables 4.A4.6 and 4.A4.7).

Taxes on vehicles reflect a variety of influences beyond the obvious need to raise revenue. Geographic, industrial, social, energy, transport and environmental policy considerations have all had an influence on the level and structure of taxation. Most of them (except more recent pollution-related taxes) were instituted in a time when cars were considered luxury items. Wider ownership of cars in recent decades has reduced the progressivity of those taxes (many low income households have at least one car today). In most cases current taxation schemes are used to influence consumer or business behaviour. More recently, energy and environmental considerations have led to an adjustment of taxation according to the fuel efficiency of vehicles, CO_2 and other polluting emissions, town planning and transport policies, including the introduction of road or urban tolls.

In most countries total taxes on vehicles result from a combination of one-off (on purchase or import) and recurrent (on ownership or use) taxes as well as from a mix between *ad valorem* (on the price) and specific taxes (taking into account polluting emissions, weight, engine power, number of axles, age, fuel efficiency, equipment, suspension, cylinder capacity, number of seats, type of fuel, electric propulsion and distance covered).

Although this chapter only focuses on taxes on sale/registration and use of motor vehicles (Tables 5.A5.1 and 5.A5.2), these taxes should not be regarded in isolation from other tax bases and rates. A number of other elements should also be taken into consideration such as insurance premium taxes, specific road tolls (bridge of motorway tolls), fuel taxes (see Chapter 4), energy taxes and a number of direct tax components such as the personal tax treatment of company cars (Harding, 2014).

5.2. Car taxation and polluting emissions

Governments have developed policies for reducing motor vehicle pollution for about forty years by imposing technical norms to the car industry. For example, in the European Union (EU) polluting emissions have been regulated since 1970 and a series of amendments have been issued since then to gradually tighten the limit values. The current norms set maximum emissions of carbon monoxide (CO), Volatile Organic Compounds (VOC), nitrogen oxides (NO_x) and particles. It resulted in the Euro 6 (setting lower emission limits for the registration and sale of new types of cars and vans as of 1 September 2015) and in the Euro VI standards for heavy duty vehicles. Emissions of carbon dioxide (CO_2) have also been targeted by the European Commission since 2007 and the EU has put in place a comprehensive legal framework to reduce CO_2 emissions from new light duty vehicles as part of efforts to ensure it meets its greenhouse gas emission reduction targets under the Kyoto Protocol and beyond. As a result of EU regulation (510/2011), the EU car manufacturers' fleet average has to be aligned with 130g CO_2/km as of 2015 and the intention is to reduce the fleet average emission to 95 grams of CO_2/km in 2021. Norms for heavy-duty vehicles (busses, trucks, etc.) will in principle also be developed as part of a comprehensive strategy to reduce CO_2 emissions.

Taxation is increasingly used to influence customer behaviour and encourage the purchase of low polluting vehicles. In 2016, more than three quarters (29 out of 35) of OECD member countries apply lower taxes or exemptions on purchase or use/ownership for vehicles according to environmental or fuel efficiency criteria (see Tables 5.A5.1 and 5.A5.2). Amongst them, 22 base purchase or annual taxes directly on polluting emissions (for example, the level of CO, CO_2, NO_x or particulate matter per kilometre) and 19 have tax rebates or exemptions for electric or hybrid vehicles. A number of EU Member States use the polluting emission norms set by the European Directives (see paragraph above) as a benchmark for their vehicle taxes although there is currently no European rule regarding car taxation.

Differentiating motor vehicle purchase taxes according to the fuel-efficiency or the polluting emissions can give potential vehicle purchasers an immediate incentive to buy a vehicle that causes relatively few emissions. Differentiation in purchase or annual registration charges on motor vehicles may also provide such an incentive, but somewhat less directly. Very high registration taxes are also likely to reduce the number of new motor vehicles purchase. However, while this would at first appear to favour environmental policy, higher purchase taxes on vehicles can cause some purchasers to defer their purchase or to purchase a used vehicle, increasing the population of older, more polluting, cars. By making assumptions regarding how far a vehicle is driven over its lifetime, one can also calculate tax rates expressed per tonne CO_2 each vehicle will emit over its lifetime. Comparisons make it clear that the tax rates applied per tonne CO_2 emitted over a vehicle's lifetime vary significantly between countries (for an in-depth study on this topic see OECD 2009).

5.3. Taxes on purchase and registration of motor vehicles

Taxes on the acquisition and registration of motor vehicles may include VAT, sales taxes, excise duties and other fees and charges associated with the registration of a vehicle. These taxes may vary considerably from one country to another (see Table 5.A5.1). They are based on a large diversity of criteria or a combination of these criteria. There are five main criteria against which the tax can be assessed:

- The price or value of the vehicle.
- The engine power or cylinder capacity.
- Environmental impact (fuel consumption, polluting emissions, the type of fuel used).
- Social considerations: exemptions for emergency vehicles, ambulances, vehicles for disabled people, vehicles for public transport, etc.
- The use of the vehicle (specific criteria apply to commercial vehicles such as number of axles, cargo room, number of seats, etc.).

A number of specific elements can further be taken in consideration for assessing the tax burden such as weight, presence of safety equipment or of air conditioning. Taxation is also adjusted according to the age of the vehicle in several countries and a specific tax applies on tyres in the United States.

The burden of these taxes may vary considerably from one country to another and sometimes between states, provinces, cities or regions in several countries. For example, a VAT rate of 8% and a 3% acquisition tax apply in Japan while a 25% VAT and a 150% registration tax applies in Denmark.

Unlike many other products, the international differences in taxation of sale and registration of motor vehicles do not give rise to cross-border shopping as motor vehicles need to be registered with a unique identification number in the principal country of use. Similarly VAT levied on the importation (or on the "acquisition" of the vehicle within the EU) will generally be due in the country of registration. Even in the integrated market of the EU there has been no harmonisation or even approximation of taxes or tax rates on motor vehicles.

Nevertheless, motor vehicle taxation can affect the functioning of the motor vehicle market. This may notably be the case for registration taxes. Generally, registration tax paid in the country of first registration is not paid back when a car is transferred from one country to another (e.g. when the owner moves from one country to another). When registration tax has to be paid (again) in the country of destination where the car is to remain permanently, double taxation occurs. In addition, large differences in tax systems reinforce car market fragmentation. Cars marketed in one country with specifications designed to meet the national tax structure (e.g. brackets of fiscal horsepower, tax policy regarding diesel) are imperfect substitutes and may not effectively compete with cars sold in another country with different tax requirements. Also pre-tax prices appear to be influenced by tax considerations. Significant tax differentials may encourage consumers in some cases to buy cars in countries where registration taxes are very high and where car manufacturers tend to offer lower prices net of taxes by compensation and import and register them in their own country. This may undermine the benefits that should derive from a competitive market for both consumers and industry.

5.4. Periodic taxes in connection with ownership or use of motor vehicles

Taxes on the use of vehicles include recurring charges levied on the right to drive on public roads, usually in the form of an annual motor tax (see Table 5.A5.2). Taxes on the operation of motor vehicles also include excise duties on fuel (see Chapter 4) and motorway charges or other road user tolls and motor fuel taxation. Recurring taxes on the ownership of motor vehicles can take many forms. The main elements used to assess these kinds of taxes are very similar to those used for assessing taxes on sale and registration such as use (commercial or not), vehicle type, type of fuel, engine size, age, emissions of pollutants and fuel efficiency.

References

Barde, J.P. and N.A. Braathen, (2005), "Environmentally Related Taxes" in *Theory and Practice of Excise Taxation*, ed. Sijbren Cnossen, 120-54. Oxford, United Kingdom.

European Commission (2005), *Proposal for a Council Directive on passenger car related taxes*, COM(2005)261final, Brussels.

Harding, M. (2014), "Personal Tax Treatment of Company Cars and Commuting Expenses: Estimating the Fiscal and Environmental Costs", OECD Taxation Working Papers, No. 20, OECD Publishing, Paris. *http://dx.doi.org/10.1787/5jz14cg1s7vl-en.*

OECD (2009), *Incentives for CO_2 Emissions Reductions in Current Motor Vehicle Taxes*, OECD Publishing, Paris *www.oecd.org/officialdocuments/publicdisplaydocumentpdf/?cote=env/epoc/wpnep/t(2009)2/final&doclanguage=en.*

Motor Vehicle Taxes Database (*www.oecd.org/env/policies/database*).

ANNEX 5.A5

Data on car taxation

Table 5.A5.1. **Taxes on sale and registration of motor vehicles**[1]

Pays	Taxes	Criteria	Rebates/Exemptions
Australia	**GST:** 10% **Luxury Car Tax:** 33% calculated on the value of the car that exceeds the luxury car tax threshold. The luxury car tax threshold is AUD 64 132 (in 2016-17), tax inclusive (including GST). **Registration fee** calculated on the tare weight of the vehicle. **Stamp duty** calculated on the value of the vehicle.	Value Weight	Emergency vehicles such as ambulances and fire engines. Vehicles modified to suit the transportation of eligible people with disabilities. Luxury Car Tax: Eligible fuel efficient cars are subject to a higher threshold known as the "fuel efficient car limit", AUD 75 375, tax inclusive for the 2013-14 financial year. Exemptions apply for emergency vehicles, vehicles modified to transport a person in a wheelchair (provided it is not GST-free), commercial vehicles primarily used for carrying goods in business or trade. Eligible tourism operators and primary producers are eligible to claim a refund of LCT paid up to AUD 3 000 for certain cars. GST: exemption is provided to veterans and persons with a disability that fulfil legal requirements.
Austria	**VAT:** 20%. **New Car Registration Tax:** while the tax base is the selling price, the tax rate depends on the CO_2-emissions of the car: (CO_2 emissions in gram/km, reduced by 90 grams), divided by 5. The rate cannot exceed 32% (which corresponds to 250g CO_2/km). For CO_2 emissions above 250g/km, the tax increases by 20 EUR for each g/km exceeding the limit of 250g/km. An amount of up to 300 EUR (no bonus possible) has to be deducted from the amount of tax calculated following the above rules. **Registration fee (tax):** fixed rate for motor vehicles registered for the state or local authorities EUR 119.80 per motor vehicle (+ up to 45 Euro processing fee for the registration office + approx. EUR 20 for other expenditures).	Value CO_2 emissions	Exemptions for demonstration vehicles, motor vehicles for driving schools, vehicles that are hired, used for guests or as taxis, motor vehicles used for short time hiring out, motor vehicles used for the transport of sick persons and for rescue services, vehicles used for the transport of corpses, vehicles used by fire brigades and accompanying vehicles for special transports. Registration fee: motor vehicles registered for the state or local authorities.
Belgium	**VAT:** 21% **Entry into Service Tax** *Federal tax:* a company car tax is based on CO_2 emissions. The deductibility of expenses, except for fuel costs, related to the use of the car (50 to 120%) is linked to CO_2 emissions. *Flemish Region:* the tax rate depends on engine power, vehicle age and environmental characteristics. It is set according to a progressive scale from EUR 41.99 to EUR 10 497.70, subject to indexation and modified on July 1st of each year according to inflation. *Walloon Region:* the tax rate depends on engine power and is set according to a degressive scale based on the age of the vehicle. For motorcycles the amount is calculated with respect to the kilowatt. For electric cars, the nominal continuous power is taken into account. If the engine power corresponds to different amounts expressed in h.p. than in kilowatt, the highest amount has to be taken into consideration. *Brussels Capital Region:* the tax rate depends on engine power and is set according to a degressive scale based on the age of the vehicle (fuel and gasoil from EUR 61.50 to EUR 4.957 and Liquefied Gas Petroleum from EUR 61.50 to EUR 4.659).	Value Age Engine power CO_2 emissions Type of fuel/gas Bonus/malus	*Flemish Region:* exemption for certain fuel types (pure electric, hydrogen-powered, plug-in hybrid (until 2021), powered by CNG/LNG (until 2021). Rebate (EUR 298.00) for cars running with Liquefied Gas Petroleum or other Gas Exemption for disabled people and for utility vehicles Exemption of the additional annual tax for utility vehicles. Rebate (EUR 298.00) for cars running with Liquefied Gas Petroleum or other Gas. *Walloon Region:* Cars emitting 145g CO_2/km and more pay a penalty with a maximum of EUR 2 500 for cars emitting more than 255g CO_2/km. The penalty is reduced when the beneficiary has at least 3 dependent children (< 25y or > 25 if legally considered a minor) or for cars with gas-powered engines. For certain categories of old-timers and for cars owned by leasing companies the bonus/penalty is reduced to 0. Exemption from the eco-malus for utility cars. *Brussels Capital Region:* exemption for disabled persons. Rebate (EUR 298) for cars running with Liquefied Gas Petroleum or other Gas.

Table 5.A5.1. **Taxes on sale and registration of motor vehicles**[1] *(cont.)*

Pays	Taxes	Criteria	Rebates/Exemptions
Canada	**GST:** 5% **HST:** 13%, 14% or 15% for sales in the participating provinces. The following provinces have harmonized their provincial sales taxes with the federal Goods and Services Tax and therefore levy a rate of GST/HST of: New Brunswick, Newfoundland and Labrador, Ontario: 13%; Prince Edward Island: 14%; Nova Scotia 15%, Québec applies GST at a rate of 5% and Québec Sales Tax at a rate of 9.975%. **Provincial tax rates** are applicable for sales made in provinces not applying HST. **Automotive Air Conditioning Tax:** CAD 100 per unit. **Tax on Fuel Inefficient Vehicles:** vehicles with a weighted fuel consumption rating of 13 or more litres per 100 kilometres (55% city and 45% highway) are subject to an excise tax at the following rates: – at least 13 but less than 14 litres per 100 kilometres, CAD 1 000; – at least 14 but less than 15 litres per 100 kilometres, CAD 2 000; – at least 15 but less than 16 litres per 100 kilometres, CAD 3 000; and – 16 or more litres per 100 kilometres, CAD 4 000.	Value Fuel efficiency Air conditioning	**Rebate of GST/HST – Specially Equipped Motor Vehicle:** to purchasers of specially equipped motor vehicles for persons with disabilities. The rebate is only available on the GST/HST paid on the portion of the purchase price that is attributable to the special features. **Rebate of Excise Tax on Fuel Inefficient Vehicles – Specially Equipped Van:** to end-users of vans equipped with a device designed exclusively to assist in placing a wheelchair in the van without having to collapse the wheelchair.
Chile	**VAT:** 19% (used cars are exempt with some exceptions). **Registration fees payable to Civil Registry:** first registration fee, new plate fee, fee for transfer and registration of vehicles. **Tax on transfer of used motor vehicles (levied by municipalities):** 1.5% of the value of the vehicle.	Value Fixed fee	-
Czech Republic	**VAT:** 21% **Registration fee:** motorcycles CZK 300 or 500 (depending on cylinder capacity); Other motor vehicles CZK 800. The fee includes the registration plate. Permit fee on non-standard motor vehicles.	Value Cylinder capacity	
Denmark	**VAT:** 25% **Vehicle registration tax:** payable on first registration of the vehicle. Graduated tax rates according to the value of the vehicle (with lower rates for commercial vehicles) from 105% to 150% (on the remainder above DKK 82 800) for private vehicles and from 0% to 50% (on the remainder above DKK 17 500) for commercial vehicles.	Value Utilisation Safety equipment Anti-pollution equipment	**Rebate for low fuel consumption vehicles:** Registration tax is reduced by DKK 4 000 for every kilometre the vehicle can run in excess of 16 km with 1 litre of petrol or in excess of 18 km with 1 litre of diesel. A supplement of DKK 1 000 is payable for cars for every kilometre less than 16 km (petrol) or 18 km (diesel) they can run on one litre of fuel. **Traffic Safety Equipment:** Motor vehicles with major traffic safety equipment receive a deduction in the value liable to registration duty up to DKK 13 370. Motor vehicles with minor traffic safety equipment receive a deduction between DKK 200 and DKK 600.
Estonia	**VAT:** 20% **Vehicle registration fee (State fee):** Vehicle – EUR 130; Temporarily imported vehicle – EUR 335.	Value Type of vehicle	

Table 5.A5.1. **Taxes on sale and registration of motor vehicles**[1] *(cont.)*

Pays	Taxes	Criteria	Rebates/Exemptions
Finland	**VAT:** 24% **Vehicle Registration Tax** is based on CO_2 emissions. Rates vary from 4.4% of the general consumer price of the vehicle for cars emitting 0g/km or less to 50% for cars emitting 360g/km or more. **For delivery vans** there is a deduction based on maximum laden weight of the vehicle for vans over 2 500 kg. **For motor cycles** varies according to the cylinder capacity, between 9.8% and 24.4%, and the base is general retail value.	Value CO_2 emissions Utilisation Cylinder capacity Type	**Exemption** for disabled people, taxis, motor homes, cars used for veterinary purposes, rescue vehicles and funeral cars.
France	**VAT:** 20% **Tax on Registration Certificates** or regional tax on certificates is based on engine power and CO_2 emissions. Rates vary between EUR 27 and EUR 46 per horsepower according to the region. CO_2 Emission component of the tax varies from EUR 0 for vehicles emitting less than 160g CO_2/km to EUR 2600 for vehicles emitting more than 250g CO_2/km. The rate is reduced by half for some vehicles depending on their nature (trucks weighing more than 3.5 tons, motorcycles) or age (more than 10 years old). **Additional Lorries Tax** is levied on the regional certificate tax for lorries according to their weight (from EUR 38 for less than 3.5 tons to EUR 305 for more than 11 tons or trailers and buses for public transport of passengers). **Company car tax** is based on CO_2 emissions. Tax rates vary from EUR 2 for each gram emitted for cars emitting 100g CO_2/km or less to EUR 19 for each gram emitted for cars emitting more than 250g CO_2/km.	Value Engine power Weight Utilisation Age CO_2 emissions Type of fuel Electric propulsion Bonus-malus	**Exemption for new demonstration models** weighing less than 3.5 tons, state vehicles, certain motorcycles **Rebate for electricity or gas propelled cars:** from 50% to 100% of the Tax on Registration Certificates. **Rebate for Ethanol propelled cars:** the Tax on Registration Certificates is reduced by 50% for cars that run with E85 fuel (super ethanol). **Bonus-malus system:** a premium is granted for the purchase of a new car when its CO_2 emissions are 125 g/km or less. The maximum premium is EUR 5000 (below 60 g/km). A malus is payable for the purchase of a car emitting more than 155 g CO_2/km. The maximum tax amounts to EUR 2.600 (above 245 g/km).
Germany	**VAT:** 19%	Value	
Greece	**VAT:** 23% **Registration tax:** rate varies. From 5% to 346% of the taxable value (wholesale price) for passenger cars according to cylinder capacity and anti-polluting technology (polluting emissions). From 5% – 26% of the taxable value for lorries – trucks etc. according to cylinder capacity and mass (less or more than 3.5 tons). Rates are increased by 30% for vehicles that do not meet EU Directives'/Regulations' emissions requirements. From 0% to 25% of the taxable value for motorcycles according to cylinder capacity. **Registration tax for buses** depends on the number of seats. **Luxury tax:** rate varies from 10% to 40% according to taxable value.	Value Weight Cylinder capacity Polluting emissions Number of seats Electric propulsion	**Exemptions from registration tax:** Cars used by public authorities. Cars with hybrid motor technology or those with electric motors. Cars used by disabled persons. Cars used by parents having at least three (3) children. Ambulances used by public hospitals. Cars used by people who have moved their normal residence to Greece. Cars donated to the Greek Police, Fire Brigade or Greek Coast Guards. **Exemptions from luxury tax:** Taxis, caravans, ambulances, hearses, cars with electric motors. Cars used by disabled persons having complete paralysis of the lower limbs with disability percentage of 80% or 100% and disabled persons having ambilateral amputation of their lower limbs. Cars donated to the Greek Police, Fire Brigade or Greek Coast Guards.

Table 5.A5.1. **Taxes on sale and registration of motor vehicles**[1] *(cont.)*

Pays	Taxes	Criteria	Rebates/Exemptions
Hungary	**VAT:** 27% **Registration Tax**: from HUF 45 000 to HUF 400 000 on new passenger cars according to engine type (diesel or petrol) and engine cylinder capacity, and from HUF 20 000 to HUF 230 000 on motorcycles according to engine cylinder capacity. For cars with lower environmental category of engine higher rates are levied (400, 600, 800 or 1200% higher), but rate is reduced according to a scale based on age (until 90%). Reduced rate is levied to hybrid cars and HUF 0 is levied to electric cars. **Transfer of motor vehicles:** the rate of duty shall be determined based on the capacity of motor vehicle's engine (in kW). The tax rate is from HUF 300/kW to HUF 850/kW depending on the age of the vehicle (the older the vehicle, the less is due).	Engine type Cylinder capacity Engine power Polluting emissions Type of fuel Age Electric propulsion	**Reduced registration tax** for cars with hybrid engines or with gas-powered engines (HUF 76 000) and for cars with electric engines (HUF 0).
Iceland	**VAT:** 24% **Vehicle Registration Fee** of ISK 15 000 on initial registration and ISK 2 630 for subsequent changes. **Motor vehicle excise duty:** based on CO_2 emissions ranging from 0-65%. **Excise duties on motor vehicles other than private automobiles** Large goods vehicles, large special purpose vehicles, tractors, agriculture trailers, large snow-mobiles, amphibious vehicles, competition cars and motorbikes, vehicles for transport of disabled persons, rescue vehicles and large coaches is none. Small goods vehicles, small special purpose vehicles, vehicles over 40 years old, motor vehicle bodies 13%. Small coaches, motorbikes, other vehicles 30%.	Value CO_2 emissions Electric propulsion	**Temporary VAT exemption** at import and domestic sales of electric-, hydrogen or plug-in hybrid vehicles.
Ireland	**VAT:** 23% **Registration Tax**: the registration tax is based on CO_2 emissions. Rates vary from 14% of the value of the car for cars with CO_2 emissions of up to 80 g/km to 36% for cars with CO_2 emissions above 225 g/km. Specific rate applies to vehicles designed and constructed for the carriage of goods and having a maximum mass not exceeding 3.5 tonnes with more than 3 seats and motor caravans (13.30% of the value with a minimum of EUR 125); new motor cycles and used motor cycles (EUR 2 per cc up to and EUR 1 per cc above 350cc); commercial vehicles and "vintage" (over 30 years old) vehicles (EUR 200).	Value CO_2 emissions Type Age Type of fuel Electric propulsion	**Relief for hybrid electric vehicles:** with a maximum tax relief of EUR 1500. **Relief for plug-in hybrid electric vehicles:** with a maximum tax relief of EUR 2500. **Relief for series production electric vehicles:** subject to a maximum of EUR 5000. **Remission/repayment for vehicles specially adapted for disabled persons** subject to a maximum of EUR 10 000, EUR 16 00 and EUR 22 000 for a disabled driver and EUR 16 000 and EUR 22 000 for a disabled passenger. The amount is depended on the adaptations carried out on the vehicle.
Israel[2]	**VAT:** 17% **Purchase Tax**: Private and commercial vehicle weight not exceeding 3500 kg are taxed at 83% of the value; Additional luxury tax is levied on the value of the vehicle that exceeds 300 000 NIS, according to the following formula: 20%* (vehicle price – 300 000)/vehicle price; Taxi < 3 500 kg – 8%; Taxi > 3 500 kg – 0%; Commercial vehicles over 3500 kg are taxed at 72% of their value but not eligible for a grant.	Weight Polluting emissions Power Electric propulsion	**Rebates according to the polluting emissions:** vehicles weighing up to 3500 kg benefit of a rebate on the Purchase Tax according to their degree of pollution. There are 15 levels of polluting emissions that are set by a "Green Score" (weighting the emission of five major pollutants). Rebate is up to the amount of 16 384 NIS. **Hybrid vehicles** – Pollution level 1 or 2 – 1. battery capacity > 3 KWH and green score < 100 – 20% 2. others are taxed at a rate of 30%. **Electricity powered vehicles** are taxed a rate of 10% of their value depending on the customs and purchase tax rate. There is no luxury tax on hybrid vehicles and electronic vehicles.

Table 5.A5.1. **Taxes on sale and registration of motor vehicles**[1] *(cont.)*

Pays	Taxes	Criteria	Rebates/Exemptions
Italy	**VAT:** 22% **Registration Tax** (IPT): EUR 151 for cars < 53 kw , EUR 3.5 per kw for cars > 53 kW. For other vehicles, such as, for instance, buses, tractors and lorries with trailer, the tax is determined on the basis of their engine power, weight, number of seats or other criteria. Provinces may increase the rate up to a maximum of 30%.	Vehicle Type Engine power Polluting emissions Weight Number of seats	**Rebate for disabled people, voluntary associations, motorcycles, sale of used cars by private individual to car dealers:** 100% relief of the Registration Tax. Reduced registration tax: historic and special vehicles.
Japan	**VAT:** 8% **Automobile Acquisition Tax (Prefecture):** 3% of purchase price (2% for commercial and light vehicles).	Value	Special measures of reduced automobile acquisition tax. Vehicles with small burden of environment, barrier-free buses and taxis, trucks with collision damage alleviation brake control device, etc., buses for ordinary passengers used on the bus routes provided for in prefectural ordinance.
Korea	**VAT:** 10% **Special Excise Tax:** from zero to 5% of the manufacturer's price according to cylinder capacity. **Education Tax:** 30% on the amount of Excise Tax. **Acquisition Tax:** 2-7% of the retail price excluding VAT.	Value Cylinder capacity Electric propulsion	**Exemptions from special excise tax and education tax:** – Cars used by disabled persons. – Ambulances used by hospitals. – Cars used for transportation business(public passenger transportation only). – Cars used for car-rental business. **Exemptions from acquisition tax:** – Cars used by disabled persons. – Cars used by parents having at least 3 children. – Small cars for non-commercial activities. **Rebate for hybrid and electricity powered vehicles:** relief of the Special excise tax (not exceed KRW 1 000 000(hybrid), KRW 2 000 000(electricity powered)).
Latvia	**VAT 21%** **Registration Tax:** for passenger cars from 2009 is based on CO_2 emissions. The lowest rate EUR 0.43 for each gram CO_2 per km (CO_2 emissions up to 120 g CO_2/km) and the highest EUR 7.11 for each gram CO_2 per km if CO_2 emissions exceed 350 g CO_2/km. Passenger cars registered before 2009 is taxed depending on age of vehicle and motor capacity. Registration tax for motorcycles is EUR 0.14 per each cc of motor capacity.	CO_2 emissions Age of vehicle Motor capacity Electric propulsion	**Exemptions form registration tax:** – cars and motorcycles that are older than 25 years; – cars with an electric motor (electromobiles); – special passenger cars (for example, ambulances, motor caravans, hearses); – cars that are specially equipped for carrying disabled persons in wheelchairs.
Luxembourg	**VAT:** 17% **Registration Tax:** the tax is calculated per 100 cm^3 according to the following formula: Tax = a * b * c, where a = CO_2 emissions component; b = multiplier (= 0.9 for cars using gasoil & 0.6 for cars not using gasoil). c= additional multiplier when CO_2 emissions > 90 g/km (= 0.5 plus 0.1 per additional 10 g/km).	Value CO_2 Emissions Type of fuel Electric propulsion	**Bonus system:** purchasers of new hybrid cars emitting less than 60g CO_2/km and electricity powered vehicles are entitled to a bonus of EUR 5 000.
Mexico	**VAT:** 16% **New vehicles tax:** from 2% to 17% plus a no movable fee according to vehicle value. For vehicles whose price is higher than MXN 660 255.71 (for 2016), there is an additional discount consisting in the reduction of the tax according to the 7% of the difference between the sales price and the threshold mentioned above. The update of the limits of the tax tariff is made every year.	Value Electric propulsion	Exemption of 100% in New Vehicles Tax to vehicles with value up to MXN 222 032.19. Exemption of 50% in New Vehicles Tax to vehicles with value from MXN 222 032.20 to MXN 281 240.78. Exemption of 100% in New Vehicles Tax for hybrid electricity powered vehicles.

Table 5.A5.1. **Taxes on sale and registration of motor vehicles**[1] *(cont.)*

Pays	Taxes	Criteria	Rebates/Exemptions
Netherlands	**VAT:** 21% **Registration Tax:** for passenger cars, it is fully based on CO_2 emissions and the type of motor fuel used. Vehicles with a CO_2 emission of 0g/km are in any case exempt from the registration tax. For passenger cars, the registration tax is progressive and varies between EUR 175 and EUR 478 per g/km exceeding the level of 1g/km. Passenger cars using diesel are charged with an additional EUR 86.43 per g/km exceeding the level of 67 g/km. Registration tax for motorcycles and delivery vans is based on the value of the vehicle.	CO_2 Emissions Motor fuel Value Electric propulsion	**Zero-emission (e.g. electricity powered vehicles)** are exempt from Registration Tax **Other examples of exemption are:** delivery vans owned by entrepreneurs and used for business purposes for at least 10%;. **Tax refunds are provided for vehicles such as**: vehicles used by fire brigades, vehicles used by the police, funerary vehicles, vehicles used for the transport of prisoners, vans used by disabled persons, (animal) ambulances, taxis and vehicles that are used for secure transport.
New Zealand	**GST:** 15% **Registration Fee** on initial registration: rates vary depending on the cylinder capacity and type of vehicle and whether registration is f or 6 months or a year. For private passenger, petrol driven cars this ranges from NZD 291.08 to NZD 462.30.	Value Cylinder capacity	
Norway	**VAT:** 25% **Registration Tax**: rates vary according to weight, engine performance (KW), CO_2.emissions and NO_x- emissions. When CO_2.emissions information is not stated, the tax is calculated based on cylinder capacity instead of CO_2.emissions.	Weight Engine performance CO_2 emissions NO_x emissions Type of fuel Electric propulsion	**Electricity powered vehicles** are exempt from Registration Tax. **Hybrid vehicles** (both electric and combustion engine) have a rebate. The engine performance of the electric engine and 10 pct. of the total weight are not included in the tax base. For plug-in hybrid cars the weight deduction is 26%. **Flexifuel vehicles** (can use fuel with at least 85 pct. ethanol) have a rebate of 10 000 NOK per vehicle.
Poland	**VAT:** 23% **Excise-Duty** is levied on passenger cars prior to their first registration due to their sale, intra-community acquisition and import. The excise tax rates for personal cars depend on engine capacity and amount to: – for passenger cars with engine cubic capacity over 2000 cm^3 – 18.6%, – for others – 3.1%.	Value Cylinder capacity	
Portugal	**VAT:** 23% **Vehicle excise duty** varies according to the following formula and rates, Cylinder capacity x rate – fixed rebate (as at 31 March 2016). Vehicles up to 1000 cc = number of cc x EUR 0.95 – EUR 737.00. Vehicles from 1001 to 1250 cc = number of cc x EUR 1.03 – EUR 740.55. Vehicles above 1250 = number of cc x EUR 4.84 – EUR 5 362.67. There are other rate brackets for light commercial vehicles and some segments of combined (passenger and freight) vehicles.	Value Engine capacity CO_2 Emissions	**Rebates according to CO_2 Emissions (as at 31 March 2016)** Rebate is calculated according to the formula (grams CO_2/km) x rate – fixed rebate **Petrol Vehicles** EUR EUR Up to 99 4.00 370.00 From 100 to 115 7.00 650.00 From 116 to 145 45.49 5 110.00 From 146 to 175 53.00 6 180.00 From 176 to 195 135.00 20 450.00 Above 195 178.00 28 900.00 **Diesel Vehicles*** Up to 79 5.00 380.00 From 80 to 95 20.30 1 600.00 From 96 to 120 68.58 6 228.00 From 121 to 140 152.10 16 380.00 From 141 to 160 169.15 18 800.00 Above 160 232.33 28 950.00 *Light passengers diesel vehicles with particle emissions equal or above 0.002 grams/km have a penalization of EUR 500 on the amount of tax.

Table 5.A5.1. **Taxes on sale and registration of motor vehicles**[1] *(cont.)*

Pays	Taxes	Criteria	Rebates/Exemptions
Slovak Republic	**VAT:** 20%	Value	**Disabled persons:** rebates in administration fees are applied for disabled persons.
	Administrative fees: First record of vehicle in to Slovak cars register shall be registration fee payable by the first owner of a motor vehicle, If the engine capacity is up to 80 KW (apply for new, imported and used cars): EUR 33, First record of vehicle in to Slovak cars register shall be registration fee payable by the first owner. If the engine capacity is in excess of 80 KW and up to 86 KW (apply for new or imported cars): EUR 167, in excess of 86 KW up to 92 KW: EUR 217, in excess of 92 KW up to 98 KW: EUR 267, in excess of 98 KW up to 104 KW: EUR 327, in excess of 104 KW up to 110 KW: EUR 397, in excess of 110 KW up to 121 KW: EUR 477, in excess of 121 KW up to 132 KW: EUR 657, in excess of 132 KW up to 143 KW: EUR 787, in excess of 143 KW up to 154 KW: EUR 957, in excess of 154 KW up to 165 KW: EUR 1 157, in excess of 165 KW up to 176 KW: EUR 1 397, in excess of 176 KW up to 202 KW: EUR 1 697, in excess of 202 KW up to 228 KW: EUR 2 047, in excess of 228 KW up to 254 KW: EUR 2 467, in excess of 254 KW: EUR: 2 997. First record of electric car in to Slovak cars register shall be registration fee payable by the CO_2 first owner of a motor vehicle: EUR 33. Any other record (second, third and so on…) of vehicle in to Slovak cars register shall be registration fee payable by the current owner: EUR 33. Registration fee for assigning and releasing of a licence plate number: EUR 16.50 per one plate number (i.e. EUR 33 for 1 vehicle).	Engine power	**Other exemptions:** state authorities, higher territorial units, budget organisation, diplomats, court of justice, prosecution, police, Slovak red cross and legal person owned by state authority (100% of shares).

Table 5.A5.1. **Taxes on sale and registration of motor vehicles**[1] *(cont.)*

Pays	Taxes	Criteria	Rebates/Exemptions
Slovenia	**VAT:** 22% **Motor vehicle tax** is paid for passenger motor vehicles, motorcycles and camper vans, which are put into circulation in Slovenia for the first time; imports and acquisitions from other EU Member States are also taxed. The tax base is the selling price of an individual motor vehicle, excluding VAT and this tax. The tax rate is determined according to environmental criteria (CO_2, Euro emission standards) and the rates are determined from 0.5% to 28% for petrol cars and from 1% to 31% for diesel cars. Passenger cars with cylinder capacity over 2500 cm^3 are subject to the additional tax. Rates vary from 8% (2500 cm^3 and more) to 16% (4000 cm^3 and more). For diesel cars particulate matter (PM) emissions are also considered. Tax rates for motorcycles and camper vans are set upon engine power in the range from 1.5% to 5% for motorcycles and 6% to 18% for camper vans. Motorcycles with cylinder capacity over 1000 cm^3 are subject to the additional tax of 5%. Motor vehicle tax is levied only at the time of first registration of a vehicle and not on an annual basis. **Environmental tax** for pollution of the environment with used motor vehicles is paid for passenger motor vehicles, motorcycles, camper vans and vehicles for the carriage of goods, which are put into circulation in Slovenia for the first time; imports and acquisitions from other EU Member States and imports from third countries are also taxed. The basis for calculating the environmental tax is the mass of a motor vehicle. The amount of tax is determined by the government each year according to the costs of handling used motor vehicles deregistered from traffic on the territory of Slovenia in the previous year. The environmental tax is paid in certain amount per kilo of vehicle and is a precondition for registration. For the year 2015 the amount of tax hasn`t been determined and it amounts to 0 EUR/kg. Environmental tax is levied only at the time of first registration of a vehicle and not on an annual basis.	Value Selling price CO_2 emissions Particulate matter emissions EURO emissions standards Engine power Cylinder capacity Weight	**Tax exemptions (motor vehicle tax):** – vehicles acquired for transport of families with three or more children; – vehicles purchased for carrying disabled people; – vehicles intended for: 1. Official use by diplomatic and consular representations accredited to Slovenia; 2. Official use by international organisations, if so stipulated by international treaties binding on Slovenia; 3. Personal use by foreign staff of diplomatic and consular missions, accredited to Slovenia, including their family members; 4. Personal use by foreign staff of international organisations, including their family members, if so stipulated by international treaties binding on Slovenia; – used vehicles (old-timers); – vehicles imported on a temporary basis (the temporary change of residence of the vehicle's proprietor who does not maintain his permanent residence in Slovenia); – sports vehicles that have not been adapted for road use and are intended only for driving on circuits; – transfer of vehicles in the case of reorganizations of vehicle's proprietor; – emergency rescue motor vehicles used for transport of victims and patients; – leasing of the vehicles. **Environmental tax**: no exemptions.
Spain	**VAT:** 21%. **Vehicle Registration Tax (VRT)** is based on CO_2 emissions. Rates vary from 0% (up to 120 g CO_2/km) to 14.75% (200 g CO_2/km and more).	Value CO_2 emissions	**VRT exemptions**: taxis, driving school vehicles, rental service vehicles; vehicles acquired and used by disabled people; vehicles with special diplomatic registration; transfer of vehicles in the case of change of residence of vehicle's proprietor.
Sweden	**VAT:** 25%	Value	
Switzerland	**VAT:** 8% **Acquisition Tax** on new vehicles (up to 1 600 kg and all passenger cars up to 3 500Kg): 4% of purchase price. No registration tax (but small fees for number plates and registration papers).	Value Electric propulsion	**Electrically powered vehicles** are exempt from acquisition tax.

Table 5.A5.1. **Taxes on sale and registration of motor vehicles**[1] *(cont.)*

Pays	Taxes	Criteria	Rebates/Exemptions
Turkey	**VAT:** 18%. **Special Consumption Tax** (SCT) is payable on first acquisition of vehicles (importation, acquisition by public auction, acquisition from those who carry out motor vehicle trade, inception of use, capitalisation or registration in the name of those who carry out motor vehicle trading). **Motor vehicles:** proportional duty is applied. For motor vehicles under CN Code 87.02 and designed for transport of passengers, tax rate is 9% for minibuses, 4% for minibuses and 1% for buses. Passenger cars and other motor vehicles: designed for transport of passengers excluding those under CN Code 87.02 and placed under CN Code 87.03 and having a max. weight of 3.5 tons and passenger carrying capacity less than 50% of max. load capacity. Vehicles with a max. loading capacity not over 850 kg and having an engine capacity below 2000cm³ are subject to the SCT at a rate of 15% and the ones with a max. loading capacity over 850 kg and having an engine capacity below 2800cm³ are subject to the SCT at a rate of 15% and SCT rates for others vary from 45% to 145% according to their engine capacity. Tax rates applied to electric cars vary from 3% to 15% according to electric engine capacity. **For motor vehicles designed for transport of goods** and placed under CN Code 87.04 and have a max. loaded weight not over 4700 kg and have a seat other than the driver's seat or have side windows other than those besides the driver's seat, SCT rate is 10% for the ones with an engine capacity not over 3000 cm³, 52% for those with an engine capacity over 3000 cm³ but not over 4000 cm³ and 75% for those with an engine capacity over 4000 cm³. Tax rate for those provided with a covered body and have a max. loading capacity under 620 kg is 10%. For others 4%. **The tax on motor cycles** varies from 8% to 37% according to the cylinder capacity. Tax rates applied to electric motor cycles vary from 3% to 37% according to electric engine capacity.	Value Cylinder capacity Weight Customs category Electric propulsion	**Rebate for disabled people:** disabled people are exempt from the Special Consumption Tax.
United Kingdom	**VAT:** 20% **Vehicle First Registration Fee:** a flat rate fee of GBP 55.0 is payable on the first registration or licensing of a motor vehicle in the United Kingdom.	Value	**Rebate for disabled people:** disabled people are exempt from the Vehicle First Registration Fee. **Other exemptions:** Vehicles previously registered in Northern Ireland. Vehicles registered for off road use. Crown Exempt Vehicles. Historic vehicles previously registered with the old Local Authorities (late conversions). Imported vehicles previously registered under the Personal Export Scheme and New Means of Transport Scheme. Visiting Forces Vehicles.

Table 5.A5.1. **Taxes on sale and registration of motor vehicles**[1] *(cont.)*

Pays	Taxes	Criteria	Rebates/Exemptions
United States	**A Gas guzzler tax:** is imposed on the manufacturer or importer of a vehicle whose combined city and highway fuel efficiency is less than 22.5 miles per gallon. The tax varies from USD 1 000 to USD 7 700 depending on the fuel efficiency. **A tax** of 12% of sales price is imposed on the first retail sale of a truck that is suitable for use on a highway and weights more than 33 000 pounds. **A tax is imposed on the sale of tyres for highway vehicles**. A tax is imposed on taxable tyres sold by the manufacturer, producer, or importer at the rate of 9.45 cents (4.725 cents in the case of a bias ply tyre or super single tyre) for each 10 pounds of the maximum rated load capacity over 3 500 pounds. State and local governments impose a one-time sales tax and/or title fee.	Fuel efficiency Value Weight Tyres	The gas guzzler tax is widely applied and must be paid by vehicles sold to the federal government, state and local governments, and non-profit educational organizations. Vehicles used for police, other law enforcement purposes, or firefighting purposes or as ambulances are exempt. Limousines weighing more than 6 000 pounds or designed to carry more than 10 people are exempt. Tyres for use on local and school buses or for the exclusive use of the Department of Defence or the Coast Guard are exempt.

1. This table does not include customs duties; specific regimes for second-hand cars (e.g. margin scheme, old timers); diplomatic sales; export/import and transit schemes and insurance premium tax.
2. Israel: The statistical data for Israel are supplied by and under the responsibility of the relevant Israeli authorities. The use of such data by the OECD is without prejudice to the status of the Golan Heights, East Jerusalem and Israeli settlements in the West Bank under the terms of international law.

Source: National delegates; position as at 1 January 2014.

Table 5.A5.2. **Taxes on ownership or use of motor vehicles**[1]

Country	Taxes	Criteria	Rebates/Exemptions
Australia	The States and Territories levy fees for annual registration, third party compulsory insurance and drivers' licenses. Fees for commercial vehicles are generally higher than the fees for private vehicles. In most States, fees for trucks vary depending on the type of vehicle and the gross vehicle mass. Licence renewal fees vary to reflect validity periods from one to five years.	Commercial/private use Gross vehicle mass	
Austria	Motor vehicles above a permissible gross weight of 3.5 tonnes: Motor Vehicle Tax based on the weight of the vehicle (from EUR 1.55 to EUR 1.90 per month and ton depending on the weight). Motor vehicles up to and including a maximum permissible gross weight of 3.5 tons: Motor Vehicle Insurance tax based on engine power in kilowatt (cars) or cubic capacity (motorbikes). For cars: gradual tariff from EUR 0.62 to 0.75 per month and kw. For motorbikes: EUR 0.025 per month and by cubic centimetre.	Weight Engine power Cubic capacity	Vehicles used by diplomatic missions and consular offices; armed forces; police; fire brigade; ambulances; mountain rescue; electrically propelled vehicles; self-propelled working machines; trial moving vehicles; taxi services; mopeds and motorcycles with a cubic capacity of maximum 100 CC; vehicle used solely in agricultural production and forestry; vehicles used for disabled persons.
Belgium	**Annual Road Tax:** *Walloon Region and Brussels Capital region:* the tax rate depends on fiscal h.p. and cylinder capacity and is set according to a progressive scale from EUR 77.35 to EUR 1 979.60. For vehicles above 20 h.p. (more than 41 cylinder capacity) an additional amount of EUR 107.98 by h.p. is levied. Vehicles of more than 30 years old (25 years old in the Brussels Capital Region) are subject to an annual tax of EUR 35.10. *Flemish Region:* the tax rate depends on fiscal h.p. and cylinder capacity and is set according to a progressive scale from EUR 70.32 up to EUR 1 799.52. For vehicles above 20 h.p. (more than 41 cylinder capacity) an additional amount of EUR 98.04 h.p. is levied. Vehicles of more than 25 years old are subject to an annual tax of EUR 35.10. As from the fiscal year 2016 the tax will be modulated depending on the CO_2 emission, the euro standard and the type of fuel (except for leasing cars). *Flemish and Walloon Region:* a "compensation tax" is levied on cars entirely or partially powered by Liquefied Gas Petroleum. This tax is calculated on a progressive scale depending on the engine power from EUR 89.16 to EUR 208, 20 **Eurovignette:** the tax will be abolished as of 1 April 2016 and replaced with a kilometre charge.	Engine power Cylinder capacity Fuel used Electric propulsion	All regions provide exemptions for cars used by public authorities, vehicles for disabled people and war invalids, agricultural vehicles, rescue vehicles, trial moving vehicles, ships and little boats, taxi services, mopeds and motorcycles with a cylinder capacity of maximum 250 CC. Rebates for the salaried transport of persons; vehicles used for road haulage in the ports. *Flemish Region:* as of fiscal year 2016 a tax reduction of EUR 100 is applicable to cars running on Liquefied Gas Petroleum. Exemption is provided to cars using certain fuels: pure electric, hydrogen-powered, plug-in hybrid (until 2021), CNG/LNG (until 2021).
Canada	All provinces impose annual fees for the use of motor vehicles. In general, the fees depend on the type of vehicles and in most cases on the weight of the vehicle.	Type Weight	
Chile	Annual Motor Vehicle Tax (levied by municipalities) for the use of motor vehicles on public roads depending on the commercial value of the vehicle. Lightweight vehicles: depending on the commercial value of the vehicle. Passenger vehicles: fixed fee. Cargo vehicles: according to loading capacity.	Commercial value Fixed fee Loading capacity (trucks)	

Table 5.A5.2. **Taxes on ownership or use of motor vehicles**[1] *(cont.)*

Country	Taxes	Criteria	Rebates/Exemptions
Czech Republic	The road tax is imposed on all road motor vehicles and their trailers registered and operated in the Czech Republic if they are used by: – taxpayers of corporate income tax (except of vehicles used by public benefit taxpayer for activities which are not subject to corporate income tax); – taxpayers of personal income tax to the activities or in direct connection with that activities from which he has income from an independent activity under the Act on income tax. Vehicles with a total permitted weight above 3.5t registered in the Czech Republic and determined solely for freight transport are always liable to road tax. As regards passenger cars the tax base shall be the engine's cylinder capacity in cubic centimetres, with the exception of electric-driven passenger cars; As regards semi-trailers and other motor vehicles the tax base shall be: – the total of the maximum permitted weight on axles in tonnes and the number of axles of semi-trailers; – in the case of other vehicles the maximum permitted weight in tonnes and the number of axles. The annual tax rate of passenger cars varies from CZK 1 200 to CZK 4 200 and in the case of other vehicles vary from CZK 1 800 to CZK 44 100.	Cylinder capacity (passenger cars) Type of propulsion Type of fuel Total max. permitted weight on axles and number of axles (semi-trailers) Max. permitted weight and number of axles (other vehicles)	Tax Exemption: vehicles usually with less than four wheels (motorcycles); vehicles used by diplomatic missions and consular offices (where there is a reciprocal arrangement); vehicles ensuring domestic line passenger transport, vehicles operated by the armed forces and civil defence; vehicles which are state mobilisation reserve or emergency reserve; vehicles of the Police of the Czech Republic; fire protection vehicles; ambulances; mining and mountain rescue vehicles; gas emergency service and power engineering emergency service vehicles. Special road sweeping vehicles; special single-purpose vehicles (e.g. vehicles used in road marking) and vehicles belonging to road authorities or to persons authorized by road authorities exclusively used to maintain land communications, except for passenger cars, electrically propelled vehicles, hybrid driven vehicles, vehicles using as fuel either LPG or CNG or vehicles equipped with an engine determined by his producer for combustion of E85. Tax reduction (25% to 100%) for vehicle exclusively used for carriage in the combined transport for which railway transport or inland waterway transport is made use of. The tax rate is reduced for the period of 108 months from the date of the first registration of vehicle (for the first 36 months by 48%, for the next 36 months by 40% and for the next 36 months by 25%.
Denmark	**Passenger cars semi-annual tax**: the tax is based on fuel consumption, with different rates for petrol/diesel. Rates range from DKK 310 (> 20km/l) up to DKK 10830 (< 4.5km/l) for petrol cars, and from DKK 130 (> 32.1km/l) up to 16 100 (< 5.1km/l) for diesel cars. **Lorries' annual tax:** Vehicles registered for the first time until 24 April 2007: the charge for private use is DKK 1 060 annually for cars with total permissible weight (tpw) up to 2000 kg and DKK 5 920 annually for cars with tpw between 2000 and 4000 kg. Vehicles registered on 25 April 2007 or after: the charge for private use is DKK 5920 annually for cars with total permissible weight (tpw) up to 3000 kg and DKK 17 590 annually for cars with tpw between 3000 and 4000 kg. For cars used for both private and commercial purposes the rates are 50%. Cars used exclusively for commercial purposes are free of charge.	Fuel efficiency Weight (for lorries)	
Estonia	Heavy goods vehicle tax. Varies from 0 to 232.60 (per quarter) EUR depending on the combination of following factors: weight range (12 tonnes to 40 and more tonnes), axel combination (2, 3, 4, 2+1, 2+2, 2+3, 3+2, 3+3), type of suspension (air, other).	Weight range, Axle combination, Type of suspension	Exemptions apply for Defence Force, Defence League, Enforcement Force and Rescue Service Heavy goods vehicles and Local Authority, NGO, Foundation and Business vehicles intended for rescue operations.
Finland	The annual tax for passenger cars and delivery vans is based on CO_2 emissions. If the car does not have emission data in the Vehicular and Driver Data Register, the tax is based on the total mass of the vehicle. Tax rates vary from EUR 106.21 for vehicles emitting from 0g CO_2/km up to EUR 654.44 for vehicles emitting 400g CO_2/km or more. For diesel passenger cars and vans there is a tax on driving power based on total mass of the vehicle. This is applied on other cars and vans using less taxed fuels than petrol as well. For lorries there is an annual tax based on maximum gross weight, number of axles and use of trailer.	CO_2 emissions Weight Number of axles (lorries)	

Table 5.A5.2. **Taxes on ownership or use of motor vehicles**[1] *(cont.)*

Country	Taxes	Criteria	Rebates/Exemptions
France	Tax on business passenger cars: up to 7 HP: EUR 1130; more than 7 HP: EUR 2440. An annual tax is payable by owners of vehicles emitting more than CO_2 190g/100km.	Engine power Electric propulsion Type of fuel	Exemptions: – Cars more than 10 years old; – Cars used for public passenger transport, cars used for leasing or sale, – Electrically or gas propelled cars (for mixed oil and gas propelled vehicles exemption is reduced by half). Vehicles that can use both petrol and GPL are exempt at rate of 50%.
Germany	For passenger cars being firstly registered since 1 July 2009, the Motor Vehicle Tax is based mainly on CO_2 emissions. It consists of a base tax (according to cylinder capacity) and a CO_2 tax. The rates of the base tax are EUR 2 per 100 cc (petrol) and EUR 9.50 per 100 cc (diesel) respectively. The CO_2 tax is linear at EUR 2 per g CO_2/km. Cars being firstly registered before 1 July 2009 are taxed according to their polluting emissions (EURO-Norm) and cylinder capacity.	Polluting emissions Cylinder capacity CO_2 emissions	Cars with CO_2 emissions below 95 g/km are exempt from the CO_2-element. Only the base tax is due. Exemption for pure electric cars for ten years after the first registration, if the car is registered between 18 May 2011 and 31 December 2020.
Greece	Annual road tax on private passenger cars registered for the first time in Greece before 31.10.2010 (as well as those with international initial registration before 2002), and also motorcycles regardless of their date of registration: based on cylinder capacity from EUR 22 to EUR 1 380.For the above category, there is an extra criterion of years of circulation of cars. Private passenger cars and taxis registered for the first time in Greece, after 1.11.2010: based on CO_2 emissions from EUR 0 to EUR 3.72 per gram of CO_2. Annual road tax on trucks based on gross weight and on buses on the number of seats.	Cylinder capacity CO2 emissions Electric propulsion Gross weight (trucks) Number of seats (buses)	The main exemptions are: Cars used by public authorities, municipalities, ambulances etc, Cars used by disabled persons and members of foreign diplomatic services; Electric cars, Hybrid cars registered until 31.10.2010, with engine displacement under 1.549 cc , Private passenger cars, registered after 1.11.2011 ,with CO2 emissions under 100g/km Motorcycles up to 300 cc cylinder capacity used in order to replace old technology ones (replacement should take place up to 31.12.2009). For motorcycles with cylinder capacity over 300 cc used in order to replace old technology motorcycles exemption applies for 5 years only following the date of first registration of the new motorcycle. Cars and motorcycles, registered with a valid permission of circulation, may be imported for a limited period up to six months per year, by the customs procedure of temporary importation.
Hungary	Motor vehicle tax levied according to capacity of engine (in Kw) of passenger cars and motorcycles. The tax base for busses, semi-trailers and caravans is the unladen weight of the vehicle. For lorries the tax is based on net weight plus 50% of cargo weight. The tax rate for passenger cars and motorcycles is from HUF 140/kW to HUF 345/kW depending on the age of the vehicle (the older the vehicle, the less is due). For lorries, busses, semi-trailers the tax rate is HUF 850/100 kg of the tax base, if the vehicle is equipped with road-saving axles. The tax rate for other lorries, trailers is HUF 1380/100 kg.	Engine capacity Weight (for lorries) Type of axles (for high-duty vehicles) Electric propulsion	Exemption for vehicles: – owned by budgetary agencies, religious organisations, – owned by social organisations, foundations if this organisations do not have to pay tax on profit, – used for public transport or fire service, – owned by a person who is seriously handicapped, or used for transporting seriously handicapped person under age 18, or used for transporting seriously handicapped person who is under guardianship because of his/her legal incapacity, – passenger cars equipped with environment-saving engine.

Table 5.A5.2. **Taxes on ownership or use of motor vehicles**[1] *(cont.)*

Country	Taxes	Criteria	Rebates/Exemptions
Iceland	A disposal charge of ISK 350 is levied on each vehicle for each six-month period. This charge is payable for fifteen years from the date of the first registration of the vehicle in Iceland, except when the vehicle is already 25 years old at the beginning of the payment year. The charge is an environmental tax that is intended to finance the disposal of the vehicle at the end of its useful life. Once the vehicle is delivered for scrap, a ISK 20 000 refund will be paid to the owner. Motor vehicles fuelled with diesel in excess of 10 tonnes are subject to a special weight/distance tax, calculated on the basis of the weight of the vehicle and the number of kilometers driven. Owners of diesel vehicles that weigh less than 10 tonnes do not pay a weight/distance tax. A semi-annual road tax on passenger cars is levied based on the vehicle's carbon dioxide emissions declared by the car manufacturer for combination of city and road driving. Where emission data are not available, the tax rate is based on the weight of the vehicle. The semi-annual road tax is ISK 130 for each gram of carbon dioxide emission for emission above 121 grams, in addition to the minimum fee which is ISK 5 415 ISK.	Weight Distance CO_2 emissions	
Ireland	Road Tax on private cars based on CO_2 emissions. Rates vary from EUR 120 (for 0g CO_2/km) to EUR 2350 (above 225 g CO_2/km). Tax on commercial vehicles based on net weight: from EUR 333 (< 3000 kg) up to EUR 5195 (> 20 000 kg).	CO_2 emissions Weight (commercial vehicles) Electric propulsion	Electrically propelled vehicles: EUR 120 flat rate – private and EUR 92 flat rate – commercial not over 1 500kg
Israel (b)	Annual licensing fees: private and commercial vehicles weighing up to 3500 kg total:the vehicles are sorted into seven groups (generally the price). The annual licensing fees are reliant upon the year of vehicle production, and the group the vehicle belongs to The annual licensing fees range between NIS 718 to NIS 4 535. Commercial vehicles above 3.500 kg, motorized by diesel, have a different tariff.	Price Age Category	Vehicles for disabled person, diplomats, United Nations Organisations, specific charity institutions.
Italy	Annual Ownership Tax: From EUR 2.58 per KW to EUR 4.95 per KW according to engine cylinder capacity and polluting emissions. Regions are entitled to vary the national rate. A surtax on use of cars and vehicles intended for the transport of persons or goods applies at a rate of EUR 20.00 for each KW exceeding 185 KW in engine power. Such surtax is reduced after five, ten or fifteen years from the construction of the vehicle by 40%, 70% and 85%, respectively.	Engine power Polluting emissions Electric propulsion	Exemption for historical vehicles over 30 years old; vehicles over 20 years old are exempt only if recognised as being of special historical or collectors' interest; flat rate road tax on vehicles over 30 or 20 years old if still running on public roads. An exemption of 100% from ownership tax is allowed for electric, LPG and CNG vehicles in the first 5 years (from the first registration) and an exemption of 75% afterwards in many regions. 100% exemption also applies to vehicles for disabled persons.
Japan	Motor Vehicle Tonnage Tax(National)(N.B. *Commercial vehicles): levied according to weight , the tax rate are for passenger vehicles from JPY 4 100 per 0.5 ton up to JPY 6 300 per 0.5 ton(from JPY 2 600 up to JPY 2 800); for lorries from JPY 3 300 per 0.5 ton up to JPY 6 300 per 0.5 ton(from JPY 2 600 up to JPY 2 800). Automobile Tax(Prefecture): levied according to cylinder capacity for passenger vehicle from JPY 29 500 up to JPY 111 000 (from JPY 7 500 up to JPY 40 700). Lorries: (e.g.4-5 tons maximum load) JPY 25 500 (JPY 18 500). Buses: (e.g.41-50 passengers capacity) JPY 49 000(JPY 17 500). Light Vehicle Tax (Local): levied on light vehicles and motorcycles according to cylinder capacity and standards.	Weight Cylinder capacity Impact on the environment	Special measures of reduced Motor Vehicle Tonnage Tax. Vehicles with low impact on the environment, barrier-free buses and taxis, trucks with collision damage alleviation brake control device, etc. Special measures of refunded Motor Vehicle Tonnage Tax. Used vehicles properly scrapped before the expiry date of valid period of inspection certificate. Special measures of reduced Automobile Tax and Light Vehicle Tax. Vehicles with low impact on the environment.

Table 5.A5.2. **Taxes on ownership or use of motor vehicles**[1] *(cont.)*

Country	Taxes	Criteria	Rebates/Exemptions
Korea	Automobile Tax: rates are applicable according to cylinder capacity from KRW 80 per cc up to KRW 200 per cc for non-commercial vehicles; and from KRW 18 per cc to KRW 24 per cc for commercial vehicles.	Cylinder capacity	Full exemption for disabled persons
Latvia	**The annual tax** for passenger cars registered after 2005 is based on gross weight, motor capacity and maximum motor power, but annual for passenger cars registered before 2005 is based only on gross weight. The annual tax for motorcycles is based on motor capacity, for heavy goods vehicle is based on gross weight and number of axes and type of suspension if gross weight exceeds 12 000 kg.	Weight (passenger cars and heavy goods vehicles) Motor capacity (passenger cars and motorcycles) Maximum motor power Number of axes and type of suspension (heavy good vehicles) Electric propulsion	The main exemptions are for: – a car, motorcycle, tricycle or quadricycle, the owner, holder or driver of which is a disabled person; – a vehicle, the owner, holder or driver of which is a representative of a diplomatic, consular or international organisation or a person who has diplomatic or consular privileges and immunities; – an emergency vehicle; – vehicles having been registered or being registered with the status of historic motor vehicle; – electric mobiles.
Luxembourg	Automobile Tax: the annual circulation tax is based on CO_2 emissions. Tax rates are calculated by multiplying the CO_2 emissions in g/km with 0.9 for diesel cars and 0.6 for cars using other fuels respectively and with an exponential factor (0.5 below 90 g/km and increased by 0.1 for each additional 10 g of CO_2 /km). Tax on heavy vehicles (also known as "Eurovignette") is levied on vehicles (lorries) with a gross weight of 12 tons or more for the use of motor ways. Tax also varies according to Euro norms.	CO^2 emissions Electric propulsion	Exemptions: vehicles for disabled people; historical vehicles; cars used by public authorities; electrically propelled cars
Mexico	Starting 2012, the tax on ownership was eliminated as a Federal Tax. State governments may impose a tax on ownership and/or periodic registration. Registration fee is near to MXN 400 in most states and Tax on ownership usually goes from 3% to 19% based on value, type of vehicle and number of passengers.	Value Type of vehicle Number of passengers Electric propulsion	Some states exempt hybrid and electric vehicles used for public passenger transport. Some states provide a subsidy of 100% for vehicles any value.
Netherlands	Motor vehicle tax is based on the dead-weight and the type fuel used. There is a Provincial surtax. Tax on heavy vehicles (also known as "Eurovignette") is levied on vehicles (lorries) with a gross weight of 12 tons or more for the use of motor ways in the Netherlands. Tax also varies according to Euro norms (diesel category).	For motor vehicle tax: Fuel used Weight Region (province) CO_2 emissions For tax on heavy vehicles: Number of axles Polluting emissions	Vehicles with a CO_2 emission of 0 are exempt. Low-emissions vehicles (CO_2 is not exceeding a level of 50 g/km) pay 50% of the taxes. **Other examples of exemptions are:** (Animal) ambulances; vehicles used by fire brigades; vehicles used by the police/defence; funerary vehicles; vehicles used to clean, maintain or construct roads; taxis and vehicles older than 40 years. Other special regimes apply such as reduced tax rate for delivery vans owned by entrepreneurs and used for business purposes for at least 10% and for vans equipped for and used by disabled persons.
New Zealand	Annual licensing fees: vary depending on the type of vehicle. The licensing fee for private passenger, petrol driven cars is NZD 280.55.	Vehicle type	
Norway	Annual tax: NOK 3 655 for diesel cars without factory-fitted particle filter and NOK 3 135 for other cars; NOK 1 920 for motorbikes; NOK 1 120 for caravans and NOK 445 for moped, tractors, electric vehicles, etc.	Vehicle type Electric propulsion Particle filter	

Table 5.A5.2. **Taxes on ownership or use of motor vehicles**[1] *(cont.)*

Country	Taxes	Criteria	Rebates/Exemptions
Poland	Annual Motor Vehicles Tax levied at municipal level on heavy goods vehicles of maximum permissible gross laden weight over 3.5 tons, road and ballast tractors, trailers and semi-trailers and buses.	Weight Type of vehicle Number of passengers for busses	Vehicles under possession of diplomatic representations, consular offices and other foreign missions. Transport vehicles constituting mobilisation supply. Special vehicles and vehicles used for special purposes. Historic vehicles.
Portugal	Annual State and municipal tax due by the ownership of the vehicle, it was reformed on 1st of July of 2007 for passengers vehicles and mixed use cars with gross weight not exceeding 2500 Kg, if registered after the reform, tax rate is based on motor capacity and CO_2 emissions and for vehicles registered since 1981 up to the reform rates vary depending on motor capacity or voltage, date of registration and fuel type. Vehicle excise duty on lorries above 2.5 tonnes used in public and private transport of merchandise.	Motor capacity CO_2 emissions Electric propulsion Weight Number of axels Vehicle type and fuel Type of suspension	Vehicles owned by the State (central, regional or local administration), fire brigades, foreign States, diplomatic and consular missions, international organizations, specialized European agencies and disabled persons; vehicles seized by the State for as part of a criminal procedure. Are also exempt ambulances, passengers vehicles destined to rental or taxi services, tractors, funerary vehicles, non-motorized vehicles that are purely electric or moved by renewable energies.
Slovak Republic	**Motor Vehicle Tax** is imposed only on vehicles used for business purposes. Rates vary depending on type, weight, cylinder capacity and number of axles (for utility vehicles and buses) of the vehicle.	Usage Vehicle type (passenger cars) Weight Cylinder capacity (utility vehicles and buses) Number of axles Polluting emissions	The vehicles exempt from the motor vehicle tax are the following: a) vehicles the documents of which name as the vehicle holder the higher territorial unit to the budget of which the motor vehicle tax is transferred; b) vehicles of diplomatic missions and consular corps, provided that reciprocity is guaranteed.
Slovenia	**Circulation tax** (levied on an annual basis) – an annual fee for the use of road transport vehicles is paid once a year for the use of motor vehicles and trailers in Slovenia by vehicle owners. The fee is paid at the time of renewal of registration certificate. By paying an annual duty a person acquires the right to use a registered vehicle in road traffic for the next 12 months. The amount of tax depends on the category of the vehicle and is proportionate to the duration of the registration period in a certain year.	Cylinder capacity, Engine power, Weight Polluting emissions Electric propulsion Type of suspension Number of seats	Tax exemptions: Vehicles exclusively using electricity for power, tractors and tractor trailers, motorcycles, three-wheeled cycles with engine capacity up to 50 cc and light four-wheeled cycles, light trailers with maximum permissible weight up to 750 kg, motor vehicles registered to the Slovenian Army, Civil Protection, Mountain Rescue Service, Ecological Laboratory with mobile unit, police and fire-fighting vehicles, ambulances, motor vehicles and trailers registered for diplomatic and consular missions, vehicles owned by certain international organizations, and vehicles used for the transport of disabled persons. Tax reduction for low polluting trucks Trucks of category N1: tax reduction for EURO 5 (-25%) and EURO 6 and higher (-35%) and tax increase for EURO 3 (+10%), EURO 2 (+20%), EURO 1 (+30%) and EURO 0 or lower (+40%); Trucks of category N2, N3 and buses (M2, M3): tax reduction for EURO 5 (-25%) and EURO 6 and higher (-35%) and tax increase for EURO 3 (+10%) EURO 2 (+20%), EURO 1 (+30%) and EURO 0 or lower (+40%) Tax reduction for buses and trucks with air suspension (-15%) Tax reduction for old-timers (-80%) and vehicles acquired for transport of families with four or more children (-50%).
Spain	Motor Vehicle Tax (levied by municipalities) based on engine power for passenger cars, passenger capacity for buses, loading capacity for trucks and cylinder volume for motorcycles.	Vehicle type Engine power Cylinder capacity	**Tax exemptions:** Official vehicles belonging to public bodies of diplomatic offices, ambulances, vehicles adapted to disabled people, public transport vehicles over nine seats, tractors and other vehicles of agricultural use; historic vehicles.

Table 5.A5.2. **Taxes on ownership or use of motor vehicles**[1] *(cont.)*

Country	Taxes	Criteria	Rebates/Exemptions
Sweden	The annual circulation tax for cars from 2006 and later or, older cars that meet at least Euro 4 exhaust emission standards, is based on CO_2 emissions. Also campers, light goods vehicles and light buses that are taken in to use in 2011 or later are taxed based on the CO_2 emissions. The tax consists of a basic rate of SEK 360 plus SEK 22 for each gram CO_2 the vehicle emits above 111 g/km. If the vehicle can be driven with diesel fuel this sum is multiplied by 2.37. For vehicles that can be driven with alternative fuels, the tax is SEK 360 plus SEK 11 for each gram CO_2 the vehicle emits above 111 g/km.	Weight CO^2 emissions Type of fuel. Electric propulsion	An exemption from annual circulation tax applies to green cars during the first five years. The exemption applies to cars, campers, light goods vehicles and light buses with low emissions of CO_2 in proportion to the vehicles weight. The vehicles emissions of CO_2 shall not exceed a calculated value; (95 + 0.0457 x (the vehicles weight in kg – 1 372)). For alternative fuel vehicles the value is calculated; (150 + 0.0457 x (the vehicles weight in kg – 1 372)). Electric cars shall not consume more electricity than 37 kWh/100 km.
Switzerland	**Cantonal (provincial) level:** The annual motor vehicle tax depends on the weight or engine volume of the vehicle. **Federal level:** Use of Swiss motorways (first and second-class motorways) has been generally subject to charge. The charge is levied in the form of the motorway charge sticker, which costs CHF 40. The obligation to display a motorway charge sticker generally applies to motor vehicles and trailers with a total weight of up to 3.5 tons each. This group comprises primarily passenger vehicles, motorbikes, vans, trailers, etc. Motor vehicles and trailers with a total weight exceeding 3.5 tons (so-called heavy vehicles) require a motorway charge sticker if they are not subject to the heavy vehicle charge. These include, for example, heavy utility vehicles (e.g. crane lorries). The performance-related heavy vehicle charge (LSVA) depends on the total weight, polluting emissions and kilometres driven in Switzerland. It is levied on all motor vehicles and trailers that have a total permissible laden weight of more than 3.5 tons, are used to transport goods, are registered in Switzerland or abroad and are driven on the Swiss public road network. The lump-sum heavy vehicle charge (PSVA) is levied in the form of a lump sum on heavy motor vehicles for the following vehicle types that are driven on the Swiss public road network: heavy passenger vehicles, heavy campervans, motor-homes and caravans, vehicles used for transporting passengers (coaches, buses), tractors and motor carriages, motor vehicles for fun fairs and circuses. Other motor vehicles for the carriage of goods and with a maximum speed of 45 km/h.	Weight Engine volume Kilometres driven Polluting emissions Electric propulsion	A reduced rate of the motor vehicle tax usually applies to electric and agricultural vehicles.
Turkey	Motor Vehicle Tax levied on all motor vehicles – based on weight, type and cylinder capacity. Paid as two equal instalments per annum by registered owner.	Weight, Vehicle type Cylinder capacity Electric propulsion	Electrically propelled passenger cars are not subject of the tax
United Kingdom	VED on lorries is set according to the number of axles, weight and type of vehicle. Cars that are presented for registration in the UK on or after 1 March 2001, on the basis of a type approval certificate specifying a carbon dioxide (CO_2) emission figure, attract a rate of Vehicle Excise Duty (VED) according to the amount of CO_2 emitted and the type of fuel used. These cars fall within a 13-banded graduated VED system. The bands are labelled A-M, with band A containing the least polluting vehicles and band M comprising of vehicles that have high CO_2 emissions. Full details can be found at *www.direct.gov.uk/Motoring.* For private cars which do not fall into the above graduated VED system there is a two-tier threshold: vehicles not over 1549cc pay an annual rate of duty of GBP 145, and those over 1549cc pay a rate of duty of GBP 230.	Vehicle type CO_2 emissions Type of fuel Electric propulsion	Tax exemption applies to vehicles for disabled people, historic vehicles constructed before 1.1.1975, limited use vehicles, agricultural machines, mowing machines, steam powered vehicles, electrically propelled vehicles, and electrically assisted pedal cycles. Vehicles belonging to public bodies such as ambulances, fire engine, police cars, etc.

Table 5.A5.2. **Taxes on ownership or use of motor vehicles**[1] *(cont.)*

Country	Taxes	Criteria	Rebates/Exemptions
United States	A tax is imposed on the use of trucks weighing 55 000 pounds or above. For those trucks (except logging trucks) weighing no more than 75 000 pounds, the tax is USD 100 per year plus USD 22 for each 1 000 pounds in excess of 55 000 pounds. For those trucks weighing more than 75 000 pounds the tax is USD 550. For logging trucks, the tax is USD 75 per year for trucks weighing at least 55 000 pounds plus USD 16.50 per 1 000 pounds in excess of 55 000 pounds. For logging trucks weighing more than 75 000 pounds the tax is USD 412.50. A credit may be claimed for the tax in the following year if the vehicle was driven 5 000 miles or less (7 500 miles or less for agricultural vehicles.). State and local governments may impose a periodic registration, operators' license, parking and inspection fees as well as property taxes.	Weight (for trucks)	

1. Excluding insurance premium tax.
2. Israel: The statistical data for Israel are supplied by and under the responsibility of the relevant Israeli authorities. The use of such data by the OECD is without prejudice to the status of the Golan Heights, East Jerusalem and Israeli settlements in the West Bank under the terms of international law.

Source: National delegates; position as at 1 January 2016.

ANNEX A

Countries with VAT*

Almost all countries levy general consumption taxes i.e. taxes on the sale of most goods and services to consumers. In the vast majority of those countries, this tax is a VAT i.e. a tax collected at all stages of the processes of production and distribution of goods and services, accumulation of the tax being prevented by allowing businesses to deduct the tax they incur on their inputs from the tax they collect on their outputs. A minority of countries apply retail sales taxes, i.e. single-stage taxes on goods and services supplied to final consumers. All OECD countries levy VAT, except the United States, where resale sales taxes are levied at sub-national level (see Chapter 1).

As of 1 January 2016, 167 countries and territories in the world have implemented a VAT.

Countries and territories operating a VAT

No.	Country	Implementation	Rates 2016 (%)		
			Standard	Lower	Increased
1	Albania	1995	20.0	0.10	
2	Algeria	1992	17.0	0, 7	
3	Andorra	2013	4.5	0, 1, 2.5	9.5
4	Antigua and Barbuda	2007	15.0	0, 12.5	
5	Argentina	1974	21.0	2.5, 5, 10.5	27
6	Armenia	1993	20.0		
7	Australia	2000	10.0	0	
8	Austria	1973	20.0	10, 13	
9	Azerbaijan	1992	18.0		
	Bahamas	2015	7.5		
10	Bangladesh	1991	15.0	0 - 7.5	10 - 500
11	Barbados	1997	17.5	0, 7.5	
12	Belarus	1991	20.0	0, 909, 10, 16.67	
13	Belgium	1971	21.0	0, 6, 12	
14	Belize	2006	12.5	-	
15	Benin	1991	18.0	0	
16	Bolivia	1986	13.0	0	
17	Bosnia Herzegovina	2006	17.0		
18	Botswana	2002	12.0	0	
19	Brazil	1964	17, 18	4, 7, 12	25

* The acronym "VAT" refers to any national tax that embodies the basic features of a value added tax as described in Chapter 1, by whatever name or acronym it is known *e.g.* "Goods and Services Tax" ("GST")

Countries and territories operating a VAT *(cont.)*

No.	Country	Implementation	Rates 2016 (%)		
			Standard	Lower	Increased
20	Bulgaria	1994	20.0	9	
21	Burkina Faso	1993	18.0	0	
22	Burundi	2009	18.0	0, 10	
23	Cambodia	1999	10.0		
24	Cameroon	1999	19.25	0	
25	Canada	1991	GST: 5.0 HST: 12/13/14/15		
26	Cape Verde	2004	15.0	0	
27	Central African Republic	2001	19.0	5	
28	Chad	2000	18.0	0	
29	Chile	1975	19.0		
30	China (People's Republic)	1994	17.0	13	
31	Colombia	1983	16.0	0, 5	
32	Commonwealth of Dominica	2006	15.0	0, 10	
33	Congo (Democratic Republic)	2012	16.0	0	
34	Congo (Republic)	1997	18.0	0, 5	
35	Cook Islands	1997	15.0	0	
36	Costa Rica	1982	13.0	5, 10	
37	Croatia	1998	25.0	5, 13	
38	Cyprus[1]	1992	19.0	0, 5, 9	
39	Czech Republic	1993	21.0	10, 15	
40	Denmark	1967	25.0	0	
41	Djibouti	2009	10.0		
42	Dominican Republic	1983	18.0	0, 16	-
43	Ecuador	1982	12.0	0	
44	Egypt	1991	10.0	5	15, 20, 30
45	El Salvador	1992	13.0	0	
46	Equatorial Guinea	2005	15.0	0, 6	
47	Estonia	1991	20.0	0, 9	
48	Ethiopia	2003	15.0	0	
49	Faroe Islands	1993	25.0	0	
50	Fiji	1992	15.0	0	
51	Finland	1994	24.0	0, 10, 14	
52	Former Yugoslav Republic of Macedonia	2000	18.0	5	
53	France	1968	20.0	2.1, 5.5, 10	
54	Gabon	1995	18.0	0, 5, 10	
55	Gambia	2013	15.0	0	
56	Georgia	1993	18.0	0	
57	Germany	1968	19.0	7	
58	Greece	1987	23.0	6, 13	
59	Ghana	1998	15 + 2.5	0, 3, 5	
60	Grenada	2010	15.0	10	20
61	Guatemala	1992	12.0	0	
62	Guinea	1996	18.0	0	
63	Guinea-Bissau	2001	15.0	0, 10	20
64	Guyana	2007	16.0	0	
65	Haiti	1982	10.0		
66	Honduras	1964	15.0	-	18
67	Hungary	1988	27.0	5, 18	
68	Iceland	1990	24	11	
69	Indonesia	1985	10.0		10 – 200
70	Iran	2008	6.0 + 3.0		12+3, 20 (5 or 10)
71	Ireland	1972	23.0	0, 4.8, 5.2, 9, 13.5	
72	Isle of Man	1973	20.0	0, 5	

Countries and territories operating a VAT *(cont.)*

No.	Country	Implementation	Rates 2016 (%)		
			Standard	Lower	Increased
73	Israel[2]	1976	17.0	0	
74	Italy	1973	22.0	0, 4, 5, 10	
75	Ivory Coast	1960	18.0	0, 9	
76	Jamaica	1991	16.5	2, 10	21.5, 25
77	Japan	1989	8.0		
78	Jersey	2008	5.0	0	
79	Jordan	2001	16.0	0, 4, 8	16, 20, 24
80	Kenya	1990	16.0	0	
81	Kazakhstan	1992	12.0	0	
82	Korea (South)	1977	10.0		
83	Kosovo	2001	16.0	8	
84	Kyrgyzstan	1999	12.0	0	
85	Lao (People's Democratic Republic)	2010	10.0	0	
86	Latvia	1995	21.0	12	
87	Lebanon	2002	10.0	0	
88	Lesotho	2003	14.0	0, 5	15
89	Liechtenstein	1995	8.0	2.5, 3.8	
90	Lithuania	1994	21.0	5, 9	
91	Luxembourg	1970	17.0	3, 8, 14	
92	Madagascar	1994	20.0	8	
93	Malaysia	2015	6.0		
94	Malawi	2002	16.5	0	
95	Maldives	2011	6.0	-	12
96	Mali	1991	18.0	5	
97	Malta	1999	18.0	0, 5, 7	
98	Mauritania	1995	16.0	-	18
99	Mauritius	1998	15.0		
100	Mexico	1980	16.0	0	
101	Moldova	1998	20.0	8	
102	Monaco	1968	20.0	2.1, 5.5, 10	
103	Mongolia	1998	10.0		
104	Montenegro	2003	19.0	0, 7	
105	Morocco	1986	20.0	0, 7, 10, 14	
106	Mozambique	1999	17.0		
107	Namibia	2000	15.0		
108	Nepal	1997	13.0		
109	Netherlands	1969	21.0	6	
110	New Zealand	1986	15.0	0	
112	Nicaragua	1975	15.0	0, 7	
113	Niger	1986	19.0	0, 5	
114	Nigeria	1994	5.0	0	
115	Niue	2009	12.5	0	
116	Norway	1970	25.0	0, 10, 15	
117	Pakistan	1990	17.0	0, 2	18.5, 21, 22, 25
118	Panama	1977	7.0		10, 15
119	Papua New Guinea	1999	10.0	0	
120	Paraguay	1993	10.0	5, 2	
121	Peru	1991	16.0 + 2.0		
122	Philippines	1988	12.0	5	
123	Poland	1993	23.0	0, 5, 8	
124	Portugal	1986	23.0	6, 13	
125	Puerto Rico	2016	10.5 + 1.0	4	
126	Republic of Congo	2012	16.0	0	
127	Romania	1993	20.0	5, 9	

Countries and territories operating a VAT *(cont.)*

No.	Country	Implementation	Rates 2016 (%)		
			Standard	Lower	Increased
128	Russia	1991	18.0	10	
129	Rwanda	2001	18.0	0	
130	Saint Kitts and Nevis	2010	17.0	0, 10	
131	Saint Vincent and the Grenadines	2007	15.0	0, 10	
132	Samoa	1994	15.0	0	
133	Senegal	1980	18.0	0, 10	
134	Serbia	2005	20.0	10	
135	Seychelles	2012	15.0	0	
136	Sierra Leone	2009	15.0	0	
137	Singapore	1994	7.0	0	
138	Slovak Republic	1993	20.0	10	
139	Slovenia	1999	22.0	9.5	
140	South Africa	1991	14.0	0	
141	Spain	1986	21.0	4, 10	
142	Sri Lanka	1998	11.0	0	
143	St. Lucia	2012	15	0, 10	
144	Sudan	2000	17.0	0	30
145	Sweden	1969	25.0	0, 6, 12	
146	Swaziland	2012	14	0	
147	Switzerland	1995	8.0	2.5, 3.8	
148	Tajikistan	1992	18.0	0	
149	Taiwan	1986	5.0	0, 1	
150	Tanzania	1998	18.0	0	
151	Thailand	1992	7.0	0	
152	Togo	1995	18.0		
153	Tonga	2005	15.0		
154	Trinidad and Tobago	1990	12.5		
155	Turkey	1984	18.0	1, 8	
156	Turkmenistan	1992	15.0	0	
157	Tunisia	1988	18.0	0, 6, 12	
158	Uganda	1996	18.0	0	
159	Ukraine	1992	20.0	0, 7	
160	United Kingdom	1973	20.0	0, 5	
161	Uruguay	1972	22.0	0, 10	
162	Uzbekistan	1992	20.0	0	
163	Vanuatu	1998	12.5	0	
164	Venezuela	1993	12.0	8	27
165	Vietnam	1999	10.0	0, 5	
166	Zambia	1995	16.0	0	
167	Zimbabwe	2004	15.0	0	

1. **Footnote by Turkey:** The information in this document with reference to "Cyprus "relates to the southern part of the Island. There is no single authority representing both Turkish and Greek Cypriot people on the Island. Turkey recognizes the Turkish Republic of Northern Cyprus (TRNC). Until a lasting and equitable solution is found within the context of United Nations, Turkey shall preserve its position concerning the "Cyprus issue".
   Footnote by all the European Union Member States of the OECD and the European Union: the Republic of Cyprus is recognised by all members of the United Nations with the exception of Turkey. The information in this document relates to the area under the effective control of the Government of the Republic of Cyprus
2. **Israel:** The statistical data for Israel are supplied by and under the responsibility of the relevant Israeli authorities. The use of such data by the OECD is without prejudice to the status of the Golan Heights, East Jerusalem and Israeli settlements in the West Bank under the terms of international law

Source: F. Annacondia, International – Overview of General Turnover Taxes and Tax Rates, 27 International VAT Monitor 2 (2016), Journals IBFD, cited with permission of IBFD, see *http://online.ibfd.org/kbase/*, All rights reserved.

ANNEX B

Statement of outcomes on the OECD International VAT/GST Guidelines

PARIS, 5-6 NOVEMBER 2015 – OECD GLOBAL FORUM ON VAT

We, the high-level officials of 104 jurisdictions and international organisations worldwide, gathered at the third meeting of the OECD Global Forum on VAT (the Global Forum) in Paris on 5-6 November 2015 to examine the progress made towards completion of the OECD International VAT/GST* Guidelines (the Guidelines) as a global standard to address issues of double taxation and unintended non-taxation in the application of VAT to international trade.

We recall that, at its first meeting on 7-8 November 2012 in Paris, the Global Forum pledged to build the widest possible international consensus on the Guidelines with a view to achieving their endorsement as a global standard.

We also recall that, at its second meeting, on 17-18 April 2014 in Tokyo, the Global Forum:

- welcomed and endorsed the first three chapters of the Guidelines, including those on the neutrality principle and on the place of taxation for cross-border business-to-business (B2B) supplies of services and intangibles, to serve as a reference point for designing and implementing legislation; and
- urged the OECD to finalise its work on the remaining chapters of the Guidelines, including to ensure the effective and coherent VAT treatment of cross-border supplies of services to private consumers (B2C), and to present the completed Guidelines for endorsement at the third meeting of the Global Forum in November 2015.

Against this background and in light of our discussions at the third meeting of the Global Forum, we:

- welcome the approval by the OECD Committee on Fiscal Affairs (CFA) on 7 July 2015, of the complete consolidated set of Guidelines, including the new elements of the Guidelines developed since the second Global Forum meeting in April 2014, with OECD and G20 countries working together on an equal footing. These new elements include recommended rules and implementation mechanisms for the effective and coherent

* Value Added Taxes (VAT) are also referred to as "Goods and Services Tax" (GST) in many jurisdictions. For ease of reading, this statement hereafter refers to VAT to cover all value added taxes, by whatever name, in whatever language, they are known.

VAT treatment of supplies of services and intangibles to private consumers (B2C), which will facilitate the efficient collection of VAT due on these transactions, thus helping jurisdictions to prevent distortion of competition between domestic and foreign suppliers;

- welcome the active involvement of an increasing number of countries beyond the OECD and G20 and of the global business community in shaping the outcomes of this work, notably through the participation in consultations on discussion drafts, in seminars and workshops and in the meetings of the Global Forum on VAT;
- welcome the inclusion of the Guidelines on the application of VAT to cross-border supplies of services and intangibles in the Base Erosion and Profit Shifting (BEPS) package that was endorsed by the OECD Council on 1 October 2015 and that was delivered to G20 Finance Ministers on 8 October 2015;
- endorse the complete consolidated set of Guidelines as standards for the VAT treatment of international trade in services and intangibles, to serve as a reference point for designing and implementing legislation with a view to minimising the potential for unintended non-taxation and double taxation;
- look forward to the development of an OECD Recommendation in 2016 that will embody the complete set of Guidelines and that will be open to adherence by all interested non-OECD Members;
- urge the OECD to develop implementation packages to support the effective and consistent implementation of these Guidelines, and to work on areas that are not yet covered by these Guidelines. This work could include research and analysis of approaches to improve neutrality and overall performance of VAT systems, such as through the design and implementation of efficient VAT refund mechanisms and risk assessment processes. This work could also include the development of a possible framework for the exchange of information and enhanced administrative co-operation in the area of VAT. Future work could also focus on the application of VAT to cross-border trade in goods, including on the collection of VAT on low value imports, and on good practices to address compliance issues. Work might also need to be developed on the interaction between VAT and the international direct tax framework, notably in the area of transfer pricing; and
- look forward to the design of an even more inclusive framework to support and carry out this work with the involvement of all interested countries and jurisdictions, particularly developing economies, on an equal footing.

Global Forum website on *www.oecd.org/tax/consumption/vat-global-forum.htm.*

ANNEX C

Exchanges rates

Exchange rates

Country	Currency	PPP rate[1]	Market rate[2]
Australia	AUD	1.49	1.33
Austria	EUR	0.82	0.90
Belgium	EUR	0.82	0.90
Canada	CAD	1.25	1.28
Chile	CLP	392.30	654.32
Czech Republic	CZK	13.18	24.59
Denmark	DKK	7.50	6.73
Estonia	EUR	0.56	0.90
Finland	EUR	0.93	0.90
France	EUR	0.82	0.90
Germany	EUR	0.79	0.90
Greece	EUR	0.61	0.90
Hungary	HUF	133.86	279.19
Iceland	ISK	142.20	131.90
Ireland	EUR	0.85	0.90
Israel*	ILS	3.88	3.89
Italy	EUR	0.75	0.90
Japan	JPY	105.33	121.00
Korea	KRW	891.25	1 331.31
Latvia	EUR	0.51	0.90
Luxembourg	EUR	0.90	0.90
Mexico	MXN	8.26	15.87
Netherlands	EUR	0.83	0.90
New Zealand	NZD	1.47	1.43
Norway	NOK	9.80	8.06
Poland	PLN	1.80	3.77
Portugal	EUR	0.59	0.90
Slovak Republic	EUR	0.50	0.90
Slovenia	EUR	0.60	0.90
Spain	EUR	0.67	0.90
Sweden	SEK	9.13	8.43
Switzerland	CHF	1.28	0.96
Turkey	TRY	1.27	2.72
United Kingdom	GBP	0.69	0.65
United States	USD	1.00	1.00

Note on exchange rates: Cross-country comparisons of thresholds or tax amounts expressed in national currency require their conversion into one single currency. By convention, the currency used in this publication is the United States Dollar (USD). Two rates can generally be used for converting national currencies into USD: (1) market rates, which are currency exchange rates observed on the markets (the rate used in this publication is the average rate for 2015 as published in the OECD Monetary and Financial Statistics). (2) the purchasing power parity rates (PPP) for GDP, which equalise the purchasing power of different countries by eliminating differences in price levels between them; they show the specified number of monetary units needed in each country to buy the same representative basket of consumer goods and services that costs USD 1 in the United States. PPP exchange rates (for 2015) are used for Tables 1.A1.10 (Chapter 1) and 2.A2.3 (Chapter 2) as they provide for a better comparison of the value of VAT relief thresholds. Market exchange rates are used for the other tables as they allow easier comparison of prices and the level of taxes in countries.

Note on Israel: The statistical data for Israel are supplied by and under the responsibility of the relevant Israeli authorities. The use of such data by the OECD is without prejudice to the status of the Golan Heights, East Jerusalem and Israeli settlements in the West Bank under the terms of international law.

1. Purchase Parity Rates (PPP) for GDP 2015. Accessed on 1 July 2016. For further detail see *www.oecd.org/std/ppp*
2. Average market rates 2015. OECD Monthly Monetary Statistics. For further details see stats.oecd.org.

Source: OECD.

ANNEX D

Cigarettes – Most sold brands (MSB) in OECD Countries

Cigarettes – Most sold brands (MSB) in OECD Countries

Country	MSB 2014
Australia	Winfield
Austria	Marlboro
Belgium	Marlboro
Canada	NA
Chile	Belmont
Czech Republic	Red &White
Denmark	Prince
Estonia	Marlboro
Finland	L&M
France	Marlboro
Germany	Marlboro
Greece	Marlboro
Hungary	Sopianae
Iceland	Winston
Ireland	Silk Cut
Israel	Marlboro
Italy	Marlboro
Japan	Mevius
Republic of Korea	Esse
Luxembourg	Marlboro
Mexico	Marlboro
Netherlands	Marlboro
New Zealand	Holiday
Norway	Prince
Poland	L&M
Portugal	SG
Slovakia	Goden Gate
Slovenia	Boss
Spain	Ducados
Sweden	Marlboro
Switzerland	Marlboro
Turkey	Winston
United Kingdom of Great Britain and Northern Ireland	Marlboro Red Kingsize
United States of America	NA

Source: World Health Organisation (WHO)/national delegates.

ORGANISATION FOR ECONOMIC CO-OPERATION AND DEVELOPMENT

The OECD is a unique forum where governments work together to address the economic, social and environmental challenges of globalisation. The OECD is also at the forefront of efforts to understand and to help governments respond to new developments and concerns, such as corporate governance, the information economy and the challenges of an ageing population. The Organisation provides a setting where governments can compare policy experiences, seek answers to common problems, identify good practice and work to co-ordinate domestic and international policies.

The OECD member countries are: Australia, Austria, Belgium, Canada, Chile, the Czech Republic, Denmark, Estonia, Finland, France, Germany, Greece, Hungary, Iceland, Ireland, Israel, Italy, Japan, Korea, Latvia, Luxembourg, Mexico, the Netherlands, New Zealand, Norway, Poland, Portugal, the Slovak Republic, Slovenia, Spain, Sweden, Switzerland, Turkey, the United Kingdom and the United States. The European Union takes part in the work of the OECD.

OECD Publishing disseminates widely the results of the Organisation's statistics gathering and research on economic, social and environmental issues, as well as the conventions, guidelines and standards agreed by its members.

OECD PUBLISHING, 2, rue André-Pascal, 75775 PARIS CEDEX 16
(23 2016 35 1 P) ISBN 978-92-64-26404-5 – 2016

www.ingramcontent.com/pod-product-compliance
Lightning Source LLC
Chambersburg PA
CBHW061212240926
51846CB00006B/1197